# Revitalizing the Institution of Marriage for the Twenty-First Century

# Revitalizing the Institution of Marriage for the Twenty-First Century

*An Agenda for Strengthening Marriage*

EDITED BY
*Alan J. Hawkins, Lynn D. Wardle,
and David Orgon Coolidge*

FOREWORD BY
*Linda J. Waite*

PRAEGER

Westport, Connecticut
London

Library of Congress Cataloging-in-Publication Data

Revitalizing the institution of marriage for the twenty-first century : an agenda for strengthening marriage / edited by Alan J. Hawkins, Lynn D. Wardle, and David Orgon Coolidge ; foreword by Linda J. Waite.
    p.  cm.
   Includes bibliographical references and index.
   ISBN 0–275–97272–0 (alk. paper)—ISBN 0–275–97273–9 (pbk. : alk. paper)
   1. Marriage—United States.  I. Hawkins, Alan J.  II. Wardle, Lynn D.  III. Coolidge, David Orgon.
   HQ536.R456  2002
   306.81′0973—dc21     2001036320

British Library Cataloguing in Publication Data is available.

Library of Congress Catalog Card Number: 2001036320
ISBN: 0–275–97272–0
    0–275–97273–9 (pbk.)

First published in 2002

Praeger Publishers, 88 Post Road West, Westport, CT 06881
An imprint of Greenwood Publishing Group, Inc.
www.praeger.com

Printed in the United States of America

The paper used in this book complies with the Permanent Paper Standard issued by the National Information Standards Organization (Z39.48–1984).

10 9 8 7 6 5 4 3 2 1

**Copyright Acknowledgment**

The editors and publisher gratefully acknowledge permission for use of the following material:

Excerpts from *Songs for the Bride: Wedding Rites of India* by William G. Archer. Copyright © 1985 by Columbia University Press. Used with permission.

# Contents

Foreword: Marriage Myths and Revitalizing Marriage      vii
    *Linda J. Waite*

Introduction      xiii
    *Alan J. Hawkins*

1. The Social Costs of De-Institutionalizing Marriage      1
    *Steven L. Nock*

2. Community Involvement and Its Limits in Marriage      15
    and Families
    *Margaret F. Brinig*

3. The Language of Health Versus the Language of Religion:
    Competing Models of Marriage for the Twenty-First Century      29
    *Don S. Browning*

4. A Plea for Greater Concern About the Quality of Marital
    Matching      45
    *Norval D. Glenn*

5. Why Covenant Marriage May Prove Effective as a Response
    to the Culture of Divorce      59
    *Katherine Shaw Spaht*

6. Good Incentives Lead to Good Marriages      69
    *Allen M. Parkman*

10827 /

7. Strengthening Couples and Marriage in Low-Income
   Communities                                                    79
   *Theodora Ooms*

8. Promoting Marriage as a Means for Promoting Fatherhood         101
   *Wade F. Horn*

9. Reflections on the Nature of Marriage                          111
   *Brian Bix*

10. Adoption by Unmarried Cohabitants, Same-Sex Couples,
    and Single Persons in Europe                                  121
    *Rainer Frank*

11. Assisted Reproductive Technology (ART) and the Family:
    Risk or Revival?                                              133
    *Ruth Deech*

12. Marriage and Belonging: Reflections on *Baker v. Vermont*     145
    *David Orgon Coolidge*

13. Marriage Policy and the Methodology of Research on
    Homosexual Parenting                                          155
    *Robert Lerner and Althea K. Nagai*

14. Institutionalizing Marriage Reforms Through Federalism        167
    *Lynn D. Wardle*

15. Fixing the Family: Legal Acts and Cultural Admonitions        177
    *Carl E. Schneider*

16. The Limits of the Law and Raising a Sentiment
    for Marriage                                                  185
    *Laurence C. Nolan*

17. A Marriage Research Agenda for the Twenty-First Century:
    Ten Critical Questions                                        195
    *David Popenoe*

Index                                                             207

About the Editors and Contributors                               213

# Foreword: Marriage Myths and Revitalizing Marriage

## Linda J. Waite

As a society, we are basically conflicted about marriage. On the one hand, we say that having a happy marriage is an important personal goal. On the other hand, we say that it shouldn't matter if other people do not want marriage for *themselves*. We say that it is fine if single people have sex, but *not* fine if either of them is married to someone else. We say that people should be able to have children when they aren't married, but *not fine* if our daughter does it. Almost all of us say that *our* marriages are very happy, but almost half of us divorce at least once. Understandably, then, we are ambivalent about making divorce more difficult.

What's going on here? I believe we have been naïve. Sold a bill of goods. Misinformed. We have accepted myths about marriage that are based on fantasy or politics, not on facts. We have allowed these myths to permeate our culture, the messages we send to others, the choices we make, and those we encourage others to make. The following six myths and our belief in them do a lot of damage.

1. *Marriage is just a piece of paper.* It's how you feel that matters, not whether you signed a form in a government office, according to this myth. Getting married makes no difference to your relationship, how it develops, or how long it lasts. So why bother? Not true. Getting married, making a public, legally binding promise—to stay together forever, to support each other, to be faithful—matters. It makes relationships more likely to last and so a better "investment." Promising to stay together allows partners to grow *together,* support each other, and count on that support. Religious beliefs and values undergird marriage for many couples, giving the union support

and meaning beyond their personal feelings of the moment. Getting married even changes sexual behavior, increasing fidelity and sexual satisfaction.

2. *Marriage matters for children (maybe) but not for those without kids at home.* Marriage improves childrens' lives, true. But it also transforms the lives of men and women, both parents and nonparents, making them healthier, happier, wealthier, and more satisfied with sex.

3. *Marriage puts women at risk of domestic violence.* In fact, being *unmarried* puts women at greater risk of violence, both in and outside the home. Married women (and men) are less likely to be assaulted by either strangers or those they know than single women and men. Women are less likely to be hit, slapped, or beaten by their husbands than by their ex-husbands, boyfriends, ex-boyfriends, or cohabiting partner. Getting married ties men and women into a network of family and friends who seem to discourage violence.

4. *Marriage is a personal relationship. No one matters in a marriage but the two people in it and no one (including the state) should be allowed to interfere.* Marriage *is* a personal relationship, but it is much more. Marriage is a legal contract, a civil status, a religious union. Spouses have rights and responsibilities that come only with marriage, toward each other, toward their children, toward their communities, and toward the government. When marriage fails or fails to form, families have a much harder time and succeed less often. When families fail, communities and government struggle to pick up the pieces.

5. *Marriage may be good for men, but it is bad for women.* According to this myth, marriage makes women into domestic drudges, damages their emotional health, and ruins their careers. Marriage makes men into the king of the castle, with health and happiness from power at home and the services of a wife. If this was ever true, it certainly is not today. Most married women work for pay, most husbands share housework and childcare tasks with their wives, and spouses most often *share* decisionmaking and power. So contemporary marriages improve the physical health, happiness, and emotional well-being of *both* women and men.

6. *Divorce is usually the best solution if couples can't seem to get along, even if they have kids.* Although research evidence contradicts this statement, most adults think it is true. It has, I think, become almost a moral imperative to seek divorce as a solution to unhappiness in marriage, so that the children do not grow up with a poor or flawed model of loving relationships. The best current research does suggest that if a marriage is characterized by high levels of conflict, either physical or verbal, children are better off if the marriage ends. But in marriages that are boring or not emotionally fulfilling or strained but not highly conflictual, children are better off if their parents stay together. And relatively *few* divorces end the kinds of high-conflict marriages that damage children; most—70 percent or more—end marriages that are *good* for children, even if imperfect. More-

over, when unhappily married couples stick it out through rough times, a large majority find marital happiness again within five years.

These myths lead to many of the wrong choices and many of the wrong policies. As a first step toward revitalizing marriage, we must replace these myths with an understanding of the institution of marriage and the ways it works its magic.

Marriage is a legally binding contract, backed by the force of religious principle and civil law. Because husband and wife have promised to join together to form a new family, they can plan their futures together. This pledge to work as a team for the rest of their lives allows spouses to specialize. Each person can pick some of the tasks of everyday life, get good at them, and do them for the family. And, just like countries that specialize in producing different goods and services, spouses produce more if they divide things up and then share than they would if they both did everything for themselves. So, married people produce more than they would if they were not married.

Married people also benefit from the economies of scale of sharing a home with someone else. A couple needs only one couch, one TV, one refrigerator. They can share heat and light. So, it costs less to live with another person. Of course, other people are also troublesome and irritating, at least at times, and might want to watch a different program than you do. But stable bonds of affection tip the balance away from the costs and toward the rewards of living with others. Cohabiting couples get most of the same economies of scale as married couples. But cohabiting couples almost always marry or split up within a few years, economies of scale notwithstanding.

Marriage includes a promise of mutual support, regardless of what happens. So marriage makes a man and woman into a two-person insurance pool, providing a level of protection that money cannot buy. If one spouse becomes ill or disabled, the other generally fills in, doing tasks around the house, working more to replace lost earnings, providing physical care and moral support. In most contemporary marriages, husband and wife both help support the family with their earnings. Dual-earner families have a sort of built-in unemployment insurance, so a job loss, while a crisis, is not as devastating as it would be to a family with one earner.

Wives and husbands also offer each other a sympathetic ear, a sounding board, a confidant. This social support, along with the knowledge that one is loved and valued, contributes to the high levels of emotional well-being and happiness of married people. Since spouses benefit directly from the career and earnings success of their partner, husbands and wives are both well positioned and highly motivated to help each other with work. These efforts contribute to the "marriage premium" in earnings for men. Married women also see a gain in their earnings, but only if they are childless; married mothers seem to use their husband's earnings to "buy" time with children.

If marriage is such a great deal, then why do so many marriages end in divorce? And why are a third of all children in the United States now born to unmarried women? Why do most couples cohabit before they marry? Why does marriage need "revitalizing"?

The answers are complicated, interwoven with other large-scale changes in our society and the world in general. The sexual revolution, huge advances in reproductive technology, the movement of women into the labor force, no-fault divorce, and the increasing social acceptance of divorce all played a role. And changes in one arena often lead to further changes in another. The shift to no-fault divorce *caused* an increase in divorce rates that reduced the stability of marriages generally. Increasing divorce rates cause married couples to be more reluctant to have a(nother) child, a child who would have helped hold their marriage together. Increasing acceptability of divorce seems to lead to a decline in the happiness of marriages. And women's move into paid employment contributed to and resulted from rising divorce rates and the declining stability of marriages.

This volume, *Revitalizing the Institution of Marriage for the Twenty-First Century,* brings together a first-class group of social thinkers, commentators, scholars, and policy analysts from the social sciences, law, religion, and public policy. They assess the forces that are undermining and weakening the institution of marriage. They present and critique a series of suggestions for revitalizing the institution of marriage, from using marriage to promote fatherhood through programs to strengthen marriage in low-income communities. The authors of the chapters in this volume represent the most creative, thoughtful, informed, and insightful social thinkers of our time. Many lead or are involved in efforts to strengthen marriage, through legislative and policy initiatives, social action programs, campaigns of public information, and religious- or community-based efforts. All write and speak widely on marriage and what we can do to strengthen this foundational institution.

The movement to strengthen marriage arrives hand-in-hand with efforts to reform welfare. Former National Fatherhood Initiative president Wade Horn and Urban Institute economist Isabel Sawhill point to recent statistics that 40 percent of children in the United States live apart from their fathers and that up to 60 percent will live in fatherless households by the time they reach age 18. They argue that "By focusing so heavily on moving mothers into the workforce, states have neglected to work on the equally important task of increasing the number of two-parent families."[1] Many children born to unmarried mothers are, in reality, born into two-parent families—cohabiting families. And many if not most stepfamilies begin when a woman with children begins living with a new man. If these families make the transition to marriage, their chances of success are decent, but few remain together as cohabiting partners over the long run.

Revitalizing marriage is a tremendously important goal, one with enormous implications—for our society, our communities, our families, and our children. This volume gives us the facts, the ideas, the arguments, and the suggestions to guide our efforts to reach that goal. It is a valuable resource—as is the institution of marriage—for all of us.

## NOTE

1. Wade F. Horn and Isabel Sawhill, "Making Room for Daddy: Fathers, Marriage and Welfare Reform." Paper presented at The New World of Welfare: An Agenda for Reauthorization and Beyond, Washington, D.C., February 1–2, 2001.

# Introduction

## Alan J. Hawkins

As the twenty-first century dawns, marriage is at an important historical crossroad, and scholars are debating its future. Virtually all scholars agree that marriage has experienced significant changes over the last one hundred years that make it less stable and enduring.[1] Furthermore, scholars and practitioners agree that helping individuals and couples build stronger, healthier, mutually satisfying relationships is a worthy endeavor. And researchers have contributed much to our knowledge of how to build and sustain intimate relationships.[2] But specifically promoting marriage—rather than helping couples build loving relationships of any form—is another matter altogether. Scholars differ on whether the institution of marriage deserves our support. Many scholars in the social sciences and the law no longer view marriage as a unique and vital institution that is the foundation of individual, family, community, and societal well-being. Instead, they view marriage primarily as a personal lifestyle choice—only one of a number of viable relationship forms that are capable of promoting personal well-being and deserving societal support. From this perspective, sexual unions are seen ultimately as a private contract whose terms should be set only by the partners themselves. Moreover, privileging marriage over other forms of intimate union may even be harmful to these other unions. Other scholars, however, point to the solid data that suggest marriage matters a great deal to the health and well-being of men, women, children, communities, and societies. In addition, these scholars stress that many of the personal and social goods that arise from marriage can be attributed to the institutional dimension of marriage, a dimension that could be lost in a view of marriage as a private rather than public concern.[3]

Throughout history, societies have placed a large burden on marriage. We have expected marriage to regulate sexuality, protect and socialize children, and create the fundamental social and economic units of our societies. Recently, we have added more personal demands: marriage should provide emotional and psychological benefits and meet the more prosaic needs for daily companionship, goals that can be hard to meet for many couples.[4] In short, we expect an awful lot from marriage. Against this daunting set of expectations, it should not surprise us that historians can point to flaws and shortcomings in this institution across time and space.[5] These flaws and changing social norms about intimate relationships provide intellectual fodder for the argument that we are rapidly approaching a post-marriage era in which the way we accomplish the important societal tasks historically assigned to marriage must be reexamined and reworked to manage the inevitable force of social change. Although the social and legal mechanisms that would replace marriage are not well articulated or understood, proponents of a post-marriage culture accept their inevitability; those who would resist such inevitable forces are anachronistic, even quixotic.[6]

Many scholars believe, however, as the contributors to this volume do, that this assessment of marriage is too pessimistic and too rash. Despite its warts and weaknesses, they argue, marriage remains a dynamic institution in our society, able to meet the challenge of revitalization. They note the empirical evidence that married people become happier, healthier, wealthier, and more successful, even when controlling for a basketful of confounding variables.[7] They observe that the divorce rate has leveled off and even declined slightly.[8] Social demographers are revising downward the oft-projected 50 percent failure rate for first marriages. These more optimistic scholars see the continuing popularity of marriage reflected in both attitude and behavior; a good marriage remains the most important goal of young adults, and only a tiny fraction of adults choose not to marry.[9] Even in the face of marital failure, most divorced individuals eventually remarry. Recent research documents that even fragile families—poor, unmarried, new parents—hope for a lasting marriage despite the daunting economic and social barriers they face.[10] More optimistic scholars also point to a growing grass-roots marriage movement that is making an impact by promoting education, therapy, policy, and broad cultural change to strengthen marriage.[11] Of course, looming in the background is the evidence that children have not fared well in a culture experimenting with forming, maintaining, and dissolving intimate unions.[12]

Given these signs of vitality in the institution of marriage, particularly in the face of dramatic cultural changes and unresolved problems, the contributors to this volume share a belief that marriage deserves our best efforts to revitalize it instead of a conscious agenda of benign neglect or an active plan to pull the plug and let it die. Moreover, the contributors to this volume espouse a perspective that strengthening marriage as an institution, and not just a relationship, matters. The contributors have different and sometimes divergent perspectives on how to revitalize the institution of marriage. Nevertheless, they are uniform in their analysis that a better understanding of the institutional nature of marriage is crucial to revitalizing it.

The distinction between an institutional and a relational perspective of marriage is not just semantics; it guides how we approach the task of revitalizing marriage. The relational perspective emphasizes the relationship skills individuals need to build satisfying marriages and other intimate relationships, primarily communication and problem-solving skills. Accordingly, it focuses on the private, interpersonal nature of intimate unions. From this perspective, the task at hand is to give people the abilities needed to make them better intimate partners. Although this perspective acknowledges that marital relationships are part of a broader culture that influences our abilities to build loving, stable unions, its emphasis and hope are on reinforcing couples against harmful, external forces with a "relational technology" that effectively shields their union from damage and empowers mutually satisfying partnerships. And with its focus on relationships, the social, institutional, and legal frameworks that surround intimate relationships become less important. What matters is function, not form.

In contrast, an institutional perspective of marriage emphasizes that marriage is embedded in our culture and intertwines our public and private lives. While acknowledging the critical need to assist couples with better relationships skills, especially in times of significant social transition, the institutional perspective stresses that marriage is as fundamentally social as it is profoundly personal; as much a public act as a private relationship; and as much a societal good as an individual benefit. From this perspective, the question of how best to revitalize marriage must include an examination of the institution, of the public nature of marriage. Both relational and institutional perspectives will be needed to revitalize marriage. But an institutional perspective, I believe, has received less attention and is less understood both by scholars and the general public. Moreover, from an institutional perspective, interventions with "relational technology" to strengthen marital relations may ultimately fail without a vital institution of marriage to support them. Indeed, the relational perspective risks reducing marriage to a personally defined relational contract rather than the rich social institution it must be to support strong marriages. As Linda Waite observes, we have a tendency "to conceptualize marriage as an external, structural category and to look beneath the piece of paper for the 'real' reasons married people appear happier and healthier. But in American society, marriage not only names a relationship but it creates a relationship between two people, one that is acknowledged, not just by the couple itself, but by the couples' kin, friends, religious community, and larger society."[13]

The institutional perspective focuses on the social norms, policies, and legal frameworks that define and encompass our concept of marriage, and the institutional and cultural forces that work with and against it. These factors, which are external to the relationship itself, are at the core of what marriage means. When individuals choose to marry, they are joining a distinctive and important public institution as much as they are separating from others to create a unique and private partnership. Institutional membership comes with obligations. Granted, most initiates or new "citizens" of marriage have an incomplete understanding of the full responsibilities their membership implies. But in myriad formal and informal ways, members of the institution of marriage are taught and reminded of these obligations by a society that depends heavily on the goods that marriage produces. And, over time, most learn the fuller, deeper meanings of what it means to belong to marriage, not just to have an intimate relationship. Although almost all married people occasionally experience as a burden this fuller meaning associated with membership in the institution of marriage, most also come to sense the richer, transcendent possibilities of their membership obligations.

This perspective—that the institution of marriage matters and that it should be revitalized for a new century and a changing social environment—forms the foundation for this volume. We bring together the work of respected legal scholars and social scientists to articulate why we should care about strengthening the institution of marriage, what we can do, and what challenges we will face. The combination of social scientists and legal scholars in a volume on marriage is unique and overdue. Social scientists close to the data on the importance of marriage struggle to translate their work into public policy and law. Law and policy are two of the most powerful tools we have for shaping and supporting the institution of marriage. Furthermore, legal scholars close to the laws and legal processes that define and configure marriage search for the theory and data to bolster their efforts to strengthen the institution in the face of forces pushing in the opposite direction. And as several of our contributors note, legal reform and cultural shifts will be interdependent. We believe those who study marriage and professionals who influence policy and law on marriage will be more effective in their work as they allow both social and legal thinking to guide their efforts.

## CHAPTER SUMMARIES

*Chapter 1*. Steven L. Nock begins the volume with a sociological primer that articulates what it means to view marriage as a social institution, and identifies significant social costs of continuing the trend of de-institutionalizing marriage. "Unless we discover an equally effective and economical form of social control, and until we are willing to accept the collective costs of doing so, we should be very cautious of de-institutionalizing marriage." He argues that revitalizing marriage will require accepting reasonable boundaries around the marital relationship formed by social norms and laws to distinguish it from other unions, and granting unique legal, economic, and social benefits to married couples, which goes against current social and legal trends. These distinctions, however, are generally supported, he argues, because people sense the collective benefits enjoyed by a society with strong and stable marriages.

*Chapter 2.* Margaret F. Brinig offers an important caveat, however, to emphasizing the institutional nature of marriage. An emphasis on the social and institutional boundaries that encompass marriage must be careful not to overstep the limits of autonomy that are also essential to sustaining marriage. Brinig describes many ways that communities contribute to healthy marriages. But noting recent legal cases in which extended family and the state interjected themselves into the affairs of a married couple, she argues that "the usefulness of outsider involvement is limited. In legal terms, we reach these limits when third-party claimants assert rights to access spouses and children in ways that conflict with the autonomy families need." She cautions that when the rights of outsiders—even concerned and loving outsiders—are legally asserted as part of the family system (which rests primarily on moral obligations), they can cause serious problems, including weaker marital relationships.

*Chapter 3.* Don S. Browning explores these moral obligations that frame marriage, obligations that are richly articulated in our religious traditions. He strengthens our understanding of an institutional perspective of marriage by focusing specifically on the cultural need to sense the deeper meaning of marriage and not just the healthy outcomes of good marriage. "Strengthening marriages in our time . . . is mainly a [cultural] task of deepening and reformulating our understanding of the meaning of marriage," he asserts. This deeper meaning of marriage cannot be accomplished on narrowly empirical grounds, he argues. It will require supplementing secular, social science perspectives intended to strengthen marriage with religious classics that offer "thicker" moral perspectives on the meaning of marriage. Secular, health perspectives alone do not present a commanding cultural vision of what marriage is. Revitalizing marriage will require trusting our best religious traditions to be "the carriers of our positive cultures of marriage and family and the various languages of commitment that have energized these institutions."

*Chapter 4.* Norval D. Glenn focuses on a more prosaic yet important way to strengthen marriage. He argues that the process of entering into the institution of marriage has become less effective over the last few decades. If marriage is to be strengthened, attention must be given to the problem of creating better marital matches and studying the barriers to good matching. A primary requirement for good marital matching is "the opportunity for those 'on the market' to get to know a large number and variety of prospective spouses, and to get to know them well enough to assess their desirability on the basis of more than just their most obvious and readily observable characteristics." But contrary to prevailing common logic, Glenn indicts cohabitation as a kind of premarital entanglement that works against good circulation in the marriage market. Another difficulty is the less active participation by trusted long-term friends and family members in the marriage-partner evaluation process. Glenn urges scholars to attend once again to the important role of good matches in creating stronger marriages.

*Chapter 5.* Even with better matches, however, if our cultural understanding of marriage does not include a strong sense of permanence, the institution will diminish. Katherine Shaw Spaht's chapter is centered on the loss of permanence as an integral element of the definition of marriage. "Until policy makers alter the present legal structure of marriage by repealing unilateral no-fault divorce law and restoring permanence to marriage, it will be difficult to convince future generations that the marriage vow is the strongest, most important commitment a person makes during his or her lifetime." But the general repeal of unilateral, no-fault divorce is unlikely. Spaht proposes another, more feasible option. She argues that optional covenant marriage legislation—passed in three states—can do much to revitalize marriage with the sense of permanence. "Covenant marriage offers an opportunity to change the dominant paradigm of marriage, to change the 'definition' of marriage from a casual companionate relationship to a serious and sober lifetime commitment."

*Chapter 6.* A rational-choice framework is central to Allen M. Parkman's analysis of how to reform divorce and revitalize the institution of marriage. Instead of the emphasis on legal options for marriage suggested by Spaht, Parkman emphasizes incentives. As an economist and legal scholar, he points to shifts in the incentives people face for joining and maintaining their membership in the institution of marriage as the culprit for a decline in the institution. "Some fundamental changes in society have reduced the incentives for people to marry and, among those who marry, these incentives have resulted in less durable marriage." Specifically, Parkman criticizes the change from essentially a mutual consent divorce framework to a unilateral, no-fault divorce framework that permits the divorcing spouse to ignore many of the costs of divorce to family members. Parkman advocates a combination of no-fault, fault, and mutual consent grounds for divorce, but the primary grounds should be mutual consent, especially when children are involved in the relationship.

*Chapter 7.* Theodora Ooms also is drawn to an analysis of marital incentives, but in service of a different issue. She investigates how we can strengthen marriage in low-income communities where the institution of marriage has become anemic due in large part to the weak incentives to marry. Ooms argues that the marriage movement has inadvertently ignored the needs and circumstances of the poor, and especially the African-American poor. With the exception of some recent welfare reform policies, she argues that "most of the legal reforms and program initiatives currently being proposed to revitalize and strengthen marriage are not likely . . . to have any significant impact on marital stability and quality, or nonmarital childbearing among the poor." Ooms examines the barriers to strong and stable marriages that exist in low-income communities. But, more important, she also explores opportunities to strengthen marriage in this population. Her analysis is more optimistic than many would think. She notes that if we ignore marriage among the poor, we overlook a potent asset for improving the lives and prospects of society's most vulnerable children.

*Chapter 8.* Wade Horn also calls for the revitalization of marriage to improve the well-being of the next generation. He reviews the sober data on the consequences of fatherlessness in our society, asserting that the question is no longer whether fathers matter to children's well-being but what can be done to bind fathers and children together in contemporary society. He analyzes three common responses to the problem of father absence—child-support enforcement, noncustodial father visitation, and cohabitation—ultimately rejecting each as capable of serving well the interests of children. The answer, Horn contends, is marriage, which is "a much more effective glue for binding fathers to their children." Of course, strengthening marriage "is not as simple as pointing young couples to the altar and insisting they marry. We do not need more bad marriages. What we need is more healthy, mutually satisfying, equal-regard marriages." Horn recommends a new commitment of both public and private resources aimed at strengthening marriages before they begin, at regular intervals along the way, and when couples are in trouble. Children will be the primary beneficiaries of this commitment.

*Chapter 9.* Brian Bix is also concerned about marriage as an institution to promote children's well-being. He builds an argument for differentiating between marriages that do and do not have children so that more responsibility can be placed on parents. Bix notes that "while we have the same institution for couples who have children as for those that do not, many people think quite differently about the two kinds of marriages." He argues that much of the concern about strengthening marriage is connected to the potential harm of divorce to children. When children are involved in a marriage, "we want parents to try harder, to hold on longer, to feel a stronger sense of duty and commitment, for the sake of the children." He does not detect, however, an equally strong call to duty and sacrifice directed to couples when no minor children are involved. Strengthening the institution of marriage may be facilitated by distinguishing between marriages with and without dependent children, asking those with children to

accept greater responsibilities for sustaining their marriages and more restraints on dissolving them, while allowing greater freedom for married
individuals without children to pursue their personal preferences.

*Chapter 10.* European nations have gone further than the United States
in providing some legal status to different kinds of intimate unions, although
they have not as yet distinguished between marriages with and without
children, as Bix suggests. But as Rainer Frank points out, many would be
surprised to learn that European countries still put much stock in the institution of marriage and protect it with law and policy because it is still
the best situation for raising children. This is made clear in his analysis of
adoption in Europe and how it applies to unmarried cohabitants, same-sex
couples, and single people. Frank points out that "adoption is an institution that is intended to serve exclusively the interests of the child and to
be for its protection; it does not consider the interests of the adoptive parents, even when they may have the understandable human desire to make
by way of adoption a public statement that the child is theirs." Marriage
in Europe retains an important status under the law, especially in relation
to children. Those who look to Europe to show us the way to a post-
marriage society will be disappointed by Frank's analysis.

*Chapter 11.* Adoption laws govern the process of legally binding biologically unrelated children to parents. The emerging field of assisted reproductive technology (ART) is resulting in new ways of creating families.
Although adoption laws generally reinforce the institution of marriage, Ruth
Deech invites us to explore the effects of ART on marriage and family. "The
complex interaction between ART, marriage, and contemporary notions of
the family may be summarized as follows: traditional notions about marriage and the need for marriages to produce children encouraged investment in and acceptability of ART, which in turn contributed to the growing rejection of marriage as the only valid union." The original success and
excitement with ART involved its ability to help infertile married couples
"complete" their families. But the advancement of this technology also co-
incided with a dramatic increase in alternative family forms. Nontraditional
unions have sought legal and social validation through ART to give them
children. Deech discusses her concerns about this trend and urges caution
in how the law treats ART. There have always been legal restraints on the
freedom to reproduce as one wishes. The purposes these laws serve may
not be trivial. The existence of a dramatic, new technology does not by itself create the justification for fashioning a brave new world of marriages
and families.

*Chapter 12.* Although Frank and Deech touched on issues affected by the
increasing acceptance of same-sex unions, the next chapter addresses this
issue directly. In the United States, legalization of marriage between same-
sex couples is now a prominent judicial and political issue, one that touches
a core element of the traditional definition of the institution ōf marriage—

the sexual union of a man and woman. Hence, a volume focusing on the institution of marriage would be incomplete without attention to this critical but controversial issue. First, David Coolidge takes a direct look inside the majority opinion of *Baker v. Vermont,* in which the Vermont Supreme Court ruled that the legal and economic benefits of marriage must be given to same-sex couples. The goal of his chapter is to identify some of the conceptual roadblocks that stand in the way of a wholehearted legal reaffirmation of marriage as a unique community of a man and a woman. Constitutional discussions of marriage are paradoxical, Coolidge argues, in that they alternate between treating marriage as the creation of individuals and as the creation of the state. Taken alone, the first approach veers in a libertarian direction, while the second is more statist. But since courts are not philosophers, the tendencies combine into a kind of balancing act in which individual rights and state interests generate mixed levels of legal scrutiny and burdens of proof. Coolidge contends that both approaches to marriage law, alone or mixed, miss the real choice in the marriage debate: whether to adopt the classical or communitarian view. The classical view sees marriage as a unique sexual community rooted in human embodiment. The communitarian view sees marriage as a unique social community rooted in human relationships. *Baker v. Vermont* is best understood as a new, communitarian redefinition of marriage as an institution created to further purposes of the state. Although he appreciates some important aspects of this decision, Coolidge questions whether this approach creates more problems than it solves and suggests a reaffirmation of the classical approach to marriage, rooted in balancing the plurality of communities in our society that have an interest in marriage.

*Chapter 13.* The Vermont Supreme Court, in *Baker v. Vermont,* relied on scientific studies that implied children raised by same-sex couples are indistinguishable on various outcomes from children raised by heterosexual couples to support their conclusion that same-sex couples must be given access to the economic benefits of marriage. But Robert Lerner and Althea K. Nagai argue that there are serious flaws to these scientific studies. They focus primarily on the standard problem of interpreting the null hypothesis of these studies—that there is no difference between children raised by same-sex couples and children raised by heterosexual couples—and show that none of the studies has the statistical power needed to safely interpret the null hypothesis. "The history of social science research on challenging, sensitive issues such as this one indicates that seldom do the findings of the first wave of research studies survive unchallenged when more sophisticated studies are done." Accordingly, they argue it is premature for courts to rely on the current body of research for clues about how children will fare in same-sex unions.

*Chapter 14.* This volume has highlighted a number of potential legal paths for revitalizing the institution of marriage. Whichever paths may be taken, however, Lynn D. Wardle reminds us of an important parameter for any reform that scholars and policy makers alike can sometimes forget—federalism, which contains a substantive constitutional limitation on the power of the national government to regulate marriage and a historic limitation on the jurisdiction of federal courts. Laws in the United States governing marriage and divorce are the province of fifty individual states, not the federal government. Wardle maintains that "federalism in family law is not a mere anachronism but is a doctrine based upon significant perceptions of the realities associated with the government of a large, heterogeneous nation. These underlying policy values include pluralism, communitarianism, experimentation, and respect for state expertise and sovereignty." Wardle argues that effective marriage law reform should occur within the limits that federalism sets on these reforms. While federalism will impede the quick enactment of national legal remedies for problems, he argues that it also increases the likelihood that reforms will be authentic, effective, and lasting.

*Chapter 15.* Two of our contributors specifically discuss the limits of law for revitalizing marriage. First, Carl E. Schneider is skeptical of the law's ability to lead the way to a revitalized institution of remarriage because marriage is predominantly a social rather than a legal institution. "In principle, law can buttress the social forces that support the institution of marriage. The law should certainly try to do so." But Schneider believes that familial institutions must rest primarily on culture, rather than law. Family law largely leaves spouses free to govern their relationship and family however they prefer (short of a few kinds of serious problems) because of our cultural ethic of privacy. Moreover, regulating private conduct is extremely hard. Strengthening marriage will be most possible in the wake of cultural reform. Schneider identifies two cultural ideologies toxic to marriage that will be particularly difficult to change: the fear of obligation and the fear of dependence. If we are to revitalize marriage, we will first need to confront these deep-seated values, modifying them for the twenty-first century. Schneider is pessimistic about the success of such an effort, but it will be necessary before any legal reform can be effective.

*Chapter 16.* Like Schneider, Laurence Nolan acknowledges that law can play a role in revitalizing marriage, but also notes its limits. For instance, a concern for the welfare of children is a reason to desire a strong institution of marriage, but this same concern also places limits on what the law can do to strengthen marriage. "Children need care and financial support whether their parents are married or not. If large numbers have children without marriage, the law may choose a policy to protect the child regardless of whether his or her parents are married." The law's concern for children's well-being in a society that increasingly separates marriage and childrearing places constraints on how far it can go to sustain marriage. Moreover, legal efforts to strengthen marriage will rub up against constitutional issues such as equal protection and the separation of church and state. Laws to strengthen marriage will require careful crafting. But law is ineffective at enforcing its rules when so many of its citizens ignore them. Therefore, like Schneider, Nolan calls on the other influential institutions of society to do the hard work of changing society's sentiments towards marriage.

*Chapter 17.* The volume concludes with a panoramic and candid analysis by David Popenoe of ten major problems we face as a society in revitalizing the institution of marriage. For instance, Popenoe notes that adolescence and young adulthood have been dramatically elongated by earlier sexual maturity and later marriage. Moreover, many of the values and behaviors of young people work against forming and maintaining stable marriages. Accordingly, he asks: "How can we best insure that the life experiences during adolescence and young adulthood will contribute to, rather than detract from, eventual marriage?" Similarly, he contends that the modern sexual revolution has generated unparalleled sexual freedom that has weakened an important basis for marriage. Arguing that it will be difficult to rebuild a strong marriage culture in our current sexual climate, he asks: "Is it possible to move toward a more culturally restrictive sexual system for both men and women and if so, how, and how restrictive should it be?" This sample of the questions Popenoe asks makes clear that as an advocate for strengthening marriage he is not ducking the tough issues. He calls for more good research to address these questions.

Popenoe's list of challenges confronting the revitalization of marriage, along with the many other ideas and proposals set forth in this volume, provide a feast of conceptual, legal, and empirical questions that need better answers and data from scholars and policy makers from many disciplines. But this banquet is not for the intellectually timid or the ideologically rigid, given the difficulty of the questions and the importance of finding workable answers. In this volume, we have approached the task of revitalizing marriage for the twenty-first century from an institutional perspective that emphasizes shaping the social norms, policies, and laws that surround marriage. Successful cultural and legal interventions may be more challenging to implement than interpersonal interventions to help couples learn better relationship skills. And surely both kinds of interventions will be needed. But relationship skills will not be enough without a strong institution of marriage.

## NOTES

1. Stephanie Coontz, *The Way We Never Were: American Families and the Nostalgia Trap* (New York: Basic Books, 1992).

2. John M. Gottman and Nan Silver, *The Seven Principles for Making Marriage Work* (New York: Crown, 1999).

3. William H. Doherty and Jason S. Carroll, "Health and the Ethics of Marital Therapy and Education," in Don Browning, John Wall, William J. Doherty, and Steven Post, eds., *Marriage and the Professions* (Grand Rapids, Mich.: Eerdmans, in press); Linda Waite and Maggie Gallagher, *The Case for Marriage* (New York: Doubleday, 2000).

4. Blaine Fowers, *Beyond the Myth of Marital Happiness* (San Francisco: Jossey-Bass, 2000).

5. Nancy F. Cott, *The Bonds of Womanhood: "Women's Sphere" in New England, 1780–1835* (New Haven, Conn.: Yale University Press, 1997); Nancy F. Cott, *Public Vows: A History of Marriage and the Nation* (Cambridge: Harvard University Press, 2001).

6. Stephanie Coontz, *The Way We Really Are: Coming to Terms with America's Changing Families* (New York: Basic Books, 1997).

7. Linda J. Waite and Maggie Gallagher, *The Case for Marriage* (New York: Doubleday, 2000).

8. David Popenoe and Barbara Dafoe Whitehead, *The State of Our Unions 2000* (New Brunswick, N.J.: The National Marriage Project, 2000).

9. David Popenoe and Barbara Dafoe Whitehead, *The State of Our Unions 1999* (New Brunswick, N.J.: The National Marriage Project, 1999).

10. Elaine Sorenson, Ronald Mincy, and Ariel Halpern, *Redirecting Welfare Policy Toward Building Strong Families* (Washington, D.C.: The Urban Institute, 2000); Morehouse Conference on African American Fatherhood, *Turning the Corner on Father Absence in Black America* (Atlanta and New York: Morehouse Research Institute and Institute for American Values, 1999).

11. Maggie Gallagher, *The Marriage Movement: A Statement of Principles* (New York: Institute for American Values, 2000).

12. Sara McLanahan and Gary Sandefur, *Growing Up with a Single Parent* (Cambridge: Harvard University Press, 1994); Judith Wallerstein, Julia Lewis, and Sandy Blakeslee, *The Unexpected Legacy of Divorce: A 25-Year Landmark Study* (New York: Hyperion, 2000).

13. Waite and Gallagher, *The Case for Marriage*, 73.

# 1

# The Social Costs of De-Institutionalizing Marriage

## Steven L. Nock

### INTRODUCTION

Marriage is much more than a relationship between two people. It is also a social institution. For purposes of understanding and analyzing marriage, this perspective is critical and offers an explanation for some of the many benefits that are known to flow from marriage. It also serves as a warning against attempting to render marriage little more than a private arrangement between two adults.

What does it mean to describe marriage as a social institution? In this chapter, I will attempt to answer that question and explore the implications of an institutional perspective for our understanding of how and why marriage matters to men and women. A marriage is a relationship defined by legal, moral, and conventional assumptions. Those assumptions do not originate in the marriage. Rather, they precede and influence it. The assumptions about marriage found in law, public opinion, religion, and conventional morality define the institution of marriage.

In the course of three or four decades, various legal and social changes have made marriage less distinct from other forms of partnerships. Alternatively, there are fewer legal and social privileges associated with being married. As I will argue, there are justifiable legal and moral reasons for treating married and unmarried adults alike. But there are enormous social costs associated with doing so. These costs, I believe, are sufficiently great to justify granting married individuals significant legal, economic, and social benefits that are denied to unmarried people.

No matter what marriage may mean to a particular man and woman, it has clear meaning to others. A married man is a husband, and a married woman is a wife. These identities are independent of anything that may happen in the marriage. They guide others in their dealings with the spouses. They also guide the spouses in their relationships with each other, with children, with relatives, with neighbors, and with everyone else. In other words, the institution of marriage influences how others view married people as well as how spouses view themselves. In this sense, marriage provides a template for a relationship. It provides patterns for domestic life. Married people have something that unmarried partners do not have; they are heirs to a vast system of understood principles that help organize and sustain their lives. They have a structure that is imposed. That structure may limit personal freedom, but it is also the source of many of the well-known benefits that flow from marriage. The boundaries around marriages are the commonly understood, allowable limits of behavior that distinguish marriage from all other kinds of relationships. The social norms that define the institution of marriage also identify married people in important ways that distinguish them from others.

My purpose in this chapter is to distinguish marriage as a relationship between adults from marriage as a social institution. The former view of marriage is increasingly reflected in law and media. Moreover, recent trends in cohabitation and unmarried childbearing suggest that growing numbers of Americans see no inherent distinction between marriage as a social relationship and marriage as an institution. There are potential costs to such trends, and my comments are intended to highlight them.

## DEFINING SOCIAL INSTITUTIONS

From an institutional perspective, a society is a cluster of institutions. Institutions are clusters of social positions (or roles). And social roles are clusters of expectations (or norms). The critical issue, therefore, is that norms, or expectations, are the basis of social life. Expectations about what is and is not appropriate behavior are one source of patterned uniformity. They are also a primary source of conformity. Simply put, social life is orderly because most people conform to social norms most of the time. Some norms are quite formal, such as laws. Most, however, are much less formal, and exist solely as agreed-on conventions. The consequence of violating such rules may be formal sanctions (as when a law is broken). But, more typically, the sanctions are informal. Indeed, the most common sanction is shame, shunning, or simple disapproval. One risks personal reputation and involvement in communal life by breaking the informal rules. These are enormous risks, and most people apparently are unwilling to take them. Social norms are best viewed as soft boundaries around an institutional realm of life. They are soft because the consequences of breaking them are most often informal. They are sometimes broken by some, but are never broken by most.

## Marriage as a Social Institution

I refer to the institution of marriage as *normative marriage* because it is defined by norms, or expectations. These, in short, define what a marriage should be. A normative definition of marriage enumerates the rules that are accepted as legitimate and binding. Such a definition, once developed, explains how and why marriages differ from all other relationships. Since there is no cultural dictionary that would provide such a definition, it is necessary to look elsewhere to find the basic rules that define the institution of marriage. Here the task is to identify the core elements that have gained a broad consensus. Clues to the meaning of marriage can be found in various measures of public opinion, in law, and in religion. I view these three sources as evidence for how Americans think marriage should be organized.

The definition of an institution draws our attention to the consensus about the norms involved. Most critically, there must be broad agreement about the outlines of any institutional framework. Legal, religious, or political pronouncements notwithstanding, an institution exists only to the extent that its outlines are viewed as legitimate. One might argue, in fact, that much of the change we have seen in family structure and function during this century is a reflection of changing beliefs about what is and what is not legitimate in the area of the family. Social institutions change slowly, as large numbers of people come to hold differing values about what is right and wrong. Although there is no simple way to assess consensus about marriage, I believe we can approach this issue by consulting law, religion, and public opinion. Doing so makes it possible to identify those aspects of marriage that are viewed as legitimate. I now turn to a consideration of those dimensions of marriage that define the institution.[1]

## Individual Free Choice and Love

The most widely shared normative aspect of contemporary marriage is the strong association between marriage and love. Mate selection in this country has increasingly become a matter of personal choice in which parents play a smaller and smaller role. The contemporary centrality of romantic love in marriage is a fairly recent norm, and historians have documented the gradual evolution of love and the decline of courtship as guiding principles in mate selection.[2]

The close association of love and contemporary marriage has important consequences for the way marriage is anticipated, understood, and experienced. Love is associated with feelings of security, comfort, and companionship.[3] Ideally, love lasts a lifetime and lovers stay committed forever. Love also implies an erotic component that means lovers experience one another's physical presence as pleasing and stimulating. Romantic love, the hallmark of American courtship (and the greeting card industry), overlooks faults and glorifies and idealizes the other person. It derives emotional gratification from sacrificing for, or providing for, one's beloved.

To the extent that marriage and love are associated, marriage also implies security, companionship, lifelong commitment, erotic attraction, idealization, and altruism. These things are expected from love and from marriage. Moreover, since mate choice is an individual decision guided by love, the significance and meaning of marriage are quite personal. The external reasons and justifications for marriage that once formed the mate-selection process are relatively insignificant. Marriage is now a reflection of personal choice. It is an expression of one's individual personality. Success and failure in marriage are personal successes or failures that cannot easily be attributed to others.

### Maturity

Marriage is associated with maturity and adulthood. American laws and customs reflect such assumptions. Since there are few generally recognizable ways of indicating that a person is mature, marriage is a sign or validation of maturity.

Domestic relations laws define an age at which individuals may marry. Throughout the United States, these minimum ages are usually 18, although marriage is permissible with the court's approval at earlier ages for various reasons. The minimum age laws for marriage presume that the parties can enter into an enforceable contract.

The minimum age at marriage is also the age at which youths are legally emancipated. Parental responsibility for care and support terminates at emancipation. Marriage, in short, may occur when parents are released from their legal obligations to their children—that is, when children are presumed to be mature and capable of self-sufficiency.

In the traditional Judeo-Christian wedding ceremony each newly married partner is described as having left the parental home and dependence on it. A new form of maturity quite different from the dependency of a child is celebrated. As in Genesis: "A man leaves his father and mother and cleaves to his wife and they become one flesh."[4]

### Heterosexuality

Laws have addressed same-sex unions and, despite concerted efforts to legalize them, people of the same sex are everywhere forbidden actually to *marry*. And while there is growing acceptance of homosexuality in general, public support for homosexual marriage has not followed (which is why Vermont refers to legal homosexual unions as "civil unions" rather than marriages). Recent attempts to sanction homosexual unions as marriages have failed in every case. The resistance is best seen as a struggle to redefine normative marriage. Indeed, sociologist James Hunter claims that homosexuality is one of a few central issues over which Americans find themselves clearly divided and competing to define what the norms of American life should be. He believes that with the possible exception of abortion, "few issues in the contemporary culture war generate more raw emotion than the issue of homosexuality [because] few other issues challenge the traditional assumptions of what nature will allow, the boundaries of the moral order, and finally the ideals of middle-class family life more radically."[5] As Hunter notes, proposals to legalize homosexual marriages are a challenge to the traditional conception of marriage. And that is the central point. Heterosexuality is part of the traditional conception of marriage.

### Gender Specialization

Marriage has traditionally defined the husband as the head of the family. A married woman assumes her husband's social and legal identity, as well as his surnames. At the same time, it is fair to say that Americans generally favor equality between the sexes. But wives and husbands occupy different positions in marriage.

The traditional assumption that husbands would be the primary breadwinners and wives the primary homemakers/child-rearers has been replaced by an assumption that men and women should share such tasks. Indeed, most married women today work outside the home, as do two-thirds (68 percent) of wives with young children.[6]

Although there is a general tendency toward less traditional marital roles, little consensus exists. National surveys show that the majority of Americans hold some egalitarian views about spouses (i.e., only a third believe that family life suffers when the wife works; only a quarter believe that the wife's job is to look after the home). However, only half believe that both spouses should contribute to family income. And four in ten Americans endorse a traditional division of roles, with the wife taking care of the home and family and the husband earning the income.[7] Such sentiments are reflected in actual behaviors.

In fact, husbands typically have earnings much greater than those of their wives, and the responsibility for homemaking and childcare actually falls disproportionately on wives today as it has for decades. Working wives contribute about 30 percent of family incomes. The percentage is only slightly higher (40 percent) in families in which the wife works full-time, year-round. The presence of children, especially preschoolers, reduces the likelihood that a wife works as well as the amount she earns if she does work.[8] Married mothers do about two-thirds of all housework. Although this is a decline over what they did a decade earlier, it is an insufficiently large decline to compensate for the increase in paid labor force time for which wives are now responsible.[9]

### Fidelity and Monogamy

In law, sex has served as the symbolic core of marriage, defining it in more obvious and restrictive ways than any other element. To understand the symbolic significance of sex, it helps to analyze sex in marriage as a form of property.

Property is not a thing in itself, but a social relationship among individuals who agree how to behave toward a particular thing. To own something does not imply a bond to that particular thing. Instead, it means that (1) you have a right to use it; (2) other people do not have the right to use it; and (3) you can call on the rest of society to enforce your rights.[10] Sex in marriage satisfies these three conditions: husbands and wives have a right to have sexual intercourse with one another, other people do not have a right to sexual intercourse with either of them while they are married, and either spouse can enlist the assistance of society to enforce his or her sexual rights (e.g., through divorce). As a form of marital property, nothing is more central, or governed by more rules, than sex.

Historically, the law has recognized the vulnerability and potential fragility of the marital relationship and protected this interest through the concept of *consortium*. "Such elements as domestic duties, interaction, affectional intimacy, love, and sexual intercourse are among the factors typically recognized under the law, and when their infringement is deemed an offense according to statute or court decision, monetary damages can be exacted."[11]

Divorce law has typically handled damage done to a marriage by one of the spouses. Laws against adultery by married spouses have been abolished in most states, and, where such laws exist, they are not enforced. Accidental or intentional damages to a marriage by third parties have been handled as consortium offenses. The most serious damage to consortium, however, has traditionally been criminal conversation, the charge brought against the lover of an adulterous spouse. Since sexual exclusivity is the core of marriage, this type of offense may threaten the marriage itself. Indeed, adultery is so serious a threat to marriage that when its discovery provokes homicide, the criminal charge may be reduced from murder to manslaughter.[12]

In a contemporary world in which as many as 40 percent of marriages are predicted to end in divorce, the norm of fidelity means that each spouse has agreed, by virtue of the marriage, to restrict themselves from engaging in sexual relations with others so long as they are married. No spouse, therefore, may legitimately pursue another person for romantic purposes while married. And that is the critical meaning of monogamy. Overwhelming majorities of Americans endorse this view in national surveys, and the incidence of infidelity is surprisingly low according to scientific studies.[13]

## Parenthood

With few exceptions, married women and men become mothers and fathers. Only one in ten (11 percent) of ever-married women are still childless by age 44. And half of all married women younger than 35 who were childless in 1990 reported that they expected to have a child at some point in the future.[14]

The close association of marriage and childbearing is the reason for the current concern over illegitimacy. Nonmarital childbirth is clear evidence of an emerging belief that parenthood is not restricted to marriage. And while the law is in broad agreement with such a view, there are good reasons to see things otherwise.

Practically, when a child is born to a married couple (or born shortly after marriage), the couple is presumed to be entitled to custody of that child. Thus, the only action that a man must take to receive custody of a child is to be married to the child's mother when the child is born (or shortly thereafter). So, while childbirth clearly resolves the maternity question, marriage is the simplest method to establish a rebuttable presumption of the more complex issue of paternity. In this sense, marriage is the most elementary method of connecting every child with an adult male who becomes socially responsible for the child.

Parental obligations are now based more on blood than marriage. And fathers who are not married may be required to provide for their children through various legal and social mechanisms. However, without a need for state involvement, the married man becomes the social father of children born to his wife. The obligations associated with custody are pervasive and, until recently, gendered. Men have been responsible for providing for their children, just as they have been responsible for economically supporting their wives. Women, on the other hand, have been responsible for the care and nurture of children.

Unmarried men who do not live with the mothers of their children, it would seem, are uninterested in assuming the social and legal role of father to their children. This may also be true of married men. However, the large difference between these two types of fathers is the automatic attribution of enduring and enforceable obligations for married men. A married man has, by virtue of his status as a husband, voluntarily assumed responsibilities associated with parenthood. He has, moreover, announced his willingness to do this by marrying his wife. His role as social father to his children is proclaimed by marriage. By his marriage, a man has made a public statement about himself as a father, or potential father, and all that goes with this role. Even if his marriage should fail, his parental obligations will not be eliminated, though they may be attenuated. Marital paternity differs from the nonmarital variety, therefore, primarily in the public statement it makes about the man.

## DE-INSTITUTIONALIZING MARRIAGE

With respect to their marriages, men and women are increasingly viewed as "spouses" rather than "husbands" or "wives." For example, the marital unit has been defined as an entity greater than either partner in it. Spouses are subordinate, in certain respects, to the unity created by their marriage. By virtue of their intimate, ongoing relationship, interdependencies develop that unite the spouses in complex and pervasive ways. Historically, the unity of marriage was achieved by abolishing the identity of the wife, who lost autonomy with respect to such things as contracts, credit, earnings, property, and child custody. The unity of the marriage has meant that spouses enjoy certain privileges not granted to unmarried persons. For example, husbands and wives have traditionally been able to refuse to testify against one another. And, as noted, the law has recognized the interests of spouses in the unity created by their marriage by compensating for loss of consortium.

In addition to a view of marriage as a unity, the law has also sought to protect the harmony of the relationship. This means that spouses are denied access to the courts in matters pertaining to their own ongoing relationships—wives cannot sue husbands; children cannot sue parents. Therefore, spouses have been enjoined from suing one another for torts such as negligence (intraspousal tort immunity). And husbands have been immune from prosecution for the rape of their wives. The justification for such intraspousal limitations and immunities is that the involvement of a third party, such as a court, in marital disputes is likely to exacerbate them and jeopardize marital harmony.

Presently, the legal trend with respect to civil suits is to eliminate intraspousal tort immunities because they deny married persons the same protection that unmarried people enjoy. Indeed, the majority of states have eliminated such immunities.[15] Similar trends are evident with respect to certain criminal acts. For example, spouse battering has now been defined as a crime in many states (especially when the wife is the victim). Until the 1970s, the husband who raped his wife typically was prosecuted on other grounds, if he was prosecuted at all. The use of force, for example, might have brought charges of assault and battery. However, since the mid- to late 1970s, most states have amended their rape statutes to permit husbands to be charged under certain circumstances. Typically, the husband and wife must be living separately (usually under a judicial decree of separation) and force must be used for a nonconsensual sexual act to qualify as rape of one's wife.

The testimonial privilege that spouses have traditionally enjoyed has meant that a spouse might refuse to testify against a partner. Immunity has not been an absolute, because spouses have been allowed to testify about injuries inflicted by the other spouse on the testifying spouse or a child. And when one spouse offered to testify against another, the issue became whether the immunity belonged to the defendant or to the potential witness.[16] However, such privileges have now been severely limited or abolished completely.

The primary concern in matters of children and childbearing today is the well being of the child. Therefore, the numerous legal disabilities suffered by illegitimate children (e.g., limits on inheritance or eligibility for government transfer payments) were declared unconstitutional by the U.S. Supreme Court in a number of decisions between 1968 and 1978. Married and unmarried childbearing are increasingly indistinguishable in law.

In general, states have amended their family laws to reflect a more gender-neutral view of the marriage relationship. This has often meant that the marriage as an entity is less central and the individuals in it more central. The model of patriarchal marriage is no longer the guide for family law. Increasingly, married persons are treated much like their unmarried counterparts in law.

## CONCLUSION

There are those who would argue that married people should be viewed as no different from unmarried people. According to this view, the rights and responsibilities of all people should be equal. Marriage should not be privileged in law or elsewhere. To confer such a privilege, some believe, will perpetuate invidious distinctions between the married and the unmarried. Indeed, there is also much evidence that marriage is being deinstitutionalized, in law most obviously, but also in popular culture. Cohabitation is no longer stigmatized. Unmarried childbearing, likewise, is increasingly common and essentially indistinguishable in law from married childbearing. I would like to conclude with some brief thoughts about the implications of such trends.

My work for the past few years has shown that marriage produces measurable and significant benefits for the adults involved.[17] Married people are healthier, happier, more successful, and more productive. Married people are more generous to others and more likely to join organizations devoted to community improvement. Married individuals continue to benefit from the assumptions made about them. Married men, especially, are viewed as more mature, independent, and trustworthy than their unmarried counter- parts. Regardless of the details of the particular relationship involved, married men and women derive significant benefits from their status. Were this not so, cohabiting individuals would be more similar to married people. A decade of research has convincingly shown this to be not so.

There is also unequivocal evidence that children fare better in marriages than in other forms of relationships. Whether a child is born to an un- married woman, or is the product of divorce, the long-term consequences are comparable. Such children are less successful as adults, have higher rates of depression and other psychological disorders, and are more likely to experience poverty and divorce. They complete fewer years of schooling and drop out of school more often than children from married households.

Finally, there is the obvious yet unknown collective cost we pay, as a society, for the de-institutionalization of marriage. The microeconomic costs are already well known: higher rates of poverty, welfare receipt, Medicaid, public assistance, hospital admissions, suicide, chronic and acute illnesses, and accidents, and lower productivity and earnings. If we were able to es- timate the macroeconomic costs of divorce, unmarried childbearing, and lower marriage rates, we would surely discover that we pay an enormous price for the retreat from marriage. Seen from this perspective, marriage is an important public health and safety issue. It is a legitimate concern of the state, and we should make every effort to promote the institution.

To grant preferential rights to those who marry and remain married, therefore, makes good sense from a public policy perspective. Whether it also accords with contemporary beliefs about fairness, equal protection, and public morality is another question entirely. My own sense is that most Americans accept a distinction between marriage and nonmarriage. And only recently have a few professionals considered things otherwise.

The view of marriage as a private contract negotiated by the spouses themselves is driven, in part, by a compassionate concern that traditional marriage denied women equal protection in law. The de-institutionalization of marriage is also a reflection of an egalitarian ethic that views unmar- ried people as no less entitled to the prerogatives of civic life than husbands and wives. In short, the move to de-institutionalize marriage is a practical consequence of the concern over equal protection.

Consider only a few of the vexing questions we now face as we consider such moral issues. Should unmarried people enjoy the same legal and social privileges granted to married adults? Should all zoning and housing laws be neutral with respect to marital status? Should children born to unmarried parents be treated the same as those born into a marriage? Should homo- sexuals be allowed to marry? Should welfare benefits be the same for married and unmarried parents? Should married people pay the same federal and state taxes as unmarried people? Should children conceived in vitro or by artificial insemination and born to a surrogate mother be treated the same as those conceived, gestated, and born in marriage? There are strong egalitarian arguments in support of each position. At the same time, each idea amounts to a significant challenge to traditional assumptions embodied in the social institution of marriage.

Is it possible to grant all individuals equal standing in law without de-institutionalizing marriage? In fact, it is not. But the institution of marriage is much more than law. Indeed, for most of human history, marriage was totally unregulated by the state.[18] Today, for almost all spouses, law assumes psychological significance in marriage only when the relationship ends in divorce. Thus, whether or not marriage is distinguished from other forms of intimate relationships in law is unlikely to affect the way people view marriage as a social institution—at least not immediately. However, the symbolic effect of de-institutionalizing legal marriage will gradually erode the social distinctions associated with marriage. Law may not be an important cause of behavior in the short term, but it is quite important in symbolizing and codifying values. For that reason, I believe the current legal project to de-institutionalize marriage is unwise.

How then are we to justify any legal distinction between married and unmarried people? There are two simple answers to this question. First, we must recognize the collective benefits all people enjoy because couples get married. I suggest that we begin with significant macroeconomic benefits (e.g., lower rates of poverty, higher adult productivity, healthier and better educated children). Second, we must recognize that married people deserve (in a moral sense) certain legal privileges in return for the sacrifices they make in their personal lives. Such legal benefits are intended to symbolize the value Americans place on marriage.

Married people are justifiably entitled to different treatment in law because marriage requires different behaviors. At a minimum, married people voluntarily limit their personal autonomy in many ways. The soft boundaries that define the institution of marriage are, essentially, self-imposed limits on behavior, or sacrifices of personal autonomy. These sacrifices are sufficient grounds for differential treatment in law. They may be regarded as a strong form of social control, voluntarily accepted by most spouses as part of their marriage vows. Unless we discover an equally effective and economical form of social control, and until we are willing to accept the collective costs of doing so, we should be cautious of de-institutionalizing marriage.

I believe it is justifiable to grant marriage legal and social privileges. I believe the collective benefits of marriage justify such a distinction. Indeed, those whose thoughts and actions influence public opinion and law have an obligation to promote marriage in this way. Presumably, most Americans accept the legal and economic privileges that are presently granted by state and federal governments to those who own their homes, to those who send their children to college, to those who save for their retirement, and those who donate to charities, to mention only a few examples. Marriage is no less beneficial to the collective health of our society than any of these other actions. Indeed, it is more so. We should keep this in mind whenever we consider the possibility of changing the institution of marriage.

## NOTES

1. Steven L. Nock, *Marriage in Men's Lives* (New York: Oxford University Press, 1998).

2. See Beth L. Bailey, *From Front Porch to Back Seat: Courtship in Twentieth-Century America* (Baltimore: Johns Hopkins University Press, 1988); Ellen K. Rothman, *Hands and Hearts: A History of Courtship in America* (Cambridge: Harvard University Press, 1984).

3. Zick Rubin, *Liking and Loving: An Invitation to Social Psychology* (New York: Holt Rinehart, and Winston, 1973).

4. Gen. 2.24 (RSV).

5. James Davison Hunter, *Culture Wars: The Struggle to Define America* (New York: Basic Books, 1989), 189.

6. Daphne G. Spain and Suzanne Bianchi, *Balancing Act: Motherhood, Marriage, and Employment among American Women* (New York: The Russell Sage Foundation, 1996).

7. General Social Surveys, 1972–1995 [machine-readable data file] (Chicago: National Opinion Research Center, 1994).

8. Suzanne Bianchi, "Changing Economic Roles of Women and Men," in *State of the Union: America in the 1990s*, ed. Reynolds Farley (New York: Russell Sage Foundation, 1995) 1:107–154.

9. John P. Robinson, "Who's Doing the Housework?" *American Demographics* 12 (1988):24–28.

10. Randall Collins and Scott Coltrane, *The Sociology of Marriage and the Family*, 3rd ed. (Chicago: Nelson-Hall, 1991).

11. William J. O'Donnell and David A. Jones, *The Law of Marriage and Marital Alternatives* (Lexington, Mass.: D. C. Heath, 1982), 66.

12. Harry D. Krause, *Family Law in a Nutshell* (Eagan, Minn.: West Publishing, 1995), 152.

13. Edward O. Laumann, John H. Gagnon, Robert T. Michael, and Stuart Michaels, *The Social Organization of Sexuality: Sexual Practices in the United States* (Chicago: University of Chicago Press, 1994).

14. Martin O'Connell, "Late Expectations: Childbearing Patterns of American Women for the 1990s," *Current Population Reports*, Series P-23, No. 176.

15. Krause, *Family Law in a Nutshell*, 137.

16. Ibid., 151.

17. Steven L. Nock, "The Consequences of Premarital Fatherhood," *American Sociological Review* 63(April 1998): 250–263.

18. Mary Ann Glendon, *The Transformation of Family Law: State, Law, and Family in the United States and Western Europe* (Chicago: University of Chicago Press, 1989).

# 2

# Community Involvement and Its Limits in Marriage and Families

## Margaret F. Brinig

## INTRODUCTION

In late 1998, the Washington, D.C.–area newspapers were full of reports about a right-to-life case involving former news broadcaster Hugh Finn, who was hospitalized in a persistent vegetative state for several years following an automobile accident. His wife, Michele, wished to discontinue life support, but several relatives, including Hugh's parents and two of his seven siblings, questioned her motives and unsuccessfully took the case through the Virginia court system. The parents contended that they would care for Hugh if Michelle no longer could. Eventually Virginia Governor Gilmore and a local delegate intervened in the case; they claimed standing because the situation did not fit the state statute authorizing termination of life support. The relatives' suit was dismissed, intravenous feeding was discontinued, and Hugh Finn died on October 9, 1998. The legislature awarded Mrs. Finn money to compensate her for the state's "frivolous lawsuit."[1]

The *Troxel* case[2] (in which grandparents sought the right to visit their grandchildren over parental objection), the Washington statute that governed *Troxel*,[3] and the saga of Cuban-born Elian Gonzales,[4] where a father's right to custody of his motherless son was arguably vulnerable to attack by more distant relatives, the Immigration and Naturalization Service, the State Department, and anti-communists in general, also illustrate both the fervor with which the broader community justifies its involvement with families and the extremes to which this involvement can spread. In constitutional language, advocates point out the rights of extended family members to continue or strengthen ties to children. On the other side, parents and spouses claim their own privacy and autonomy rights not to have outsiders second-guess or interfere with their nuclear families.

Although many writings about marriage extol its virtues as a building block of community and society, few, especially in the legal context, look at the relationship from inside out. The thesis here, however, is that good family relationships need larger communities to help them to begin right, to support them, and to keep them strong. However, I will argue that the usefulness of outsider involvement is limited. In legal terms, we reach these limits when third-party claimants assert rights to access spouses and children in ways that conflict with the autonomy families need.

This chapter begins with the description of the ways community aids—in fact is essential to—marriage. Relationships invite community recognition, or what I call covenant, when they possess characteristics of permanence and unconditional love.[5] Once the community trusts that partners view each other unselfishly and over the long run, it lends vital support, informal and sometimes formal, to the marriage. However, this community sanction and support does not give individual outsiders the power to interfere with the autonomy that married couples possess. When third parties claim "rights" in the relationship they undermine marriages.

## WAYS IN WHICH COMMUNITIES ENHANCE MARRIAGE AND PARENTING

### Informal Enhancements

#### Sources of Information about the Relationships

Our social networks educate us about our family relationships. A continuum extends from the proverbial locker-room conversation about sexual exploits to the more useful things parents teach children about relationships and parenting. This informal education goes on while we are still children, but parents remain sources of support and guidance long after we become adults. Grandparents and others in the wider community also provide cultural guidelines within which to pursue relationships as well as experience about lasting relationships. This type of help is particularly evident in African-American and first-generation American communities.

Sometimes, as the section on formalized support describes, the provision of information is more structured. In some religious traditions and even for nonreligious couples electing covenant marriage in Arizona and Louisiana, couples must attend marriage preparation classes. Generally speaking, this more formalized community involvement is designed to continue during marriage as well. With arranged marriages, the extended families not only lend their support but also screen potential marriage partners.

## *Investment*

Historically, many families seeking to immigrate to this country have first sent a potential high earner along to establish a foothold and then pay for the others' passage.[6] Such investments by families can also be made by the wider community. In the U.S. business and corporate worlds, much has been said about the ability of new Asian immigrants to pool assets and earnings to establish funds from which all community members can draw. Observers have credited much of the success of the small businesses run by first-generation Asian Americans to their cooperative financial support (along with the tremendous industry of the individuals involved).[7]

## *"Venting"*

When we've had rough days at the job, whether outside or inside the home, our families, and particularly our spouses, are helpful listeners to our complaints. Social science support for the importance of this function is quite extensive. In fact, a recent paper by Bryant and Conger[8] both reviews the literature and establishes a new point—even in marriages of more than fourteen years, relationship-specific support by outsiders significantly predicted more stable and successful marriages, while friends in common and general personal support did not.

## *Dispute Resolution*

Families often provide the best settings to resolve disputes, especially when the wider support group is brought in. The Native-American community began the Navajo Peacemaker Court in 1982 because the civil state courts were contrary to Navajo tradition of having the perpetrator and the victim directly "talk out" the problem, enlisting help from family and clans. For example, in domestic violence situations, the Peacemaker Court would restore the victim her former self—called her state of *hozhó*. The perpetrator, with the assistance of his family and clan, do the restoring.[9]

## *Conventions, Behavior Channeling, and Union Building*

As mentioned earlier, spouses, families, and the wider community are useful in establishing morals or, more broadly, culture. Culture in this sense includes such mundane items as whether and in what way to celebrate one's anniversary (hence the lists of gifts, from paper to diamonds), Valentine's Day, or Father's Day. More important, conventions and behavior-channeling include expectations about the duration of marriage; what justifies leaving or divorcing one's spouse; what kind of conduct is acceptable, what cruel. Empirical research shows, for example, that the percentage of divorced people living in the state in which a person lived when he or she was 16 predicts the age when that person will marry (a higher percentage of divorced people predicts an older age at first marriage) and even how much education a woman would receive (a higher percentage of divorce in the population predicts fewer completed years of school).[10] We know, for example, that in places where there are more births to unwed parents or more divorces, and therefore a culture of single parenting or divorce, more unwed births and divorce will occur in later periods, even holding other explanatory variables constant.[11]

### The Influence of Religious Communities on Relationships

Many observations suggest a linkage between wider community involvement and religion. In most countries religious authorities (and, in some countries, only religious authorities) can marry people. Marriages "in" a religion can subject couples to a set of ecclesiastical as well as secular rules that can strengthen the marriage. Certainly there are strong marriages that are not part of a religious tradition. But if, for example, Catholics and fundamentalist Protestants divorce at about the same rate as the general public,[12] is it strong religious tradition or personal adherence to religious tenets that is important in maintaining marital stability?

Most studies find that the stated religious preference at the time of marriage has little effect on marital stability. Two Methodists marrying, holding other things constant, will divorce about as often as two Catholics, two Jews, or two atheists. A study by the George Barna research group[13] found that born-again Christians are slightly more likely to divorce than the average American (with rates of 27 as opposed to 23 percent of a group of more than three thousand randomly selected adults). A more recent Associated Press article[14] published statistics showing that the so-called Bible Belt states had higher divorce rates than the national average. Although this piece noted that Protestants seem to divorce more often than Catholics, the difference seems to be decreasing.[15] (Catholics remarry less frequently, however.)[16]

Religious intensity seems more important than affiliation, however, so that differences in religious observance and the importance of God in one's life do affect couples' ability to stay together. Call and Heaton[17] found that when both spouses attend religious services regularly, the couple has the lowest risk of divorce, while differences in church attendance increase the risk of divorce. They posit that church attendance "can either provide a common forum for a couple's religious orientation and family commitment or become a conflict for couples who do not share the same levels of personal dedication." They note that joint participation in church gives a family a sense of purpose and similar values that increase family commitment and social integration. Like other studies, the Call and Heaton study found that all significant religious affiliation influences disappear once the authors controlled for demographic differences. They continued to find significant results in cases where the spouses differed in church activities, because "joint socialization in religious teachings that support family values and stability affirm the importance of marriage and family," and "joint participation in friendship networks provides a greater potential for interaction with friends in a context that generally supports positive communication between spouses."[18]

### Community Influence on Marriage through Community Size

Attachment to the community in which the couple lives may also influence marital stability and that is at least in part a function of community size. For example, South and Spitze found that home ownership increased marital stability because of the couples' increased long-term stakes, and that living in a large metropolitan area (whether in a suburb or central city) decreased it, because of the increased autonomy and anonymity urban areas provide.[19] Likewise, Frank Buckley and I found that divorce rates from 1979 to 1991 were higher both in metropolitan areas and in "frontier" states.[20]

### Formalized Support

#### Arranged Marriage

I have been exceptionally fortunate in reading the stories of many students who have shared with me something of their lives and their families. Two in particular have written about arranged marriages in twentieth-century America. One, a second-generation Indian American, sent me an exceptionally moving and interesting account of her arranged marriage. Not surprisingly, as an American-educated and involved young person, she was skeptical that her parents could find someone right for her. Surprisingly, she fell in love with the man they arranged for her to marry after her first year in law school, though she became acquainted with him largely over the phone and met him briefly only just before their wedding.[21]

On balance, she thinks they are more successful than many of their Western counterparts.

> There are numerous benefits of arranged marriages that may not always exist in the "love" marriage. The marriage is generally not based on fleeting sexual desires. I believe this is one of the primary reasons arranged marriages are more stable than love marriages. The husband and the wife will have similar religious backgrounds, family friends, and cultural values to rely on if their marriage is having problems. In addition, both the husband and wife's families are very supportive of the marriage because they were the ones who arranged it. An arranged marriage is not just a union between a husband and his wife, but also a union between two families.

The community's involvement in Hindu weddings and marriages is evident in "The Song of the Groom's Anointment," or "Âbtauni," that is sung in rural India when the bridegroom is rubbed with saffron prior to his returning home,[22] and illustrates the involvement of the extended family in the successful union:

> In a gold cup
> I make the saffron paste
> And rub it on the bridegroom's body
> The Brahman utters prayers,
> The women sing their joy.
> The mother wipes his mouth with her sari
> The father's sister pencils his eyes
> The elder brother's wife fans his head,
> The women sing their joy.
> The father's brother's wife wipes his mouth
> The elder sister pencils his eyes
> The mother's brother's wife fans his head,
> The women sing their joy.[23]

Similarly, a Navajo-American student wrote:[24]

From the second quarter of this century to the present, the tradition of arranged marriages has been replaced in favor of allowing couples to choose their own spouses. Interestingly, my own observation of the success of these two different marriage processes—if success is measured in longevity—has been that the arranged marriage survives longer than those based on emotion. This does not suggest that an arranged marriage is without affection; rather, people whose judgment is not "clouded" by the titillation of love make the initial decision of marriage.

In the Navajo tradition,

marriages were arranged between families, which included not only the parents, but also grandparents, uncles, and aunts of the "husband to be and wife to be." Furthermore, traditionally the bride and groom really did not have a say as to whom they would marry. Negotiations between the families included what the groom's family would give to the bride's family—horses, sheep, cows, jewelry—a sort of dowry. A date for the ceremony was chosen. More importantly, the clans of the couple were stated and approved by the family to ensure against intermarriage. "The bloodlines were kept clean and everyone was knowledgeable about the clanship system and the whole society was kept in balance in that manner."

Thus, while arranged marriages may be stable because they did not depend on expectations of romance,[25] as my students believe, perhaps the qualities of community support, interrelatedness, and approval also make a difference.

## The Rationale for Community Involvement

Does the community become involved to strengthen marriages (advancing the individual goals of the couple) or is the relationship more circular than that—one in which marriages also strengthen the community? The civil law terminology of the "marital community," like the "Little Commonwealth" of the Plymouth colonies, suggests instead that marriage and family are separate from the larger society, though mirroring it.[26]

Are community involvement and participation necessary for a strong marriage? Sociological evidence suggests that frequent contact with support mechanisms, family and community, does help marriages. Traditions after the marriage ceremony itself may not encourage such participation, while the modern emphasis on autonomy and mobility work against involvement except when the married person asks for it.

All emphasis on community runs counter to another distinctly American trend—that of family autonomy. For example, in the early Puritan colonies, families were expected to deal with their own problem children.[27] It was only if they could not that the community, through its appointed elders, would adjudge whether a son was "rebellious" and ungovernable by his parents. In a similar vein, it was the head of household (usually the husband) who was responsible for his wife's and children's attendance at church services.[28] A number of legal academics have written favorably and unfavorably about autonomy. For example, Carl Schneider has argued that courts give families autonomy particularly with respect to dealing with children, for a number of reasons, among which are the courts' relative lack of knowledge and expertise.[29] Elizabeth and Robert Scott, as part of their fiduciary principle, treat being "left alone" (autonomy) as part of the reward of good parenting.[30] However, Jana Singer criticizes at least some grants of autonomy because they give the dominant adult (usually a male) so much power over the less powerful in the household, which might lead to exploitation—physical, sexual, or financial—of the wife and child.[31]

Marriage, like adoption or biological parenting, carries with it a commitment toward permanence that places it in a different category of relational interests than if it were temporary.

A "justifiable expectation . . . that the relationship will continue indefinitely" permits parties to invest themselves in the relationship with a reasonable belief that the likelihood of future benefits warrants the attendant risks and inconvenience. There is a clear analogy between the motivational factors that influence human investment and those that influence economic investments. Jeremy Bentham believed that private ownership of property is more likely to maximize social utility than is collective ownership because "the human motivations which result in production are . . . such that they will not operate in the absence of secure expectations about future enjoyment of product." The will to labor and the will to invest "depend on rules which assure people that they will indeed be permitted to enjoy a substantial share of the product as the price of their labor or their risk of savings."[32]

One obvious way in which the state's lack of interference privileges families (abuses of that power aside) stems from the additional opportunities for agreement and growth of parenting bestowed on marriage. When others—putative fathers, grandparents, well-meaning strangers—cannot second-guess decisions, families can thrive.

One of the real hopes behind the covenant marriage movement in Louisiana,[33] and, to a less publicized extent, Arizona,[34] has been the early and continuing involvement with couples of families and, perhaps, broader communities. Those who elect the covenant marriage option in either state must undergo at least five counseling meetings with clergy or a lay professional before the wedding. The couple commits to seek out a counselor—ideally the same one—and try to resolve marriage difficulties before resorting to divorce in all but the most extreme cases. Research on divorce has found that counseling stressing communication skills is particularly effective[35] and, perhaps more important, that positive relationships with family and community strengthen marriage. For example, Lawrence Kurdek found, based on nearly four hundred couples' self-reports (holding other demographic and personality variables constant), that husbands and wives who had more stable and high-quality marriages (after a year of marriage) reported significantly better satisfaction with their level of social support.[36]

Although the principles behind the proposals in both Arizona and Louisiana are overwhelmingly supported, according to survey research, only about 40 percent of the people surveyed in Louisiana knew that the new legislation existed. When a graduate student and sociologist applied for a marriage license in one-fourth of all Louisiana counties, they found that the "Not covenant marriage" box had been checked for them in some instances, while in virtually none was the new law explained. In short, sociologist Steven L. Nock explains, "Virtually nobody hears about the option when they apply for a license. So the only people asking for covenant marriages are those who heard about it in church."[37]

These examples, not meant to be exhaustive, illustrate that community involvement strengthens marriages and families generally. On the other hand, excessive community involvement may undermine marriage.

## REACHING THE LIMIT

As might be expected, the positive reach of community involvement in marriages, and families more generally, has its limits. Outsiders threaten marriage when they interfere with autonomy; that is, when the third parties acquire legal "rights" to make decisions that should be within the province of spouses. Problems arise when persons within marriages and families begin defining their relations with spouse and family in terms of "rights" instead of feelings and moral obligations, as many have noted.[38] That was a major concern of the U.S. Supreme Court in *Michael H. v. Gerald D,*[39] a case involving a challenge to the California statutory presumption of legitimacy for children born within ongoing marriages. The challenge was brought by the birth father of a child born of the wife's adulterous relationship. Later the child herself, through a guardian, was joined as a party. Justice Scalia wrote about the child's claim: "When the husband or wife contests the legitimacy of their child, the stability of the marriage has already been shaken. In contrast, allowing a claim of illegitimacy to be pressed by the child—or, more accurately, by a court-appointed guardian ad litem—may well disrupt an otherwise peaceful union."[40] In the Court's opinion, the biological father had no protectable liberty interest in his relationship with the child, because these were limited by the "substantive parental rights [of] the natural father of a child conceived within, and born into, an extant marital union that wishes to embrace the child."[41] The biological father had no right to develop a relationship of any kind with the child.

Even if the Court had accepted Michael's claim, it might not have been the most effective channel for preserving his relationship with the child Victoria. A more successful strategy might have been to work on his relationship with Gerald and Carole, the adults involved, rather than to attempt to vindicate his constitutional rights.[42] In this sense, a limit to community involvement is reached when we are talking about relationships that are in effect "beyond law."[43] Thus, in both the unmarried-father and grandparent visitation cases we have a situation akin to the deep and thoroughly unenforceable implied contract between parent and child. Children can't assert legal rights to be nurtured or educated by their parents, though they clearly have moral ones.[44]

I suggest that autonomy also prevents granting outside "rights" in cases of nonparent visitation like *Troxel* and the other grandparent cases.[45] Because of the pluralism in American family forms, however, some interests of people who have served as stepparents, co-parents in same-sex relationships, and foster parents need to be recognized (and may be the same as parental interests under other legal doctrines like estoppel)[46] but not hardened into legal "rights,"[47] particularly when the child is in an ongoing, intact family relationship. In family law terms, granting rights to third parties disrupts the intimacy and autonomy necessary for families—marriages and children—to thrive.

## CONCLUSION

Communities are vital to marriage and parenting. Informal communities should be encouraged socially and through channeling legislation.[48] Turning these informal ties into legal rights destroys the relationships. Thus,

[w]here a right exists, we prima facie prefer the individual, as the law of substantive due process illustrates. But the rights schema is often inapposite in the family context, since there a right against the government is also a right against other family members. And because we dislike compromising a right against the government, we are inhibited from looking for ways to encourage compromises or even discussion within the family. Indeed the very appeal to law—to an external set of standards enforced by might—is atomistic in that it circumvents the (no doubt idealized) standards of family decision: private persuasion and eventual accommodation based on solicitude for the person with whom one disagrees.[49]

The Finn, *Troxel,* and Elian Gonzales situations present us with a good opportunity to reexamine the need for community involvement in families. At the same time, however, these cases demonstrate the strength of the emotions involved and the problems arising when splinters of legal rights replace more normal—and natural—bonds of affection. There are limits to legal power and limits to the explanatory power of economics. The limit of both is love.

## NOTES

1. Vrooke A. Masters and Charles Babington, "Glendenning Faults Gilmore for His Role in Finn Case; Va. Right-to-Die Battle Viewed with Dismay," *Washington Post* B1 (October 6, 1998); Steve Twomey, "The Finns Deserve True Conservatives," *Washington Post* B1 (October 5, 1998).

2. *Troxel v. Glanville,* 530 U.S. 57, (2000).

3. Wash. Rev. Code § 26.10.160(3) (1998).

4. *Gonzales v. Reno,* 2000 WL 492102 (Fla. Cir. Ct. 2000).

5. Margaret F. Brinig, *From Contract to Covenant: Beyond the Law and Economics of the Family* (Cambridge: Harvard University Press, 2000); Margaret F. Brinig and Steven Nock, *Covenant and Contract,* 12 Regent U.L. Rev. 9 (1999).

6. See, e.g., Helen Thomas, *Front Row at the White House* (New York: Scribner, 1999), 3–19.

7. Eric A. Posner, *The Regulation of Groups: The Influence of Legal and Nonlegal Sanctions on Collective Action,* 63 U. Chi. L. Rev. 133–197 (1996).

8. Chalandra M. Bryant and Rand D. Conger, "Marital Success and Domains of Social Support in Long-Term Relationships: Does the Influence of Network Members Ever End?" 61 *Journal of Marriage and the Family* (1999): 437–451.

9. James W. Zion and Elsie B. Zion, *Hozhó Sokeé—Stay Together Nicely: Domestic Violence Under Navajo Common Law,* 25 Ariz. St. L.J. 407–426 (1991).

10. Margaret F. Brinig and Steven L. Nock, "I Only Want Trust:" *Norms, Trust and Autonomy,* <http://qsilver.queensu.ca/law/isFLJune2001/paperbrinignock/htm> (seen Sept. 17, 2001), in progress. Data are from the NSFH; details available from the author, University of Iowa. The paper concerns the development and effect of trust norms on families.

11. Margaret F. Brinig and Douglas W. Allen, *"These Boots Are Made for Walking": Why Most Divorce Filers Are Women,* 2 Am. L. & Econ. Rev. 126–169

(2000); Margaret F. Brinig and F. H. Buckley, "The Price of Virtue," *Public Choice* 98 (1999): 111–129, tables 3 and 4.

12. Maja Beckstrom, "Pollster's Data Tell Churches How Their Believers Behave," *Commercial Appeal (Memphis)* 16A (August 17, 1996).

13. Ibid.

14. "Bible Belt States Struggling with Divorce," *Iowa City (Iowa) Press-Citizen* 7A (November 13, 1999).

15. William Sander, "Catholicism and Marriage in the United States," *Demography* 30 (1993): 373–384; Bob Mims, "Stats Show Mormons Buck Secularization," *Salt Lake Tribune* (March 6, 1999).

16. Barbara F. Wilson and Sally C. Clarke, "Remarriages: A Demographic Profile," 13 *Journal of Family Issues* 13 (1992):123–141.

17. Vaughn R. A. Call and Tim B. Heaton, "Religious Influence on Marital Stability," *Journal for the Scientific Study of Religion* 36 (1997):382–393.

18. Ibid., 391.

19. Scott J. South and Glenna Spitze, "Determinants of Divorce over the Marital Life Course," *American Sociological Review* 51 (1986):583–590.

20. Margaret F. Brinig and Frank H. Buckley, *No Fault Laws and At-Fault People,* 18 Int'l Rev. Law & Econ. 325–340 (1998).

21. Suhana S. Rai, Final Paper for Perspectives on the Individual, Family and Social Institutions, George Mason University School of Law, Spring, 1999. For other accounts, see Yasmin Alibhai-Brown, "Marriage of Minds Not Hearts," *New Statesman and Society* 6 (1993) 28–29; Usha M. Apte, *The Sacrament of Marriage in Hindu Society from Vedic Period to Dharm'a-sastras* (Delhi: Ajanta Publications, 1978), 37–39; Chanchal Kumar Chatterjee, *Studies in the Rites and Rituals of Hindu Marriage in Ancient India* (Calcutta: Sanskrit Pustak Bhandar, 1978), 82–84; and Bala Swaminathan, *Love Match and Arranged Marriage* (1995), available online: http://www.cs.wustl.edu/~bs/essays/marriages.html.

22. William G. Archer, *Songs for the Bride: Wedding Rites of Rural India* (New York: Columbia University Press, 1985).

23. Ibid.,177.

24. Annette Tsinnajinnie Brown, Final Paper, Perspectives in the Individual, the Family and Social Institutions, College of Law, University of Iowa, Spring 2000.

25. Not all arranged marriage forms seem more successful than love matches. A study of divorce rates in China using a 1985 survey sample from two provinces and Shanghai, including more than 13,307 women, found that the arranged marriages ended in divorce more than twice as often as so-called "free choice" marriages. Liao Cailian and Tim B. Heaton, "Divorce Trends and Differentials in China," *Journal of Comparative Family Studies* 23 (1992): 413–429, 422. See also Xu Xiaohe and Martin King Whyte, "Love Matches and Arranged Marriages: A Chinese Replication," *Journal of Marriage and the Family* 52 (1990): 709–723.

26. The "Little Commonwealth" statement comes from Governor John Winthrop's speech, A Modell of Christian Charity, in 2 Winthrop Papers 292, 294 (Mass. Histor. Soc. 1931) (sermon preached aboard *Arabella*, 1630).

27. Sutton, John R. 1981. Stubborn Children: Law and Socialization of Deviance in the Puritan Colonies, 15 Fam. L. Q. 31–64.

28. Hening [Va. Session Laws] 434 (March, 1657–1658); 2 Hening [Va. Session Laws] 165–166 (December 1662, art. IV).

29. Carl E. Schneider and Margaret F. Brinig, *An Invitation to Family Law: Principles, Processes, and Perspectives* 3.7–3.10. (St. Paul, Minn.: West, 2000); Carl E. Schneider, *Religion and Child Custody,* 25 U. Mich. J.L. Reform 879–906 (1992).

30. Elizabeth S. Scott and Robert E. Scott, *Parents as Fiduciaries,* 81 Va. L. Rev. 2401–2476 (1995). For a description of such arrangements in an unusual setting, see Irvin Altman, *Polygamous Family Life: The Case of Contemporary Mormon Fundamentalists,* 1996 Utah L. Rev. 367–391.

31. Jana B. Singer, *The Privatization of Family Law,* 1992 Wis. L. Rev. 1442–1567.

32. Bruce C. Hafen, *The Constitutional Status of Marriage, Kinship, and Sexual Privacy,* 81 Mich. L. Rev. 463–574 (1983) (footnotes omitted).

33. La. Civ. Code Ann., art. 9, §§ 102 et seq. (West 1972 & Cum. Supp. 1998).

34. Ariz. Rev. Stat. § 25-901 (1998).

35. Scott M. Stanley et al., "Strengthening Marriages and Preventing Divorce: New Directions in Prevention Research," *Family Relations* 44 (1995): 392–401, 394.

36. Lawrence A. Kurdek, "Marital Stability and Changes in Marital Quality in Newly Wed Couples: A Test of the Contextual Model," *Journal of Social and Personal Relationships* 8 (1991): 27–48, 36, 40, table 2, 45, table 4.

37. Email from Steven L. Nock, Department of Sociology, University of Virginia, March 2000, in possession of the author.

38. Mary Ann Glendon, *Rights Talk: The Impoverishment of Political Discourse* (New York: Free Press, 1991); Carl E. Schneider, *Moral Discourse and the Transformation of American Family Law,* 83 Mich. L. Rev. 1803–1879 (1985); Ferdinand Schoeman, "Rights of Children, Rights of Parents, and the Moral Basis of the Family," *Ethics* 91 (1980): 8–9; Scott and Scott, *Parents as Fiduciaries;* Lynn D. Wardle, *The Use and Abuse of Rights Rhetoric: The Constitutional Rights of Children,* 27 Loyola U. Chi. L. Rev. 321–348 (1996); Barbara B. Woodhouse, *Children's Rights: The Destruction and Promise of Family,* 1993 BYU L. Rev. 497–515.

39. *Michael H. v. Gerald D.,* 491 U.S. 110 (1989).

40. Id. at 131.

41. Id. at 127.

42. Compare this with the suggestion the plurality makes in *Troxel v. Glanville,* 120 S. Ct. 2054, 2062, for working on the relationship rather than litigating.

43. Brinig, *From Contract to Covenant,* 220.

44. Margaret F. Brinig, *Finite Horizons: The American Family?* 2 Int. J. Children's Rights 293–315 (1994) .

45. *Penland v. Harris,* 520 S.E.2d 105 (N.C. App., 1999); *Hough v. Hough,* 590 N.W.2d 556 (Iowa, 1996); *Hawk v. Hawk,* 855 S.W.2d 573 (Tenn., 1993); *In re Nearhoof,* 359 S.E.2d 587 (W.Va., 1987); *Herndon v. Tuhey,* 857 S.W.2d 203 (Mo., 1993).

46. See, e.g., American Law Institute, *Principles of Family Dissolution* § 203(a)(b) and (c) (Preliminary Draft No. 9, 1999) (de facto parents and parents by estoppel acquire some of the rights that otherwise belong only to biological or adoptive parents).

47. Scott and Scott, *Parents as Fiduciaries*, Elizabeth S. Scott and Robert E. Scott, *Marriage as Relational Contract*, 84 Va. L. Rev. 1225–1334 (1998).

48. Carol Rose, *The Comedy of the Commons: Custom, Commerce, and Inherently Public Property* 53 U. Chi. L. Rev. 711–781 (1986).

49. Schneider, *Moral Discovery*, 1857–1858.

# 3

# The Language of Health Versus the Language of Religion: Competing Models of Marriage for the Twenty-First Century

## Don S. Browning

## INTRODUCTION

Strengthening marriages must be conceived of primarily as a cultural work. It is mainly a task of deepening and reformulating our understanding of the meaning of marriage. I call this task a cultural work because it must coordinate the efforts of a number of cultural disciplines—principally religion, law, economics, education, and psychotherapy. To be successful, this work cannot proceed from a single perspective; it requires the cooperative efforts of several major disciplines, each playing a distinct role.

This task faces many challenges: putting marriage back on the agenda of these disciplines, restraining each discipline from acting as if it had the only relevant perspective, and placing the reconstruction of marriage within a sufficiently comprehensive historical, philosophical, and religious context. With regard to the challenge of proper context, the cultural work of deepening marriage cannot be done on narrowly empirical grounds or in terms of the slender ethical egoist, utilitarian, or Kantian moral philosophies that rule much of modern life. Instead, the cultural reconstruction of marriage must entail the philosophical retrieval of the marriage classics—including the religious marriage classics—of the Western world and their refinement in light of modern social science insights. These classics offer thick (in contrast to thin) moral perspectives. They provide general orientations to life (i.e., ontologies), principles of moral obligation, and tested theories of basic human needs and goods. Most modern social sciences and moral philosophies provide either inadequate ontologies, theories of obligation, and indices of human needs or surreptitiously sneak more adequate ontologies, theories, and indices into their frameworks from other sources, generally without taking responsibility for their acknowledgment or justification.

Retrieving these classics is not primarily a confessional theological task. The goal of academic discourse should not entail placing public deliberation about marriage under the control of Jewish or Christian theologies. Its goal, instead, should be to create a public philosophy about marriage—one that can give an account of the functions of religious language about marriage and how this language can be orchestrated with the descriptive and predictive concepts of the social sciences.

At present, our cultural definition of marriage is in disarray for many reasons. First, there is the post-enlightenment shift in cultural values—that is, the rise of Western individualism.[1] But individualism, whether in its expressive or utilitarian forms,[2] is not the only factor. Cultural individualism, as demographer Ron Lesthaeghe has argued, is disruptive of marriage and family because cultural individualism is reinforced by market forces.[3] Economic individualism—a combination of market rationality and cultural individualism—is a major, although not the only, feature of modernization. Modernization, however, has ambiguous consequences for marriage and families. William Goode argued in *World Revolution in Family Patterns* (1963) that the modern conjugal family helped create modernization. Thirty years later when he wrote his *World Changes in Divorce Patterns* (1993) he admitted that modernization itself was now destroying the very family form that assisted in its birth.[4]

In an effort to address the disruptions surrounding marriage, several movements have emerged to repair it without necessarily developing commanding cultural visions of marriage. These movements should be supported, but they do not address the central issue about the nature of marriage. Three such movements come to mind—the marriage education movement, efforts by religious and social liberals to make marriage an equal partnership, and new efforts to document the health benefits of marriage. In this chapter, I will discuss primarily the last of these—the emerging view of marriage as the royal road to health. The discussion should, however, have implications as well for the other two movements.

### Marriage as a Road to Health

To illustrate the health message, I will turn to the outstanding work of Professor Linda Waite, my colleague at the University of Chicago. The argument in her presidential address before the American Population Society and published as "Does Marriage Matter?"(1995) is well known. It has been extended in a book co-authored with Maggie Gallagher titled *The Case for Marriage* (2000). She summarizes existing social science data demonstrating that in contrast to never-married and divorced persons, married couples enjoy more of a wide range of goods. They have better psychological and physical health, live longer, have fewer heart attacks, have more satisfying sex, and accumulate more wealth. This is true for both men and women, although marriage is slightly better for men than women.[5] This data has generated enormous attention and increasingly is used as a justification for the institution of marriage. In contrast to recent complaints charging that marriage is a bad deal, especially for women,[6] we now have reasons to think it is a vehicle, on average, for many of the basic goods of life.

This mode of thinking is typical of much of the reasoning in the contemporary social sciences. It is similar to all social science efforts to track the individual and social consequences of particular social arrangements. It is similar to the implicit argument of McLanahan and Sandefur when they show the increased educational, marital, and employment risks to children who grow up with a single parent.[7] It is the logic of the recent Iowa State University study that contends it is not the family structure but the process of communication between divorced parents and their children that predicts outcomes for offspring.[8] A similar model of reasoning undergirds the rational-choice discussions of marriage found in the work of Nobel Prize–winner Gary Becker and the entire law and economics approach to marriage represented by such writings as Judge Richard Posner's *Sex and Reason* (1992).[9]

The health argument is important and has a place in the total cultural task of deepening and reformulating our understanding of marriage. But this language and moral logic should not be allowed to dominate completely our moral and cultural discourse about marriage. The health argument for marriage is a species of what moral philosophers call a teleological view of moral reason. There are two dominant modern models of teleological moral reason—utilitarianism and ethical egoism.[10] Modern teleological views of moral reason, in contrast to the classical teleological views of Aristotle and Thomas Aquinas, see moral reason as calculative; moral thinking is a matter of computing whether an action will produce more nonmoral good over nonmoral evil for either self or the wider community. When an action is justified because it produces more nonmoral (or premoral) good for oneself, philosophers call this thinking a brand of philosophical ethical egoism. When an action is justified because it produces more nonmoral good for the majority of the wider community, this reasoning is called a brand of philosophical utilitarianism.[11]

By the obscure words *nonmoral* or *premoral*, I do not wish to convey a meaning associated with the concept of *immoral*. Rather, the idea of nonmoral or premoral goods points to the myriad ways we use the word *good* to refer to the things and qualities of life that are pleasant, useful, or helpful for survival but that are not necessarily moral in the full sense of the word.[12] Food, wealth, health, transportation, shelter, and pleasure are goods in the nonmoral or premoral sense.[13] But such things and qualities are not moral goods as such; it would not be intelligible to speak of a moral steak, a moral automobile, or a moral house. These objects are goods that can be used either morally or immorally, depending on the intentions of the person using them and how they are organized with other goods sought by both self and neighbor.

Health is certainly one of these nonmoral or premoral goods. It is a good thing to enjoy sound health. Sex is certainly good in the premoral sense; it feels good, binds us with those who give us pleasure, and may make us healthy in other ways. Wealth is another premoral good. But we do not say that persons are moral simply because they have lots of health, good sex, and a good deal of money stashed in American or Swiss banks. We judge a person as morally good depending on how he or she resolves the inevitable conflicts between premoral goods—for example, the conflict between the good of sexual pleasure versus the good of a costly and demanding baby, between the good of wealth and that of health, or between my wealth and the wealth of others.

The language of health, unqualified by further moral elaboration, can end in justifying marriage on either ethical egoist or narrowly utilitarian grounds. The first means that marriage is good because it is good for *me*; this view has generally been seen as an inadequate moral justification for anything, let alone marriage. The second, utilitarian ground justifies marriage as a social utility, somewhat analogous to the reasons society values a gas or electric company.

Neither language constitutes sufficient grounds for the cultural renewal and reformulation of marriage. Ethical egoist views of the health benefits of marriage make it a tool for individual fulfillment and provide little that helps us understand the commitment that makes marriage last. Utilitarian arguments for marriage justify it as good public policy, thereby ignoring the delight, rapture, struggles, moral obligations, and personal dramas that customarily have been associated with marriage. Furthermore, there is something oddly violent about ethical egoist and utilitarian views of marriage, whether in their social science or moral philosophy wrapping. Ethical egoist views make marriage analogous to a risky business investment in which funds might be rapidly deposited or withdrawn, depending on one's judgment about the current prospects of maximizing one's gains—one's health. Utilitarian views end in losing the uniqueness of marriage and reducing it to one among many public goods deserving support or neglect depending on abstract calculations about its overall social utility. John Milbank has argued that the modern social sciences are, in fact, dominated by a vision (an ontology) of life that portrays it as fundamentally violent—that is, that renders all of life as motivated by selfish genes (evolutionary psychology), tension-reducing libidinal energies (the early Freud), material motivations (Marx), or hardwired egoistic and individualistic interests (rational-choice economic models).[14]

Finally, both ethical egoist and utilitarian justifications function to disconnect marriage from the classic religious and ethical languages once used and, to a degree still used, to express the reasons for marriage. However important health justifications—either individualistic or communal—are to the contemporary cultural reconstructions of marriage, when standing alone they are based on an inadequate style of moral reason. At the minimum, the contributions of the health justification for marriage must be placed within a more comprehensive cultural and moral framework.

For the cultural task of developing this more comprehensive framework, it is better to consider the religious language of Genesis, the gospel of Matthew, Ephesians, and other such texts as "classics" rather than as divine revelation. Of course, it is entirely justifiable for religious groups to treat these texts as revelation within their internal confessing and witnessing lives. As the continental philosophers Hans-Georg Gadamer and Paul Ricoeur explain, such texts and the history of commentary on them are classics because they have decisively shaped Western marriage theory and because they have been perceived as containers of truths that have repeatedly enlightened and enriched the cultural consciousness.[15]

## What Is Marriage?

I turn now to a fuller exploration of the meaning of marriage as this can be seen through the eyes of the marriage classics of Western history. I do this to advance my argument that the modern teleological justifications for marriage must be kept in close relation to the classical Western languages about marriage. This task, as I have indicated, is primarily a philosophical enterprise designed to develop a public philosophy of marriage.

The classical Western marriage language, although not beyond criticism, provides ontologies and theories of moral obligation that modern views either lack or unconsciously appropriate from sources beyond themselves. The classics of the Western marriage tradition have portrayed marriage as a multidimensional phenomenon. They have viewed marriage as a natural, religious, contractual, social, and communicative reality.[16] We must keep in mind this fuller picture as we proceed to deepen our understanding of marriage. In what follows, I will concentrate primarily on two of these five dimensions—marriage as a natural and a religious reality.[17]

### Marriage as Organizing Natural Inclinations and as Religious Reality

Antiquity's view of marriage as a natural institution comes close to the modern justification of marriage as a means to health. Marriage in much of Greek philosophy was viewed as giving form to persistent yet sometimes conflicting natural inclinations and needs. A range of natural inclinations was viewed as ordered by marriage. These included the desire for sexual union. Then there is the desire Aristotle believed that humans share with the animals: "to leave behind them a copy of themselves."[18] Following Aristotle again, marriage was seen as meeting another natural need, that is, the need to supply humans with their "everyday wants."[19] The premoral value of sexual union, the basic needs of life, and offspring were seen by ancient Greek philosophy as the natural goods—indeed the health goods—that marriage satisfies. Aristotle's teleological form of moral thinking constituted the foundation of much of later thought on marriage in the West.

Aristotle's influence came about when his views were absorbed into Christian theology, especially the writings of Thomas Aquinas. These in turn had enormous impact on Roman Catholic thought, later on Protestant thought, and finally on marriage and family law in both Catholic and Protestant countries. In Aquinas, Aristotle's views were brought together with the creation stories of Genesis 1 and 2. Genesis tells humans to "be fruitful and multiply." It also teaches that humans were made for companionship: "It is not good for man to be alone." For these reasons marriage was created: "Therefore a man leaves his father and his mother and clings to his wife, and they become one flesh."[20] Procreation, mutual helpfulness, and companionship—these were the aims of marriage in the creation story of Genesis.

But in contrast to Aristotle and the modern teleological moral tradition—whether ethical egoist or utilitarian—these premoral goods in the creation story are located within a larger narrative about God's acts in creating the world. These human needs and goods are seen as given by God, affirmed by God, and their responsible use as backed by Divine Command. Aristotle would say that humans want copies of themselves; Genesis depicts God as commanding humans to multiply. Aristotle says humans are naturally social beings; Genesis states as a pronouncement of God that "it is not good for man to be alone." Aristotle sees the bonding of male and female as a consequence of these natural tendencies; Genesis combines indicative and imperative modes by saying, "And therefore a man leaves his father and mother . . . and becomes one flesh" with his wife. Genesis provides a vision (i.e., an ontology) of the fundamental goodness of the created world, including the inclination leading to the union of man and woman, and backs this up as an expression of the will of God and therefore a moral obligation. In Genesis, the language of need and nature is placed within the larger context of the language of God's will for creation. Marriage is a product of God's command, but what God wills is also good for humans.

### Religion and Naturalism

At least from the time of Thomas Aquinas (1225–1274), the great synthesizer of Aristotelian philosophy with the Judeo-Christian tradition, marriage was often justified on two interrelated grounds. One was drawn from the Jewish doctrine of creation and grounded on the command of God. The other came from the naturalism and teleological thinking of Aristotle.[21] It is true that within the hands of Christian theologians such as Aquinas, Jewish and Christian theologies of creation provided the deeper context surrounding Aristotelian naturalism. But—and this is the point—Aquinas crystallized what had been gradually developing for centuries, that is, a double language—one religious and one philosophical or naturalistic—used to justify marriage. It is my argument that the cultural work of restoring marriage must understand how these two languages worked together in the past and use this as a model for their fruitful interaction in the future.

In much of the Western tradition, the philosophical language accounting for the natural grounds of marriage was considered vital for the clarification of the religious language. One can see this in perspectives as different as those of Thomas Aquinas, John Locke, and the Roman Catholic marriage encyclicals of Pope Leo XIII. All three retain in some manner the Jewish and Christian creation stories. Yet all three make use of a naturalistic and philosophical language as well. All of them developed a subordinate naturalistic argument for the institution of marriage similar to one first put forth by Aristotle. This naturalistic argument supplemented their view of the will of God in creation.

For instance, Aquinas taught that matrimony is the joining of the father to the mother–infant dyad. It was and is required by virtue of the long period of dependency of the human infant and child. This dependency is so burdensome to the mother that it necessitates the material and educational labors of both biologically invested procreators.[22] This partnership secures the well-being of the child and secondarily that of the mother who needs assistance. It also enhances the well-being of the father, since the child also carries the "substance" of the father. Similarly, Locke, the author of liberal family theory, wrote with special reference to humans that "the Father, Who is bound to take care for those he hath begot, is under an Obligation to continue in Conjugal Society with the same Woman longer than other Creatures."[23] Similar health- or well-being–oriented arguments for marriage can be found in the influential neo-Thomistic writings by Pope Leo XIII in the late nineteenth century.[24]

It was assumed by all three of these authors that God created humans as the kind of creatures whose infants have a long period of dependency. Nonetheless, this theological affirmation did not obscure their analysis of the concrete natural conditions that function to create matrimony at this basic level. In *From Culture Wars to Common Ground* (1997), my colleagues and I show that these naturalistic observations are consistent with contemporary evolutionary psychology's view of how long-term human pair bonding occurs.[25] But we do not argue that this naturalistic explanation should supplant cultural appreciation for the wisdom of the founding marriage myths. Rather, the naturalistic explanation (I sometimes call it a "naturalistic moment") should be viewed as an index, sign, or signal of both the realism and profundity of the founding story.

The existence and importance of this double language about marriage are generally lost on people, who tend to believe that marriage is a uniquely religious and even distinctively Christian practice. This is not true. Although I have illustrated its philosophical and naturalistic dimensions by referring to Aristotle and Locke, I could have done much the same by turning to Roman law. Religious language adds breadth, seriousness, and transcendent grounds for commitment; but it need not exclude naturalistic explanations for marriage as long as they are not made absolute or allowed to dominate the entire field of meaning of this institution.

### The Reformulation of Marriage: The Foundations of the Equal-Regard Marriage

So far, I have been discussing how religious language and naturalistic language evolved into a double language about marriage—a double language important today for a public philosophy for marriage. Such a double language would make it possible for theologians, philosophers, and social scientists to cooperate in the cultural work of reviving marriage. Religion could become a partner in this work without reducing our public language to the confessionalism of specific religious traditions or the naturalism of the social sciences. The task of this public philosophy would be to position each discipline's specific contributions so that an orchestrated and holistic cultural vision could emerge.

I have called for an interdisciplinary cultural work and a double language for the deepening and reformulation of marriage. This reformulation of marriage would involve a complex task: retaining male commitment to marriage and children but uncoupling this commitment from the lingering shadows of patriarchy. Patriarchy, of course, has been on the decline in the West for centuries—since early Christianity repudiated the double sexual standard of the ancient world, since Roman Catholic canon law required the consent of both man and woman to establish a valid marriage (thereby breaking the power of a father to select his daughter's mate), and since Locke's theories of family and marriage influenced both England and the mothers of the American Revolutionary War.[26] Women's move into the wage market and their subsequent economic independence, as economists have demonstrated, were additional blows to patriarchy.[27]

All these moves have created the need for what I have called a new "critical" familism and a new "critical" marriage culture.[28] By this I mean an equal-regard marriage where both husband and wife treat each other as equals, work for each other's well-being, and in principle give each other equal access to privileges and responsibilities of both domestic and public life.[29] This view does not mean, as some believe, that husband and wife must become identical and suppress the distinctiveness of being male and female. It means instead that a husband or wife must live by a strenuous love ethic of regarding the other with equal seriousness, just as he or she expects the other to regard them. Within such an ethic, they should work together to determine their responsibilities and privileges in light of respective talents, inclinations, and realistic constraints.

Such an ethic is not a pure fabrication of the liberal imagination—it can be buttressed by the marriage classics of the Western tradition. I believe that the seeds of the equal-regard marriage are deeply embedded within the founding marriage myths of the Western tradition. But the interpretive nurturance of these seeds needs to be sharpened, clarified, and completed. This is part of the cultural work of deepening and reformulating our understanding of marriage.

The creation stories of the Abrahamic religions suggest an ethic of equal regard. The suggestive work of scholars Phyllis Trible, Mary Stewart van Leeuwen, and Lisa Cahill[30] reminds us that in the Genesis account, both male and female are made in the image of God: "In the image of God he created them: male and female he created them." These scholars further argue that male and female in this founding story are given joint and equal dominion over the reproductive and productive responsibilities of life: "God blessed them, and God said to them, 'Be fruitful and multiply, and . . . have dominion over the fish of the sea and over the birds of the air.'"[31] Equal status before God, equal reproductive responsibilities, and equal productive responsibilities—this is the moral ontology behind the ethic of equal regard in the founding myths of the Abrahamic religions. These religions have not always been faithful to the full implications of this story, but the seeds of the equal-regard marriage are clearly there. Furthermore, it is against the background of a narrative that tells of God's primary purposes in creation that we must understand the subservience of Eve to Adam in the fall; the inequality, as this same group of women scholars demonstrates, is a consequence of human brokenness and not due to the primordial intention of God in creation.

Movement toward the deeper realization of the equal-regard marriage occurred when early Christianity brought the ethics of neighbor love ("You shall love your neighbor as yourself") directly into marriage itself: "Husbands should love their wives as they do their own body."[32] Furthermore, we now know that early Christianity must be interpreted against the background of the honor-shame ethic of much of the ancient world, especially the Roman Hellenism that surrounded it. This was an ethic of male honor associated with male agency, dominance, and sexual freedom; it also entailed an ethic of shame for women if they broke out of their confinement to the domestic realm and their restriction from public life. Early Christianity, while never completely escaping the honor-shame ethic of antique paganism, rejected the Greco-Roman double sexual standard, confined men's sexual activity to their wives, emphasized an ethic of male servant-hood, and greatly increased the stature and visibility of women.[33]

But a double language justifying the equal-regard marriage begins to emerge most strikingly, once again, with Thomas Aquinas. It was Aquinas who synthesized the Genesis accounts of how both male and female were created in the image of God with Aristotle's philosophical view of friend-ship. Marriage, for Aquinas, was partially a naturalistic process of incor-porating males into the task of raising children, as we saw previously. But marriage was also about friendship, and friendship implies equality.[34] Aquinas could simultaneously use and blend the philosophical language of friendship with the theological language of the image of God in both male and female. Of course, Aquinas was too much an Aristotelian to make this a fully equal friendship of the kind he believed possible only between free and educated males. But he did set the stage for viewing marriage as a friendship—an idea that has been developed and extended by various con-temporary philosophical and theological perspectives and is consistent with Genesis and the ethic of neighbor love applied to marriage. The idea of marriage as friendship is the precursor for understanding it as a "conver-sation," as John Milton proclaimed,[35] or as a "dialogue" as we put forth in *From Culture Wars to Common Ground*.[36] Such a view is the assump-tion behind marriage seen as communication and conflict resolution, which undergirds the present-day marriage education movement.

### The Equal-Regard Marriage and Society

Marriage as a conversation and dialogue of equal regard should not ex-clude viewing marriage in terms of its health benefits for husband, wife, and children. It does mean, however, that in the equal-regard marriage, neither husband nor wife, parents nor children, should ever be reduced to the level of being viewed primarily as instruments of health.

More concretely, if marriage is an institution of equal regard that also raises children, some dramatic changes must be made in our society. Here are a few of these changes. Education that prepares individuals for an equal-regard marriage must be widespread. Furthermore, government and market should cooperate in making it possible for couples to be simultaneously parents, wage earners, and citizens. All three roles should be possible with-out working 80 to 90 hours each week outside the home, as some parents do today. This entails institutionalizing something like the 60-hour work-week as the maximum combined time couples with children should work in the wage economy. These 60 hours can be divided as the couple sees fit—an idea we developed at length in *From Culture Wars to Common Ground*.[37] It certainly should not mean, however, that one member of the couple will work the entire 60 hours.

Supporting the equal-regard marriage means privileging marriage in a variety of cultural, political, and economic ways. It means removing all penalties—such as the so-called marriage tax. But the question of how one organizes a culture and society to support the equal-regard marriage is a huge topic and must be addressed more fully at another time.

My argument has been that the vision of life, the narratives that convey it, and the ontologies of personhood found in the key texts of the Western marriage tradition should play a role today in the cultural work of reviving the institution of marriage. This can be done best when these texts inform a public philosophy of marriage as classics—classics that have time and again proven themselves as carrying deep truths. These truths can place naturalistic discussions of the goods of marriage into wider contexts of meaning.

Justification for retaining in public discourse the mythic framework of Western family theory has several dimensions to it, more than I can cover here. But one justification has to do with acknowledging the difficulty that all thought has in escaping mythic horizons. I have spent much of my scholarly life arguing that all theories of action, including social science theories, contain within them deep metaphors about the origins, meanings, and purposes of life that generally do not have recognized themes. The social sciences are riddled with implicit metaphors (and corresponding ontologies) of strife (rational choice), harmony (humanistic psychology, Jung), life against death (Freud), care (Erikson, Kohut), husbandry (Skinner), and more.[38] These hidden metaphors function analogously to the faith stances of the classic Western religious traditions. If this is true, it seems only fair that visions of life surrounding the religious classics of the past should be allowed to continue to inform the public conversation about marriage and be tested for the ways they illuminate the full meaning of this fundamental institution that we seek to better understand.

There is a practical payoff in retaining the language of health but subordinating it to the language of commitment. We can illustrate the advantages of this intellectual strategy. Recently, I was asked by the American Assembly to co-lead, with Gloria Rodriguez, a project to reach consensus on divisive issues about the family that face our society. For nearly fifty years, the American Assembly—an organization founded by Dwight Eisenhower and located at Columbia University—has refined a productive process for illustrating how consensus on contentious issues can be achieved. The Assembly calls together sixty leaders from different sectors of society for a long weekend of discussion based on a carefully selected list of questions pertaining to the issue at hand. Project leaders—in this case Rodriguez and I—are asked to write a background book. Our book was titled *Reweaving the Social Tapestry: Toward a Public Philosophy and Policy for Families.*[39] All participants read it in advance of the meeting. The final consensus achieved at the conclusion of the four-day assembly was published under the title of *Strengthening American Families: Reweaving the Social Tapestry* (2000).[40]

This consensus reconciled typically conservative and liberal political and religious views in the contemporary American debate over the family. For instance, it emphasized the renewal of marriage as both a cultural and political agenda, generally thought to be a conservative strategy. It also, however, emphasized the importance of social and governmental supports in the areas of taxation, work and family issues, and health care—commonly thought to be liberal strategies. The hot button issues of homosexuality, abortion, and reproductive technology were addressed and progress made, even though they were not fully resolved. But they did not become obstacles to achieving consensus on a wide range of other issues.

This consensus came about because the background book argued that consensus on family issues can best be achieved by taking the various American religious and cultural traditions with seriousness and respect. These traditions—Judaism, Christianity, and increasingly Islam, Hinduism, and various neo-Confucianism—are the carriers of our positive cultures of marriage and family and the various languages of commitment that have energized these institutions. For the purposes of public policy, these traditions and their sacred texts on marriage and family should be handled as classics that have proven over the centuries to contain wisdom and power. Although these traditions do not agree on all issues and, indeed, at times require critique, there are wide areas of analogy between them on several important issues. These include the centrality of marriage for family formation, the responsibility of parents, conservative attitudes toward divorce, and the importance of children. These analogies can constitute the grounds for the rough agreements out of which a cultural consensus might evolve.

The social sciences, we argued, cannot alone generate the grounds for consensus. Their role, instead, is to clarify conflicts within and between the various traditions. Health values and the role of the social sciences in clarifying their conditions are important for achieving consensus, but they must function in a way that is subordinate to the role of specific religious and cultural traditions in formation of the common values shaping public policy.

## CONCLUSION

The context shaping the discussion of the American Assembly's deliberation on the family was formed by ideas similar to those developed in this chapter. The religions were not marginalized, but were brought directly into the cultural discussion. We recognized that the moral framework of marriage is richly articulated in our religious traditions, as is a more commanding cultural vision of what marriage is. The social sciences played a valuable role, but not in such a way as to exclude the traditions. Research on the benefits of marriage and stable family structures shed light on difficult issues and helped to build a consensus on some of them. I believe a working partnership between the language of religion and the language of social science can be a fruitful union. This union, I submit, may be productive for wider social, cultural, and political discussions on family issues confronting our society.

## NOTES

1. For perspectives that tie family disruption to the rise of individualism, see Robert Bellah et al., *Habits of the Heart* (New York: Harper and Row, 1985), 32–35, 46, 47, 142, 311; Jan Dizard and Howard Gadlin, *The Minimal Family* (Amherst: University of Massachusetts, 1990), 11–13; Edward Shorter, *The Making of the Modern Family* (New York: Basic Books, 1977), 21; David Popenoe, *Life Without Father* (New York: The Free Press, 1996), 46–48.

2. Bellah et al., *Habits of the Heart*, 32–35.

3. Ron Lesthaeghe, "A Century of Demographic and Cultural Change in Western Europe," *Population and Development Review* 9 (3) (September 1983): 429.

4. William Goode, *World Revolution in Family Patterns* (London: The Free Press of Glencoe, 1963), and *World Changes in Divorce Patterns* (New Haven: Yale University Press, 1993), 13.

5. Linda Waite, "Does Marriage Matter?" *Demography* 32 (4) (November 1995): 483–504.

6. Waite was specifically addressing Jessie Bernard's charges that modern marriage has not been good for women. See her *The Future of Marriage* (New York: World Publishing, 1972).

7. Sara McLanahan and Gary Sandefur, *Growing Up with a Single Parent* (Cambridge: Harvard University Press, 1994).

8. Ronald Simons et al., "Explaining the Higher Incidence of Adjustment Problems Among Children of Divorce Compared with Those in Two-Parent Families," *Journal of Marriage and the Family* 61 (November 1999): 1020–1034.

9. Richard Posner, *Sex and Reason* (Cambridge: Harvard University Press, 1992).

10. William Frankena, *Ethics* (Englewood Cliffs, N.J.: Prentice-Hall, 1973), 14–16.

11. Ibid., 34–43.

12. Ibid., 9–11.

13. Ibid., 9–10.

14. John Milbank, *Theology and Social Theory* (Oxford: Blackwell, 1990).

15. For the idea of the classic, see Hans-Georg Gadamer, *Truth and Method* (New York: Crossroad, 1982), 253–258; also see Paul Ricoeur, *Hermeneutics and the Human Sciences* (Cambridge: Cambridge University Press, 1981), 59–61, 62–100.

16. For similar lists, see John Witte, *From Sacrament to Contract* (Louisville, Ky.: Westminster/John Knox, 1997), 2; *Marriage: A Report to the Nation* (New York: Institute for American Values, 1995).

17. Don Browning, "What Is Marriage? An Exploration" (January 25, 2000), unpublished article prepared for a consultation on the Marriage Movement. See Coalition for Marriage, Family, and Couples Education, Institute for American Values, and Religion, Culture, and Family Project of the University of Chicago Divinity School, *The Marriage Movement: A Statement of Principles* (New York: Institute for American Values, 2000). Available online: www.marriagemovement.org.

18. Aristotle, "Politics," in *The Basic Works of Aristotle*, ed. Richard McKeon (New York: Random House, 1941), bk. 1, pt. 2.

19. Ibid.

20. Gen. 1:28, 2:18, 2:24 (NRSV).

21. For a discussion of how Aristotelian naturalism is placed in context within Judeo-Christian doctrines of creation, see Don Browning et al., *From Culture Wars to Common Ground: Religion and the American Family Debate* (Louisville, Ky.: Westminster/John Knox, 1997), 113–124.

22. Thomas Aquinas, *The Summa Contra Gentiles*, bk. 3, pt. 2, chap. 122 (London: Burns, Oates & Washbourne, 1928).

23. John Locke, "Second Treatise," *Two Treatises of Government*, ed. Peter Laslett (Cambridge: Cambridge University Press, 1991), chap. 7, ¶ 80.

24. For Leo XIII's version of the argument, see his "Rerum Novarum," in *Proclaiming Justice and Peace: Papal Documents* (Mystic, Conn.: Twenty-Third Publications).

25. Don Browning et al., *Common Ground*, 106–114.

26. Linda Gerber, *Women of the Republic* (New York: W.W. Norton, 1980), 15–23.

27. Gary Becker, *Treatise on the Family* (Cambridge: Harvard University Press, 1991), 356, 359.

28. Browning et al., *Common Ground*, 2.

29. Ibid., 273–279.

30. Phyllis Trible, *God and the Rhetoric of Sexuality* (Minneapolis, Minn.: Fortress Press, 1978), 16–19; Mary Stewart van Leeuwen, *Gender and Grace* (Downers Grove, Ill.: Intervarsity Press, 1990), 42–47; Lisa Cahill, *Between the Sexes* (Philadelphia: Fortress Press, 1985), 46–55. These views are basically confirmed by Leo Perdue's chapters in Leo Perdue et al., *Families in Ancient Israel* (Louisville, Ky.: Westminster/John Knox Press, 1997), 223–259.

31. Gen. 1:27,28 (NRSV).

32. Matt. 19:9, Eph. 5:28 (NRSV).

33. Browning et al., *Common Ground*, 141–146.

34. Thomas Aquinas, *The Summa Contra Gentiles,* bk. 3, pt. 2, p. 118.

35. John Milton, "The Doctrine and Discipline of Divorce," in C. A. Patrides, ed., *John Milton: Selected Prose* (Columbia: University of Missouri Press, 1985), 124.

36. Browning et al., *Common Ground*, 298.

37. Ibid., 317.

38. Don Browning, *Religious Thought and the Modern Psychologies* (Minneapolis, Minn.: Fortress Press, 1987).

39. Don Browning and Gloria Rodriguez, *Reweaving the Social Tapestry: Toward a Public Philosophy and Policy of Families* (New York: W.W. Norton, in press).

40. *Strengthening American Families: Reweaving the Social Tapestry* (New York: The American Assembly, Columbia University, 2000).

# 4

# A Plea for Greater Concern About the Quality of Marital Matching

## Norval D. Glenn

### INTRODUCTION

Efforts to promote stable, high-quality marriages fall into two broad categories, consisting of those aimed at (1) getting the right persons mated in the first place and (2) maintaining and improving existing marriages. Until the past two or three decades, persons and groups interested in promoting marital success extensively employed both kinds of efforts. Emphasis on promoting good marital choices was evident in marriage preparation courses and social scientific research on marital choice, while efforts to improve existing marriages were to a large extent through conventional marriage counseling.

In contrast to this earlier attention to both ways to promote good marriages, in the pro-marriage movements that emerged in the 1990s, emphasis on the importance of good initial matching seems rather weak. The primary concern is with teaching married couples good relationship skills and constructive management of conflict. Even the proponents of marriage preparation education in the secondary schools seem more interested in imparting relationship skills than in teaching students how to choose a spouse wisely. Some of the more enthusiastic advocates of relationship skills education apparently believe that almost any couple with enough mutual attraction to consider marriage can achieve marital success with sufficient motivation, effort, and access to the right kind of training.

Why pro-marriage activists show only mild concern about promoting good marital choices is not readily apparent. Possible reasons include that (1) many people have become convinced by new evidence that problems in marriages are more likely to result from poor relationship skills than from poor initial matching, and (2) the activists lack confidence that anything effective can be done to improve marital choices. Or they may be concerned that increased public discussion of the importance of good marital matching would tend to undermine marital stability by exacerbating the already widespread tendency for married persons to reconsider their marital choices.

Whatever the reasons for the lack of emphasis on marital choice may be, this neglect is hard to justify. Although stressing the ill effects of poor marital matching might have some unintended negative consequences on existing marriages, and although the importance of good initial matching relative to other influences on marital success is debatable, to my knowledge no authority on marriage has ever claimed that good matching is not important. Even if virtually any heterosexual pair with good skills and mutual attraction can have a reasonably good marriage, an equally skilled but optimally matched couple can almost certainly have a better marriage with less effort.

Therefore, in this chapter I urge that pro-marriage activists should give more attention to promoting good marital choices, not by deemphasizing other efforts to improve and sustain marriages but by a modest reallocation of energy, time, and resources. The purpose of this chapter is to instigate such a change. I also argue that entering into marriage has become less efficient and effective in contemporary American society, and I discuss what constitutes a good marital match and barriers to achieving it. I emphasize, in particular, the barrier of lack of sufficient "circulation" on the marriage "market" to allow each person to get to know a wide variety of prospective spouses and to test his or her own desirability.

## THE NATURE AND IMPORTANCE OF
## OPTIMAL MATCHING

In view of the fact that virtually everyone agrees that good marital matching is important, giving reasons for its importance may seem superfluous. However, our understanding of how and why good marital matching is important is often not sophisticated, being based on little more than the notion that spouses should have similar interests and values. Even academic discussions of the suitability of spouses to one another often seem to be based on the assumption that good matches could be made with information such as that yielded by personality tests, interest inventories, and assessments of values. Of course, such information can to some degree predict which persons will marry, and, among those who do, which ones will have successful marriages. However, the information is not powerfully predictive, and by itself can provide only limited insight into what makes a good marital match. I have devised a simple theory and conceptual scheme, an abbreviated version of which I present here, that goes beyond simple compatibility and similarity to specify more completely the nature of optimal matching.

The most popular theories of marital choice devised by social scientists all use the concept of the "marriage market" and draw a rough analogy between the search for a suitable spouse and the search for goods and services in the economic marketplace.[1] According to these theories, just as consumers try to get as much in the way of desirable goods and services as they can, given the amount of money they have to spend, persons searching for spouses try to get mates who are as desirable as possible, given what the searching persons have to offer on the marriage market.

In any subculture in one society at one point in time, there is considerable agreement about what makes a person a desirable husband or wife, and thus it is useful to conceive of "general marital desirability," or a person's average desirability to persons of the opposite sex who are on the marriage market.[2] However, the agreement on standards of desirability is far from perfect, so it is also useful to conceive of "person-specific marital desirability," or a person's desirability to a specific other person of the opposite sex. What a person on the marriage market tries to maximize, of course, is the person-specific desirability (to himself or herself) of the person he or she marries.

I need not deal here with the characteristics of marital desirability, except to point out that they go beyond the obvious ones such as physical appearance, earning ability, character, and personality. They include relationship skills and other traits that are subject to deliberate change; thus efforts to improve existing marriages are attempts to increase the person-specific desirability of the spouses to one another. Some of the characteristics that make a person desirable to a specific person of the opposite sex are intangibles not well understood by that person or by anyone else.

Although marital desirability is not amenable to precise measurement, for theoretical purposes it is useful to assume that it can be measured on a ten-point scale, varying from ten for the highest desirability to zero for the lowest. If there were no variation in standards of desirability, if there were equal numbers of men and women on the market, if the distribution of desirability were the same for males and females, and if everyone had complete knowledge of everyone else's characteristics, the tens would all end up married to tens, the nines to nines, and so forth, with the zeroes being left to one another. Fortunately, the lack of perfect agreement on standards prevents such a harsh system of mating. Even many of the people with low general marital desirability have fairly high person-specific desirability to a few people of the opposite sex. With ideal functioning of the market, most people should be able to acquire spouses whose person-specific desirability to them is at least moderately higher than their own standard of general marital desirability. In other words, they find a person specifically desirable to them who is above the general average they began with while shopping the marriage market. Among persons of low general desirability, those whose standards for person-specific desirability are most unlike the standards for general desirability—the average that others of low desirability begin to look for—are the ones most likely to be able to marry persons highly desirable to them.

The most stable and successful marriages are likely to be those in which the spouses are substantially more desirable to one another than they are to most other people. An example would be spouses who are both threes in general desirability but eights to one another. These two people are likely to appreciate one another, and neither will have abundant desirable alternatives to lure them out of or lessen their commitment to their present marriage. Conversely, those marriages in which the spouses are more desirable to many others than to one another are unlikely to succeed. A marriage with intermediate prospects for success, and likely to occur, is one in which the spouses are about as desirable to one another as they are to most other people.

A second and related requirement for a good marital match is that each spouse should get about as much in the way of person-specific desirability in a spouse as is possible, given what he or she has to offer on the market. Those who marry before adequately testing their marital desirability may settle for someone less desirable than they are able to attract. When such persons realize that they have "undersold" themselves on the marriage market, as will almost inevitably happen, dissatisfaction and withdrawal of commitment are likely.

Another useful conceptual distinction is between "real marital desirability" and "apparent marital desirability." The former is how desirable a mate the person will really be, while the latter is how desirable it appears the person will be on the basis of incomplete knowledge of his or her characteristics. Initial screening on the marriage market occurs on the basis of apparent desirability, of course, but so does the final decision to marry, because real marital desirability can be assessed precisely only after marriage. The higher the ratio of real-to-apparent desirability of each spouse when the decision to marry is made, the greater the probability of marital success.

## CONDITIONS CONDUCIVE TO OPTIMAL MATCHING

A primary requirement for good initial marital matching is the opportunity for those "on the market" to get to know a large number and variety of prospective spouses, and to get to know them well enough to assess their desirability on the basis of more than just their most obvious characteristics. Without extensive knowledge of persons of the opposite sex who are on the market, a person is unlikely ever to find and connect with one of the most suitable prospects. Furthermore, without sufficient "circulation" in the market, the person will not adequately test his or her own desirability.

A common obstacle to sufficient circulation in the marriage market and to linking up with one of the most suitable prospects is premature entanglement. This occurs when a relationship with one prospect reaches a point at which ending the relationship is difficult, but the person lacks knowledge of how desirable that prospect is relative to other prospects he or she could attract.

Entanglement must eventually occur, of course, if the person is to move toward marriage, and from that time on, the selection process is no longer a matter of mentally lining up prospects, comparing them, and selecting one from the lineup. Rather, one can then only decide to continue the relationship or withdraw from it, and if the opportunity to marry develops, to take advantage of that opportunity or not. At that point, the main comparison is with opportunities the person thinks he or she will or would have in the future. Unless the chosen person perfectly fits the chooser's image of an ideal spouse, or unless the chooser has an illusion of such a fit, the decision to marry reflects a pessimistic assessment of future opportunities. The more realistic this assessment is, the better the marital match will be. Ideally, the person making the decision will have gained enough knowledge of self and others through experience on the marriage market, and through pre-market heterosexual experiences, to make a realistic assessment.

Persons on the marriage market are highly motivated to make the market function well, but this motivation does not always lead the seekers of spouses to act wisely and rationally to achieve their ends. For instance, although the good match is one that maximizes the desirability of spouses to one another in the long run and not just at the time of marriage, persons searching for mates may focus on short-term considerations and thus on ephemeral rather than enduring characteristics of prospective mates. Furthermore, some enduring characteristics may elicit feelings of infatuation or intense feelings of romantic love, but fail to contribute much to long-term desirability.

Given the fallible judgment of persons searching for mates, the best choices are likely to be made by persons substantially influenced by friends and family members, who often can be more objective and rational about the choice. Of course, the influence of these other people is likely to improve the selection process only if the others have good judgment and sufficient knowledge of the prospects being considered.

## SOME CURRENT OBSTACLES TO GOOD MARITAL MATCHING

We do not know how well marriage markets function in the United States. Although it should be possible to study marital choice to assess the adequacy of the resulting marital matching, such research has not been done. Some facts indicate, however, that the markets are not functioning well and that poor marital matches are common. Few indicators suggest that optimal matching has been the usual outcome of the mating process any time in recent decades, and some recent changes may have reduced that probability.

Arguably, the most consequential of the several recent changes that have affected how marital matching typically occurs is the increase in the average age of the persons involved. In just one decade, from 1980 to 1990, the percentage of men under age 20 who married declined from 8.5 to 4.3 percent; the comparable percentage for women went from 21.1 to 10.6 percent.[3] The percentage of persons under age 25 who married dropped from 44.2 to 29 percent for men and from 58.2 to 39.9 percent for women. In 1990, 27.4 percent of the men and 21 percent of the women who married were age 35 or older, compared with 19.7 percent and 13.8 percent, respectively, a decade earlier. These changes, which started in the 1970s and have continued since 1990, reflect to a large extent an increase in the percentage of brides and grooms entering second and subsequent marriages. In 1970, neither spouse in 68.6 percent of the marriages had been previously married, but by 1988, that percentage had declined to 54.1 percent. (More recent data are not available, but the percentage was virtually stable during the 1980s and has probably changed little since then.) The increase in the average age of marrying persons also reflects an increase in the median age of persons entering first marriages, which went from 22.5 percent for men and 20.6 percent for women in 1970 to 26.8 percent and 25 percent for men and women, respectively, in 1997.[4]

On balance, these changes may have tended to increase the quality of marital matching; the marriages of people under 20 are notoriously unsuccessful, on the average, and there are several reasons for thinking that poor matching contributes substantially to these outcomes. Consider, for instance, that among persons on the threshold of adulthood, both the characteristics that form the basis for their own marital desirability and their standards for evaluating the desirability of others tend to be changeable. To illustrate, to the 17-year-old woman just completing high school, the popular high school athlete may seem highly desirable, even if he lacks the characteristics valued in the adult world that would make him a desirable husband. People's own desirability and their standards of desirability never become absolutely fixed, but tend to stabilize in the first few years of adulthood. Obviously, marriages formed while these characteristics are still changing rapidly are not likely to be good matches in terms of the long-term desirability of the spouses to one another. Even if these characteristics are reasonably stable, persons who marry early are unlikely to test their desirability on the marriage market adequately.

Although the decline in early marriages has almost certainly been beneficial, the increase in persons on the marriage market who are older than their middle twenties probably has not contributed to better marital matching. The data on age at marriage and divorce suggest that prospects for marital stability are enhanced little or not at all by postponing marriage beyond the middle to late twenties.[5] There is evidence that prospects for achieving highly successful marriages may be diminished by postponing first marriage beyond ages 22–23 in the case of women and 24–25 in the case of men[6]—possibly in part because conditions are typically less conducive to optimal matching at the older ages.

Conditions conducive to effective "circulation," as that term is used, are probably better in secondary schools, colleges, and universities than in any other setting in which most persons are likely to find themselves. In the recent past, a substantial proportion of people who ended their educations with high school graduation married people they had met in school, and many who went to college met their spouses there. I know of no evidence on the topic, but the increase in the average age at first marriage has likely been accompanied by a decline in marriages of persons who met in school or college. Once one goes into the adult world of work, opportunities to meet interesting and desirable persons of the opposite sex are likely to decline. Social contacts on the job are often superficial, impersonal, and with people who are not of the right age or marital status or both to be prospective spouses. There are major obstacles, including anti-fraternization rules, to romantic involvement with work associates, especially those above or below oneself in the organizational hierarchy. For many employed persons on the marriage market, the search for a spouse is restricted to leisure time, and that time is often limited for ambitious young adults starting their careers. Therefore, the movement away from school or college into full-time employment almost certainly exerts some negative influence on the effectiveness of mate-selection processes.

Another reason why postponement of marriage may lead to poorer marital matching is that the early stages of adulthood are characterized by movement—both geographic and social—away from parents, other kin, and long-time friends, and thus the longer marriage is postponed, the less likely it is that those persons will exert positive influences on marital choice. Movement away from one's geographic and social origins before a mate is selected lessens the probability that one's spouse will be a long-term acquaintance and must to some extent increase the risk of marrying someone whose apparent marital desirability is substantially higher than his or her real desirability.

An important recent trend associated with the increase in the average age of those who marry is the increase in the proportion of people who cohabit while they are on the marriage market. Among some of the more liberal and secular portions of the American population, cohabitation has become a normal and expected stage of the mate-selection process. Many students of marriage have encouraged this change because, they believe, in the language I have previously introduced, that it should lessen the ratio of apparent to real marital desirability at the time of marriage. According to this point of view, it is desirable for couples to test their compatibility, to see how they get along while living together, before they decide to marry.

However, research on cohabitation during the past decade has rather conclusively refuted the view that premarital cohabitation is an effective means to prevent inappropriate marital matches.[7] It probably does prevent some marriages that should not occur, but the divorce rate for couples who have cohabited before marriage is substantially higher than that for couples who have not cohabited. This difference, almost all scholars who have addressed the topic agree, is partially spurious; persons with values and attitudes not conducive to marital success are more likely to cohabit before marriage than others. More controversial is the view of several scholars that habits and patterns of relating developed during cohabitation have detrimental effects on marriage.

An additional reason for the negative relationship between premarital cohabitation and marital stability may be that although cohabitation prevents some inappropriate marital matches, it leads to others. As I pointed out previously, in a well-functioning marriage market, persons seeking spouses gain as much knowledge of prospective spouses as possible while avoiding premature entanglement. That entanglement inhibits obtaining knowledge about alternative prospects and initiates pressures toward marriage that are hard to resist, even if one discovers that the prospect is not as desirable as one had thought. In the case of young adults living together, these pressures may come from parents and other kin—an instance of pernicious influence from persons whose influence is typically likely to be beneficial. For lovers, "breaking up is hard to do" under any circumstances and is likely to be especially difficult when they are living together. Sometimes it may be so difficult that it is easier to marry and convince oneself that the match is not as bad as it really is. Traditionally, the momentum toward marriage was so strong that it was difficult to stop once the engagement had been announced, a milestone likely to be passed after much more deliberation than that which usually precedes the decision to cohabit.

The effects on the quality of marital matches of the increase in previously married persons on the marriage market are not clear but are likely to be negative. These persons face the selection process with more experience and maturity than they had when they first married, but it is not apparent that they are necessarily better equipped on the average than other marriage-market participants to make wise judgments and choices. They are likely to be unusually free of influences from kin and long-term friends, and their experiences with marriage that may contribute to wisdom may also leave them cynical and fearful of commitment.

The situation of single parents on the marriage market is crucially different from that of other participants, and different in ways likely to diminish their chances of making good marital matches. The most obvious handicap is that single parents have relatively little time and energy to spend searching for spouses. Perhaps equally important is that the parent and his or her child or children are on the market as a package; anyone considering marrying a single parent is contemplating taking on two roles—spouse and stepparent—and is likely to evaluate the characteristics of the prospective stepchild or stepchildren as well as those of the prospective spouse. This added complexity makes good marital matching inherently harder to achieve. Furthermore, the child or children of the single parent may participate, if only subtly, in the selection process. Whereas the influence of kin on marital choice should usually be beneficial, the influence of those lacking mature judgment may not be. Emotional attachment of children to a parent's prospective spouse may lead to premature entanglement, especially when there is cohabitation.

Whatever recent trends in the influences affecting the quality of marital choices may have been, there are strong reasons to believe that a large percentage of marital matches are falling far short of being optimal and that many people are finding it difficult to connect with appropriate mates. Although evidence from social scientific research on the adequacy of the functioning of marriage markets is lacking, informal evidence suggests a rather dismal picture. Commercial dating services have proliferated in recent years, the volume of personal advertisements in newspapers has apparently increased, and many people are resorting to the Internet to connect with potential mates, despite the lack of protection from deception and exploitation it provides. This suggests widespread unmet needs—perhaps even widespread desperation—for effective pathways to good marital matches.

## POSSIBLE STEPS TO PROMOTE GOOD MARITAL MATCHES

It is relatively easy to identify probable barriers to optimal marital matching in contemporary American society, but it is hard to discern ways to remove or lower those barriers. Many of the adverse conditions seem intractable, and many of the apparently negative trends appear inevitable and irreversible. Understandably, most attempts to improve mating processes have been aimed at individuals and not at the conditions under which they seek spouses.

The most widely advocated means of improving marital choices is through education, including marriage preparation courses and premarital counseling. Although there are limits to the extent that formal courses and counseling can impart wisdom and good judgment, a great deal more could be done through these means to promote good marital choices. For instance, while the Catholic Church has a good record of requiring and encouraging premarital education and counseling, the other Christian denominations, as a whole, have done far less. Marriage preparation courses in the public schools are rare and almost certainly of poor quality, in general, when they are offered.[8] Functional marriage and family courses at the college level attract a small but not insignificant proportion of college students, but if the textbooks available for adoption for such courses indicate their substance, they give little guidance for marital choice.[9] The potential for formal education and counseling to contribute to good marital matching is considerable but apparently largely unfulfilled. Obviously, there are opportunities for pro-marriage scholars and activists to try to reach that potential. They could, for instance, prepare or commission the preparation of educational materials on marital choice that would be sounder and more effective than those now available.[10]

The most important education about marriage and marital choice, however, is almost certainly informal and through such influences as parents, siblings, other kin, friends, and exposure to the mass media. There is little that activists can do to change the nature of many of these influences, but they can to some extent improve the quality of the media. Some exemplary work of this nature has been done, especially the report on cohabitation written by David Popenoe and Barbara Whitehead and issued by the National Marriage Project.[11] This report received widespread attention in the media and helped dispel the popular belief that the odds for marital success can be substantially improved by using cohabitation as a test for compatibility.

Helping people be wise and rational participants in marriage markets is important, but a greater potential for improving marital matching may lie in changing the way the markets operate and the conditions under which persons seek mates. Wisdom and good judgment cannot have their greatest effects if, for instance, those who possess those qualities have limited opportunities to meet and get to know prospective spouses and if their social networks do not exert positive influences on their activities and interactions that may lead to marriage. To repeat a point, if there is inadequate circulation in marriage markets, the persons who could form the best matches are unlikely ever to connect.

There has been no systematic research to assess how well the institutional mechanisms for mate selection are working, and no one has done an inventory of what religious and other organizations are doing to facilitate the circulation that is necessary for good marital matching. Sponsorship of such research is an obvious first step that could be undertaken by pro-marriage activists, and social scientists interested in marriage should plan and propose such research. We do not need formal studies of mate selection processes, however, to know that they are not working as well as they should and could.

There are some good models of what could be done to facilitate good marital matches. For instance, some religious organizations, including a good many Jewish congregations, do an exemplary job of providing opportunities for unmarried people to get to know one another under favorable conditions. The activities and arrangements for circulation offered by the Jewish organizations probably have some continuity with traditional Jewish matchmakers, and they reflect to some extent a desire to promote religious and ethnic endogamy. Without such traditions and motivations, Christian congregations and organizations would be expected to do less well, which, it seems to me, is the case.

It is easier to exhort than to implement effective programs; organizations interested in facilitating good marital matches face formidable obstacles to achieving their goal. The singles activities they promote are susceptible to the same kind of stigma that has plagued singles clubs in recent decades, namely, the image that they attract mainly losers. When matchmaking is the only or the most explicit purpose of an activity, a "meat market" atmosphere tends to emerge, and there is a risk of attracting exploitative participants. The main traditional advantage of seeking spouses at churches has been that many persons of good character and high morals are likely to be found there. This advantage is diminished when there is attraction to church activities only for the purpose of making social contacts.

In view of such problems, it is clear that good intentions are not sufficient; people and organizations that have tried to implement programs to promote optimal matching must share knowledge. A great deal of such sharing may occur informally, but there appears to be little literature on the topic. This is another area in which pro-marriage activists and scholars could contribute.

The promotion of good marriage-market circulation is in part educational, because many participants lack full knowledge of the activities in their communities that provide good opportunities to meet potential spouses. Pro-marriage activists could compile directories of the relevant organizations and distribute calendars of their activities. Reporting information on the sex ratios of the memberships of the organizations might help to rectify imbalances in the numbers of men and women.

Businesses and other employers could take steps to facilitate good marital matches among their employees, although it is arguable whether it is in their interest to do so. Much has been written about the need for family-friendly policies and practices on the part of employers, and some policies have been implemented. However, these policies generally do nothing to promote family formation among unmarried employees and fail to benefit those who are both unmarried and childless. Indeed, efforts to relieve married persons from unwanted evening and weekend work often overburden single employees and interfere with their social lives and thus their search for spouses. Furthermore, discouragement of workplace romances by employers may go well beyond what is necessary to prevent sexual harassment and promote fairness and efficiency. And when employers sponsor social and recreational activities for their employees, they do not always take the needs of single employees into account—for instance, by trying to give those who work in different departments opportunities to get to know one another.

I could continue with suggestions for ways to promote good marital matching, but my purpose here is to encourage discussion of the topic rather than to provide a blueprint for action. My ideas are embryonic, and I do not know what methods would be most effective. I am confident, however, that if pro-marriage scholars and activists were to turn their collective imagination to the topic, the quality of matching, and thus prospects for marital success, could be measurably improved.

## CONCLUSION

I conclude simply by enumerating my main propositions:

1. People concerned about promoting good marriages in the United States have recently given insufficient attention to good marital matching, that is, to getting the right individuals married to one another.

2. There is a general lack of sophisticated understanding of what constitutes a good marital match.

3. The primary requirement for a good marital match is that each spouse be more desirable to the other spouse than to most other persons of the opposite sex.

4. A second requirement is that each spouse be married to a person about as desirable to him or her as is possible given what he or she has to offer on the marriage market.

5. A third requirement is that each spouse not be substantially less desirable than the other spouse thinks he or she is when the decision is made to marry.

6. Matches with these characteristics depend on circulation among those "on the market" sufficient to allow each person to get to know a large number and wide variety of prospective spouses and to test his or her own desirability.

7. Proper functioning of marriage markets also requires avoidance of "premature entanglement," that is, relationships that are difficult to end that develop before persons have well-formulated notions of the kinds of partners they can attract and want to attract.

8. The influence of friends and close relatives often tends to prevent poor marital choices.

9. Informal evidence suggests that marriage markets are not functioning well in contemporary American society and that poor marital matches are common.

10. Recent changes that may have made good marital matching harder to achieve include (a) the widespread postponement of marriage be-

yond completion of formal education and the time when opportunities for circulation are optimal; (b) the increase in persons who have children on the marriage market; (c) restrictions on workplace romances; (d) a decline of family influences on marital choice; and (e) increased nonmarital cohabitation, which may often be a form of premature entanglement.

11. There is an unrealized potential for education to contribute to good marital matching, but education cannot substantially lower most of the barriers to good matching.

12. The greatest potential for improving marital matching probably lies in the promotion of adequate marriage-market circulation and the kinds of social ties that are conducive to good marital choices.

13. There is a need for research into the changing institutional mechanisms for mate selection and for sharing of information among organizations that have tried to promote good marital matching.

## NOTES

1. The simple theory and conceptual scheme presented here draw indirectly on the various "exchange" theories of marital choice in the literature; the most influential are in, or based on, the theories presented in Peter M. Blau, *Exchange and Power in Social Life* (New York: Wiley, 1964); George C. Homans, *Social Behavior: Its Elementary Forms* (New York: Harcourt, Brace, and World, 1961); and J. W. Thibaut and H. H. Kelley, *The Social Psychology of Groups* (New York: Wiley, 1959).

2. Just who is and is not "on the market" is not entirely clear. Some people go on the market only after they encounter a particularly attractive prospect, and even married persons may be tentatively on the market. See Bernard Farber, "The Future of the American Family: A Dialectical Account," *Journal of Family Issues* 8 (1987): 431–433.

3. U.S. Bureau of the Census, *Statistical Abstract of the United States: 1999*, 119th ed. (Washington, D.C., 1999), 111, table 158.

4. U. S. Bureau of the Census, *Current Population Reports*, Series P20-506, "Marital Status and Living Arrangements: March 1998 (Update)."

5. Norval D. Glenn and Michael Supancic, "The Social and Demographic Correlates of Divorce and Separation in the United States: An Update and Reconsideration," *Journal of Marriage and the Family* 46 (1984): 564–575; and more recent unpublished analyses of data from the General Social Surveys.

6. Analyses of data from the General Social Surveys show that persons who married at these ages were more likely to be in stable and successful first marriages than persons who married at older ages. Of course, this relationship could be spurious rather than causal; that is, the same influences could lead to late marriage and lowered prospects for marital success.

7. David Popenoe and Barbara Dafoe Whitehead, *Should We Live Together? What Young Adults Need to Know about Cohabitation before Marriage* (New Brunswick, N.J.: National Marriage Project, 1999).

8. Dana Mack, *Hungry Hearts: Evaluating the New Curricula for Teens on Marriage and Relationships* (New York: Institute for American Values, 2000).

9. For a critique of some of the books, see Norval D. Glenn, "A Critique of Twenty Family and Marriage and the Family Textbooks," *Family Relations* 46 (1997): 197–208.

10. An abundance of trade books and popular magazine articles give advice about how to find and connect with good potential spouses, which is evidence that many people feel a need for education on the topic. However, these materials, while occasionally insightful, are of uneven quality, and with few exceptions are not based on sound research or sophisticated theory.

11. Popenoe and Whitehead, *Should We Live Together?*

# 5

# Why Covenant Marriage May Prove Effective as a Response to the Culture of Divorce

## Katherine Shaw Spaht

## INTRODUCTION

Those who believe that marriage is a sacred institution, essential to the continued health of our secular liberal democracy, may not know what to make of the health of the institution today. My own conclusion is that marriage in America is in the process of collapse, which is evidenced by our current historically low marriage rate. Americans are confused about marriage—its public character, its history as an institution, and even its purpose, since the procreation and rearing of children has increasingly been separated from marriage. The only issue remaining for those of us who believe that marriage is essential is how to restore the public institution, how to recapture a cultural understanding of marriage, and precisely how to strengthen marriage in the imaginations and hearts of our citizens.

Marriage as the foundation of a stable, intact family dramatically benefits the two spouses and their children on every scale of human experience—material, emotional, physical, and psychological. As a result, a state concerned about assuring and encouraging productive, flourishing families should be motivated to promote marriage. Furthermore, the negative consequences of the failure to form families and their dissolution have an impact on state resources, existing and future. The impact should motivate a state to do more than simply promote marriage; a state should also protect marriage by examining carefully every area of law and policy that influences the family. The state should determine if the law encourages or discourages the formation of stable families anchored in lifelong marriage.

Any state that remains indifferent, if not hostile, to marriage does so at its peril and the peril of its citizens.

Although there are currently various initiatives to promote marriage at both the federal and state levels, success in restoring marriage as a robust public institution requires the rhetorical power and the coercive force of law to redefine *marriage* in the imagination of our fellow citizens. The "shrieking voices"[1] of America's most influential opinion-shapers have relentlessly assailed the traditional meaning of marriage and its definition as a legal term of art. Past generations did not require a legally binding definition of *marriage* because people instructed in the tenets of Western morality have an instinctive understanding of what the word means. The received model of marriage is grounded in universal truths, natural orders, and enduring moral boundaries. As a unique institution, marriage has traditionally been defined by three elements: (1) sexual complementarity, the "ordering" purpose of which is procreation; (2) mutual faithfulness; and (3) "the special bond of permanence conferred by God as a 'sacrament,' a gift of grace."[2]

State reform must focus on the cultural definition of marriage, which has been shaped by the "shrieking voices" in complicity with legal scholars and judges, as "a couple's relationship mainly designed for the sexual and emotional gratification of each adult."[3] The Vermont Supreme Court essentially used this cultural definition to conclude that limiting the extensive legal benefits of marriage to heterosexual couples simply cannot be justified considering the articulated purpose of marriage.[4] Needless to say, if marriage as we know it is to survive, the current definition of *marriage* needs radical alteration.

Covenant marriage legislation attempts that task by elevating marriage to the position of a serious commitment made by a couple, requiring: (1) sober deliberation about the initial decision; (2) the assumption of a legal obligation to take reasonable steps to preserve the marriage during difficult periods inevitable in any long-term relationship; and (3) the agreement to limit the grounds for divorce, thus creating a more permanent relationship.[5] Restoration of an element of permanence, combined with a societal judgment about unacceptable marital conduct (fault, such as adultery), reflects a serious intention to recapture the historical definition of marriage. A relationship of permanence with the acceptance of society's judgment of spousal conduct deserves the legal benefits and advantages attendant to marriage and, frankly, makes marriage a less attractive status for those interested in a relationship terminable at will and free of the constraints of society's moral judgment.

Even though other divorce reform efforts may restore to the definition of *marriage* an element of permanence and societal judgment about spousal conduct, covenant marriage legislation offers advantages not offered by other efforts.

### Covenant Marriage Focuses on Strengthening Marriage, Not Simply Making Divorce More Difficult

Covenant marriage legislation, unlike other divorce reform efforts, focuses on marriage itself—by educating couples about the seriousness of marriage, by equipping them with the tools for resolution of the inevitable "difficulties," and by assuring that a spouse fulfills the promises he or she makes in the process. Covenant marriage accomplishes these objectives through mandatory premarital counseling[6] and the legal obligation to work diligently at preserving the couple's marriage.[7] Combined with the understanding that a covenant marriage cannot be dissolved except for serious reasons or an extended period of living separately,[8] mandatory preliminary counseling will launch couples with an attitude averse to divorce. This attitude toward divorce, new research suggests, may serve to ensure greater marital quality and thus fewer marital difficulties.[9]

Three unique components of covenant marriage legislation make the reform effort weighty and serious: (1) the legal obligation to make reasonable efforts to preserve the marriage, including marriage counseling; (2) the "rollback" of liberal grounds for divorce, especially unilateral no-fault divorce; and (3) the reinstitution of fault by a spouse as sufficient reason to permit immediate divorce. The reinforcement of the law strengthens in advance the promise made by a spouse to take steps to preserve the marriage. In our culture, moral notions of keeping one's promises have so eroded that the coercion of law is required to assure faithfulness. Society's collective interest in preserving marriages, if only "for the sake of the children," justifies the sanction of the law.

Unilateral repudiation of a spouse for no good reason undermines social and religious condemnation of such irresponsible behavior. Eliminating no-fault divorce, which unfortunately Louisiana's covenant marriage legislation does not accomplish, and restoring a common moral code about appropriate conduct in marriage communicate society's willingness once again to judge personal behavior in the most intimate of relationships. Personal behavior within marriage affects the public. There can be no compartmentalization of a person's offensive behavior in his or her marriage. That behavior has an effect on the public. Ask the children. If the offensive behavior is adultery, ask the children of the partner in adultery.

Some scholars argue and advocate that covenant marriage legislation will become a precursor to the complete "privatization" of marriage. I surely hope not. Despite arguments for permitting private contractual arrangements of marriage,[10] I am unpersuaded. Marriage as a public institution should not be reduced to a mere contract between two parties without an agreed-on mandatory content. American society has a vital interest in strengthening marriage as it has been traditionally understood. Evidence exists that legal recognition of other relationships as equivalent to marriage erodes and undermines the institution of marriage. Furthermore, I believe that where marriage is concerned, American couples may lack the moral education necessary for considered decisions, the best of which reflect some measure of sacrifice for future transcendental good. Freedom exercised responsibly requires virtuous citizens. Privatizing or customizing marriage by permitting two people to construct the content of their marriage is fraught with peril. Marriage that lasts a lifetime, "in sickness and in health," through life's many passages, requires heroic commitment and, to some degree, legal compulsion and constraint.

### Politics Is the Art of the Possible, and Covenant Marriage Combines Elements That Appeal to Both Conservatives and Liberals

Covenant marriage legislation strategically combines concepts attractive to both conservatives and liberals—traditional marriage and choice, moral judgment about personal behavior and education. Consequently, the legislation appeals to thoughtful conservative and liberal lawmakers alike, particularly those whose secular worldview also acknowledges the undesirable consequences of the present divorce culture. For liberal lawmakers and their allies who oppose covenant marriage legislation, the law exposes the hypocrisy of liberal dogma that insists on destructive choices in the name of freedom but denies citizens a virtuous choice.[11] The hypocrisy of such a position speaks for itself, and hypocrisy remains among the most serious of moral faults.

For those who understand that moral fault extends beyond hypocrisy, the best covenant marriage legislation reintroduces or expands objective fault as grounds for immediate divorce. State law that once again willingly judges marital behavior conveys confidence in a common, objective moral code. With the recent attention given to the developing field of evolutionary psychology and its revelations about human mating behavior,[12] the case can be made in secular, scientific terms for law's first role in constraining undesirable human behavior.

At the same time, covenant marriage legislation incorporates the liberal lawmaker's panacea—education—in the form of mandatory premarital counseling, which stresses the seriousness of marriage and the expectation that the marriage will be lifelong. Another appealing component of covenant marriage for liberals is the spousal obligation to make "reasonable efforts" to preserve their marriage if difficulties arise, including marriage counseling. Of course, the counseling must be directed at preserving the marriage, which often runs counter to the training received by some therapeutic professionals.[13] Too often the psychiatrist, psychologist, or social worker focuses on the individual patient or client without concern for the community in which the person lives—the family.

## In an Increasingly Secular Nation, Covenant Marriage Legislation Invites the Cooperation and Valuable Assistance of the Church in the Work of Preserving Marriage

Unlike professional therapists, a minister, priest, or rabbi who is faithful to his or her religious tenets will counsel the value of permanent marriage. When difficulties arise and the covenant couple must take steps to preserve their marriage, proponents of covenant marriage hope that one or both spouses will seek spiritual assistance. Religious leaders are particularly well equipped to offer intensive one-on-one counseling for couples, both before the marriage and during it when difficulties arise. Of equal importance to preserving the marriage is the moral authority with which the clergy speak and their compassionate concern for the congregant's family.

Although religious officials should be suspicious of governmental intrusion, covenant marriage legislation represents an invitation to religious leaders to assist. Rather than banishing religion from the public square, covenant marriage legislation invites religion back into public life to offer a service that religion is uniquely qualified to perform—preserving marriages. Conscious of the difference between an invitation and an order, the legislation contains only the bare essentials of required content of premarital counseling. Increasingly, policy makers recognize that only the moral authority of religion can effectively solve the most stubborn of our country's social problems. So rather than further "sanitize" the already secular public square, policy makers are seeking "faith-based" organizations with which government can partner. Restoration of a public and religious partnership for the purpose of solving our country's most intractable social problems, such as the dissolution of marriages, offers hope for our children's future.

## Persuasion, Not Coercion, of the Citizenry Is the Only Effective Means to Reverse More than Thirty Years of Erroneous Social Science and Celebration of the Autonomous Self

Conservatives can no longer ignore the price of the continuous, decades-long assault on traditional moral values. The results of the assault have been devastating, but none more than the consequences of the much-touted sexual revolution, particularly for women. Adultery, which at one time was a crime, is now described as a purely "private" matter concerning the adulterer and his or her spouse, even though it often results in the breakup of families. Consistent with such a view, unilateral no-fault divorce encapsulated in legal language a process of disintegration of marriage that was no one's fault—it just happened. These views, combined with the uniquely American language of "rights," inform the conclusion that divorce for no good reason is one more individual entitlement.

Joe Loconte in his May 1998 article "I'll Stand Bayou" in *Policy Review* refers to the covenant marriage legislation as a cultural "sleeping giant." The legislation invites those who believe in lifelong marriage to, in effect, "resell its value" to a cynical citizenry. Changing the culture requires missionary work, winning over one heart (or two in the case of covenant marriage) at a time. Covenant marriage legislation not only facilitates and encourages, but also requires, evangelizing marriage. Individual Americans need to be convinced of the value of keeping one's promises, of persevering through difficult times, of personal sacrifice, and of duty to one's children, a duty to assume the role of adult by providing a stable home environment and by sparing them the vicissitudes of adult conflict.

### Covenant Marriage Offers Traditional "Communities" a Refuge from the Moral Confusion About Marriage and from the Divorce Law of a Hedonistic Postmodern America

Until this country's dominant culture changes, covenant marriage legislation permits us by agreement to create for ourselves and our families an alternative legal structure for family life that social science research supports as the ideal. The legislation "allows a minority to live their desired lives [in the case of covenant marriage consistently with society's best interests] without forcing a change in lifestyle on the majority."[14] By electing the option of covenant marriage, covenant couples offer themselves as models for a society desperately in need of moral example. A commitment to lifelong marriage requires self-sacrifice and recognition of duty to a transcendental good.

As early as 1945, the renowned French law professor Léon Mazeaud, who was a devout Catholic and extremely concerned about the future of the French family, proposed a marriage of one's choice that could be either indissoluble or dissoluble by divorce.

> The family is made of stability. All [social] cohesion resides in its perpetuity. . . . The French family is, however, an ephemeral group. It is broken up at the whim of its members. Marriage, which founds it, is provisional. It endures as long as the happiness of the spouses endures. Divorce is there in order to rupture marriage. *Born from the fight led against the church*, divorce is rooted in our laws. The debate ought to cease. It is possible to reach agreement, both in liberty and by liberty. Some want a marriage that divorce dissolves; others, an indissoluble marriage. Then let each choose! Our laws have, in succession decreed first indissoluble marriage, then dissolvable marriage. Let them [now] decree marriage dissolvable or indissoluble *according to the choice of the future spouses*! This is the solution to the problem of divorce— a facultatively indissoluble marriage. No one can protest, for each remains free to bind himself up to death or only up to divorce. *No one will protest, save for the hypocrite who, at the same time, promises his life and keeps the disposition of it.*[15]

Christopher Wolfe opines that the liberal ideal of autonomy is incompatible with the substantive moral ideal of marital fidelity "that is embraced by certain traditional communities that from one perspective are 'within' the American community and from another perspective are not."[16] Wolfe specifically mentions Catholics, but the identification of traditional "communities" could be extended to all people of deep religious faith. Gertrude Himmelfarb further expands "communities," which she collectively labels the "dissident culture," to include "those of little or no religious faith" who abide by traditional values and are unembarrassed by the language of morality.[17]

Covenant marriage legislation offers the dissident culture the opportunity to live as a traditional community under a stricter moral code reinforced by law, within the larger dominant culture that is subject only to minimal moral constraints. Covenant marriage legislation offers the opportunity to demonstrate a "better way," to lay the foundation for the reconstruction of strong and stable families.

## Covenant Marriage, Because of Its Character as Partially Status and Partially a Contract Limited in Content, Offers the Most Promise Among Divorce Reform Efforts of Surviving the "Migratory Divorce" Phenomenon

No state divorce reform effort can accomplish all that it intends if one spouse can cross the state line and, by simply establishing a new domicile, seek relief in another state with more liberal divorce laws. Because of the unique characteristics of "covenant" marriage, a court in the state with more liberal divorce laws may be compelled to reexamine the 1942 U.S. Supreme Court opinion in *Williams v. North Carolina I*,[18] which equated the issue of judicial jurisdiction with the issue of choice of law.

If a court in the state of a plaintiff's new domicile would be compelled to separate the issue of jurisdiction to render a divorce from the issue of what divorce law should be applied (choice of law), general choice of law rules would favor the application of the covenant marriage law of plaintiff's old domicile. Two reasons emerge for that favoritism: (1) the fact that the distinguishing characteristic of a covenant marriage is the parties' voluntary commitment undertaken after specific and meaningful counseling and expressed in an additional contract (the "covenant") superimposed on the traditional "marriage contract" (the exchange of vows) containing an express choice of Louisiana law;[19] and (2) the fact that the covenant marriage law does not eliminate, but simply delays, the availability of a unilateral no-fault divorce.[20] There is little question, of course, that the obligation assumed in the "covenant" to take all reasonable efforts to preserve the marriage binds the spouses even if one moves to another state; it would be considered an "incident" or effect of marriage, like spousal or child support.

Covenant marriage offers the potential for reversing Supreme Court social engineering, which as early as 1942 reduced divorce laws in the states to the "lowest common denominator." The barriers and obstacles to divorce erected by North Carolina for the protection of its citizenry crumbled in obeisance to the Supreme Court's dictate that North Carolina must give full faith and credit to a judgment of divorce rendered in the more lax state of Nevada, whose court applied its own law defining marriage down.

## CONCLUSION

For any state considering options to its current no-fault divorce law, the opportunities afforded by covenant marriage legislation should be emphasized. The combination of choice with traditional morality and of education with the restoration of moral judgment can appeal to both liberals and conservatives of good faith. Furthermore, unlike other divorce reform proposals, covenant marriage legislation requires that citizens be persuaded concerning the centrality of marriage and the importance of its permanence. The legislation invites the cooperation and support of religion in this persuasive effort. Only such a massive public relations effort can reverse decades of accelerating moral and cultural decline.

Until policy makers alter the present legal structure of marriage by repealing unilateral no-fault divorce law and restoring an expectation of permanence to marriage, it will be difficult to convince future generations that the marriage vow is the strongest, most important commitment a person makes during his or her lifetime. To persuade the skeptical it is necessary to recapture the strength of the marital commitment and its unique sacrificial quality.

Covenant marriage offers an opportunity to change the dominant paradigm of marriage, to change the "definition" of marriage from a casual companionate relationship to a serious and sober lifetime commitment. Proponents of lifelong marriage must convince Americans that marriage entails responsibility to one's spouse and unqualified responsibility to children born of the marriage. Rather than serving to denigrate marriage, as detractors often argue, covenant marriage legislation offers the potential to reshape the current American idea of marriage.

## ACKNOWLEDGMENT

Adapted from an article by the author titled *Marriage: Why a Second Tier Called Covenant Marriage?* originally published in 12 Regent U. L. Rev. 1 (1999–2000).

# NOTES

1. From T. S. Eliot, "Burnt Norton," *Four Quartets.*

2. David Orgon Coolidge, *Same-Sex Marriage? Baehr v. Miike and the Meaning of Marriage,* 38 S. Tex. L. Rev. 1, 31 (1997).

3. David Popenoe and Barbara Dafoe Whitehead, *The State of Our Unions 1999, The Social Health of Marriage in America* (New Brunswick, N.J.: The National Marriage Project, 1999).

4. *Baker v. Vermont,* 744 A.2d 864 (1999).

5. A covenant marriage cannot be dissolved quickly without proof of seriously offensive conduct by one spouse. See La. Rev. Stat. Ann. § 9:307 (West 1999).

6. La. Rev. Stat. Ann. 9:272–273 (West 1999).

7. La. Rev. Stat. Ann. 9:272–273 (West 1999).

8. La. Rev. Stat. Ann. 9:307–308 (West 1999).

9. Paul R. Amato and Stacy J. Rogers, "Do Attitudes Toward Divorce Affect Marital Quality?" *Journal of Family Issues* 69, 70 (January 1999): "Although most Americans continue to value marriage, the belief that an unrewarding marriage should be jettisoned may lead some people to invest less time and energy in their marriages and make fewer attempts to resolve marital disagreements. In other words, a weak commitment to the general norm of life-long marriage may ultimately undermine people's commitments to particular relationships."

10. Jeffrey Stake and Eric Rasmussen, *Lifting the Veil of Ignorance: Personalizing the Marriage Contract,* 73 Indiana L. J. 453 (1998); Elizabeth Scott, *Rational Decisionmaking About Marriage & Divorce,* 76 Va. L. Rev. 9 (February 1990).

11. Christopher Wolfe, "The Marriage of Your Choice," *First Things* 50 (February 1995) 37–41.

12. David Buss, *The Evolution of Desire: Strategies of Human Mating* (New York: Basic Books, 1994). See also Steven Pinker, *How the Mind Works* (New York: W.W. Norton, 1997), 425–520.

13. William Doherty, "How Therapists Threaten Marriage," *The Responsive Community* 7 (Summer): 31 (1997). But see results of a survey by the Religion, Culture, and Family Project published "The Ethics of Relationality," *Journal of Family Relations* 48 (Spring 1999): 2.

14. Jeffrey Evans Stake, *Paternalism in the Law of Marriage,* 74 Ind. L. J. 801, 807 (1999).

15. Henri Mazeaud et al., *Leçons de Droit Civil: La Famille,* bk. 1, vol. 3, no. 1415, part II at 654, titled *Solution to the Problem of Divorce,* 7th ed., ed. Larent Levenuer (1995). I am indebted to my colleague, Professor Randy Trahan, for his translation of this important work.

16. Wolfe, "The Marriage of Your Choice," 41.

17. Gertrude Himmelfarb, "The Panglosses of the Right Are Wrong," *Wall Street Journal* (February 4, 1999), A22.

18. *Williams v. North Carolina I,* 317 U.S. 287 (1942).

19. "With full knowledge of what this commitment means, we do hereby declare that our marriage will be bound by Louisiana law on Covenant Marriages." La. Rev. Stat. Ann. 9:273, 275 (West 1999).

20. Katherine S. Spaht and Symeon Symeonides, *Covenant Marriage and the Law of Conflicts of Laws,* 32 Creighton L. Rev. 1085 (1999).

# 6

# Good Incentives Lead to Good Marriages

## Allen M. Parkman

## INTRODUCTION

Many people are finding it difficult to achieve happiness through marriage and a family. This is not always a regrettable situation as we have moved from an environment in which marriage was attractive to essentially all adults to one in which sometimes that is not the case. Still, marriage is the preferred arrangement for most adults and to the extent that they are less successful in finding happiness there, that is a social tragedy. Frequently, this lack of marital success is attributed to recent changes in values associated with a shift from fulfillment within a family to an emphasis on narrowly defined personal goals. Although some may feel comfortable with this explanation, it begs the question of why values changed. If we recognize that the individual's most fundamental values are based on self-interest, which is resistant to change, then a more satisfactory explanation for these changes in behavior is that people are responding to a change in the incentives that they face. In this chapter, I will address the importance of incentives in a successful marriage, the ability of no-fault divorce to frustrate these incentives, and a reform program to improve the incentives for adults to make decisions that increase the likelihood of a successful marriage.

## THE IMPORTANCE OF INCENTIVES

Incentives are central to the rational choice framework, which is commonly used in economics and frequently in other social sciences such as sociology and political science. This model assumes that people make decisions based on their attempt to increase their welfare subject to the constraints they face. People are viewed as rational not because their decisions are brilliant, but because their actions are purposeful. In the process of increasing their welfare, people weigh the costs and benefits of alternatives, choosing the ones that they anticipate will provide them with the largest net benefits. As the costs and benefits of activities change, the incentives facing people change. This framework has been shown to explain and predict a broad range of human activities.[1] Based on this perspective, people marry when they expect the benefits of a marriage to a particular person to exceed the costs—remaining single and searching for a better spouse. Alternatively, they divorce when they conclude that the costs of this marriage exceed the benefits associated with some other living arrangement.

Incentives have had an important role in the trends we have observed among American families. Some fundamental changes in society have reduced the incentives for people to marry and, among those who marry, these incentives have resulted in less durable marriages. In addition to love and physical attraction, people traditionally married because they expected to be better off psychologically as well as having access to more goods and services. The psychological benefits came from a stable relationship, while the additional goods and services followed from the spouses assuming more specialized roles. A strong incentive for this specialization was based on their desire for children. A convergence in the opportunities available to men and women accompanied by a decrease in the desirability of children has reduced the incentives for men and women to specialize during marriage, thereby reducing the gains from marriage. The impacts of these changes need to be recognized, because they cannot be reversed. For people who do not want children and see few gains from increased specialization during a relationship or perceive few psychological gains from a stable relationship, marriage has become less attractive.

Still, most people see substantial gains to be obtained from marriage, especially if they want children and a long-term commitment to their spouse. For them, legal changes have reduced the incentives for people to focus on the best interests of their families, lessening the likelihood that their marriages will be a success. The primary legal change has been the change in the grounds for divorce from essentially mutual consent—fault divorce— to permitting either spouse to dissolve a marriage unilaterally—no-fault divorce.[2] The fault grounds were normally adultery, desertion, or cruelty, while the no-fault grounds are usually irretrievable breakdown or incompatibility. Divorces granted on the fault grounds were usually based on mutual consent, so that the crucial negotiations between the spouses tended to confront the spouse wanting the divorce with the costs of divorce, especially to the other spouse and to their children. These costs were financial as well as psychological. Without a compensation package to cover those costs, the divorced spouse would be expected to be reluctant to participate in the divorce. Unilateral, no-fault divorce often permits the divorcing spouse to ignore some of the costs of divorce at the expense of the divorced spouse and their children.

Consequently, the grounds for divorce had important effects on the incentives influencing the decisions that people made in an attempt to have a successful marriage. If someone expected to be able to control when and if their marriage dissolved—as they tended to do with mutual consent divorce—their self-interest suggested that a long-term commitment to their marriage was appropriate, and personal sacrifices—such as limiting a career—that benefited others within the family were likely to result in reciprocal actions by the spouse and children then or later. As marriage has become a less stable institution—due in part to unilateral, no-fault divorce—the incentives for people to make these commitments and sacrifices have been reduced. People have responded by focusing more on their own self-interest and less on the best interest of their families.

This shift in behavior has erroneously been attributed to a change in values. In contrast to the irreversible social changes already noted, these legal changes can be reversed. A combination of no-fault, fault, and mutual consent grounds for divorce will increase the incentives for people to make decisions that increase their welfare and the welfare of their families.

## Why Do People Marry?

The importance of incentives in a successful marriage becomes more apparent if we recognize that there is more to that success than just love and physical attraction. Additional benefits follow from opportunities within a relationship for economies of scale, specialization, and insurance. Traditionally, the decision for a couple to live together was synonymous with the decision to get married. That is no longer the case. Before the broad availability of contraceptives, it was uncommon for couples to live together without being married because regular sexual relations usually resulted in parenthood. Social mores tended to require marriage as a prerequisite for regular sexual relations because the children were potential burdens on society if the parents did not marry. Society responded by placing a significant social stigma on premarital sex. With effective contraceptives, living together does not have to lead to children and, therefore, cohabitation has often been separated from the decision to get married.

### Incentives to Live Together

Therefore, a first step toward marriage is the recognition that a couple is better off living together than living on their own. Living together provides opportunities for economies of scale, specialization, and insurance.

Households provide opportunities for economies of scale that are not available to someone living alone. The size of a comfortable house does not normally increase as much as the increase in the number of occupants; thus the cost per occupant falls as the number of occupants increases up to some point. In addition, some commodities consumed in a household are public goods, which are special cases of commodities with economies of scale: A public good can be consumed by additional people at little or no additional cost; further, people cannot easily be excluded from the enjoyment of the commodity. A private good, by way of contrast, is costly to provide to additional people and people can be excluded from enjoying it. A television set can be a public good; an apple exemplifies a private good. Most households can reduce the number of public goods relative to the number that they would have if the members were living on their own.

Economists have also recognized that there are gains from specialization when people live together.[3] Specialization increases the welfare of individuals by expanding their access to goods and services as they become more efficient in their production. When people cook more frequently, they become better cooks. The activities in which people specialize tend to be based on comparative advantage, which exists when two people have levels of productivity that vary among activities. A stronger person might focus on activities such as shoveling snow, for example, while his or her partner might accept responsibility for paying bills due to a bad back or a greater talent for financial management.

The last reason that people benefit from living together is insurance. People generally do not like uncertainty, so they frequently buy insurance because they prefer certainty—a fire insurance premium—to uncertainty—having a house that has been destroyed by a fire. Economists call this characteristic of human behavior "risk aversion," concluding that increased certainty can contribute to people's welfare. Because insurance cannot be purchased to cover all uncertain future events, people frequently have to make other arrangements to avoid uncertainty. People may prefer a current known situation to an uncertain future.

*Incentives to Marry*

Although we have identified numerous reasons why adults benefit from living together, we have not established a clear reason—other than one based on romance—that would explain why they marry. Some of the benefits from living together are enhanced by a more formal, long-term arrangement that traditionally has been provided by marriage. Marriage is especially important if a couple wants children, but it can be a response to other, often psychological, inducements. Still, most adults want children and children present substantial opportunities for a couple to enhance their welfare through economies of scale and specialization. In addition, marriage can be viewed as providing more substantial insurance than that available to couples who are living together.

There are economies of scale in parenting because children are a public good: they can be enjoyed by both parents at no more cost than if only one parent is present and, if the relationship continues, it is difficult to exclude a parent from that enjoyment. A more formal arrangement such as marriage increases the likelihood that the parents will continue to live together, thereby being able to take advantage of these important economies of scale.

The specialization that results from parenthood can have longer-lasting effects than those commonly associated with people living together. Increased specialization within a relationship can impose long-term costs on a party. A couple can often avoid this type of specialization until they have children. They can maintain their careers while dividing the responsibilities within their household. Children change this situation by increasing the pressure for a couple to specialize within their relationship. The arrival of children usually results in one parent increasing the emphasis that he or she places on household activities. The parents may be tempted to share the responsibility for childrearing. However, on closer inspection most conclude that it is less costly to the couple for just one parent to alter his or her employment than for both to alter their employment. Higher-paying jobs often require unexpected overtime and travel. If both parents reject that type of employment, they may be worse off than if only one parent—usually the one with the higher income-earning potential—makes that choice and the other, if he or she is employed, accepts employment that accommodates child care or devotes full time to household and children.

Although this specialization is usually in the best interest of the parents and their children while a relationship lasts, it can be revealed as costly if the relationship ends. Skills developed in one household may have little value in another relationship and even less value in the marketplace, leaving a spouse who has emphasized domestic work vulnerable at divorce. Although this can be a problem in a marriage of short duration, it is particularly a concern in longer marriages. If spouses specialize in earning income, that skill will be intact if the relationship ends. Those persons would lose their share of the household commodities provided by their spouse, but those commodities may have decreased in value after any children have grown up and left the home. During the relationship, the spouses who worked in the home may have developed skills to produce household commodities that do not have substantial value outside their relationship. Their income-earning capacity has deteriorated because of their working primarily at home. Traditionally, spouses were reluctant to make the sacrifices associated with specializing in domestic activities during marriage unless they had the expectation of a long-term relationship; marriage was associated with that expectation.

Another anticipated benefit from marriage as a long-term relationship is insurance against the uncertain future. While marriage can provide insurance against the potential costs of parenthood previously noted, it can also be important for couples without children. Seldom does a relationship permit both parties to pursue the careers that they would have pursued without the relationship. Frequently, promotions require a relocation that requires other parties to make a sacrifice either in career or lifestyle. Alternatively, as the incomes of the parties increase, they may decide that they want a more leisurely lifestyle. Just as with parenting responsibilities, it may not make sense for both parties to adjust their careers. Marriage can provide some insurance for a person who limits a career. Last, there are important psychological benefits from predictability with marriage, providing insurance that encourages a commitment by both parties.

In summary, economists note that marriage is not the only choice for adults. Because of economies of scale, specialization, and insurance, people gain from living together but not necessarily marrying. A more formal, long-term arrangement such as marriage has usually been associated with children who magnify the gains from economies of scale and specialization. Insurance also provides an incentive for people to marry.

## THE DECLINE IN THE ATTRACTION OF MARRIAGE

The gains from marriage are not static. Fundamental changes have occurred in essentially all industrial nations that have reduced the gains from marriage. Most obvious has been a reduction in the gains from specialization. The increase in women's wages and opportunities reduced their dependence on men for income and the expansion in the availability of laborsaving devices in the home reduced men's dependence on women for domestic services. Particularly important in the decline in the gains from marriage has been a reduction in the desirability of children. The benefits of parenthood have declined for some adults, as children are no longer a major source of domestic labor or retirement income. Meanwhile, the costs of children have risen. The primary factor has been the increase in the earnings available to women outside the home. Either some income has to be sacrificed so that a parent can remain at home or arrangements have to be made for child-care services. Higher incomes also provide adults with options such as travel that often are restricted by children. With the lower benefits and higher costs of children, it is no surprise that people are electing to have fewer children and, increasingly, some couples are deciding not to have children. Without children, couples lose gains from economies of scale and specialization; they are more limited and so is the attraction of marriage.

As marriage became less attractive, some people initiated legal changes that have had an independent effect that has reduced the gains from marriage. Because of the reduction in the gains from marriage, the likelihood increased that at least one spouse would ultimately conclude that he or she would be better off if the marriage was dissolved. In the process of dissolving their marriages, many people concluded that there were obvious problems with the existing fault grounds for divorce because they were perceived to be hypocritical, restrictive, and unfair. A movement developed to make it easier for spouses to divorce, with all the states either replacing the fault grounds with no-fault grounds or adding no-fault grounds to the existing fault grounds between 1969 and 1985.

The problem with no-fault divorce is that its repercussions are subtle. It is subtle because the primary reaction has been a reduction in the commitment by adults to their families. But there may be a way to enhance commitment.

### A Program to Improve Incentives

A combination of divorce grounds based on no-fault during the initial phase of marriage, mutual consent for established marriages, and fault grounds for abusive marriages will provide a major improvement in the incentives that face adults who want to marry.[4] States have traditionally been reluctant to become involved in the normal interactions during marriage and that position is supported here. Still, the state's role in protecting children is obvious, so it is appropriate for states to have statutes that establish rules for protecting children during and after a marriage. It is important to recognize that the conditions that accompany the dissolution of marriage have far greater effects on the quality of the marriage than has been commonly accepted, as they strongly influence the commitment that spouses make to marriage.

#### Mutual Consent Divorce

Under this proposal, mutual consent would be the primary ground for divorce. An established marriage should only be dissolved if both spouses agree that it is a failure. Knowing that the ground for divorce for established marriages is mutual consent would encourage spouses to make sacrifices that benefit their marriage. Meanwhile, not all established marriages are successful and if a couple is questioning the durability of their marriage, mutual consent would increase the incentives for them to recognize and place a value on the collective benefits and costs of marriage and, potentially, divorce. Under mutual consent divorce, a party who does not want a divorce would have an incentive to require compensation for its costs as a basis for agreeing to the divorce.

One of the attractive aspects of mutual consent divorce is the increased likelihood that both parents will address the costs incurred by their children due to a divorce. These costs go far beyond just maintenance, which is covered by child support. If the divorcing spouses are forced to recognize the full costs of their divorce, some parents might be able to make their marriage work and thereby provide benefits to their children.[5] The parents who expect custody of the children after a divorce are most likely to recognize the costs that the children will incur.

Another attraction of mutual consent divorce is the incentives it creates for couples to consider the rules that are appropriate for their marriage. If people who were considering marriage knew that mutual consent was the primary ground for dissolving an established marriage, that knowledge might increase the incentive for them to negotiate premarital agreements. With mutual consent divorce, the dissolution of marriage would be based on the parties' criteria rather than those of the state. Any agreement by the spouses should nevertheless be subject to regulations that attempt to protect the interests of any children.

Mutual consent is not a perfect solution. It can result in the continuation of a marriage if one party wants to ignore the costs imposed on the parties by the marriage. This can occur when a spouse is opposed to a divorce under any circumstances. However, people can be surprisingly rational even when dealing with emotional issues such as marriage and divorce. In most divorces, at least one spouse initially wanted the marriage to continue, but when the collective benefits of divorce exceed the costs, social welfare is increased by a divorce. Under those circumstances, the parties have incentives to construct an agreement that leaves them both better off. The large number of divorces based on mutual consent under the fault grounds illustrates the willingness of spouses to negotiate even under trying conditions.

### No-fault Divorce

No-fault divorce is still attractive during the early period of a marriage. Mutual consent divorce gives substantial power to spouses who do not want a divorce. To limit abuse of this power, it would appear to be prudent to permit no-fault divorce when the potential costs of divorce are likely to be low, as they tend to be early in a marriage and when there are no children. Early in marriage, a couple is still involved in an evaluation process. During this period of evaluation, no-fault divorce should continue to be the grounds for divorce, giving the parties incentives to investigate their commitment to their relationship.

Eventually, at least one spouse may make sacrifices based on a long-term commitment to the marriage and then the grounds for divorce should shift to mutual consent. These sacrifices will usually occur because a spouse is limiting a career or the couple is having a child. Recognizing that the grounds for divorce are going to change under certain circumstances—a relocation, a child, or potentially a specified time period—will force a couple to reevaluate their commitment to each other. If they are uncomfortable with the restrictions that will accompany mutual consent divorce, they can mutually agree to maintain no-fault grounds for divorce.

*Fault Divorce*

Fault divorce can also still have a role in dissolving marriages. Mutual consent can create problems when someone is "driven out" of a marriage rather than wanting out. Being driven out of a marriage raises concerns similar to those addressed with the fault divorce statutes. Under fault divorce, the "guilty" spouse did something that gave the "innocent" spouse a right to dissolve the marriage. Fault divorce is still appropriate when there is clear evidence of fault such as abuse of a spouse or any children.

In summary, mutual consent as the ground for the dissolution of most marriages is not a perfect solution to problems facing the family, but it is superior to the alternatives, especially no-fault divorce for all marriages. Most important, it creates incentives for spouses to make decisions based on the best interests of the family rather than taking a narrow focus on themselves. No-fault divorce early in marriages provides spouses with an incentive to evaluate their commitment to each other at a fairly low cost. The potential for a fault divorce creates incentives for spouses to avoid socially unacceptable behavior.

## CONCLUSION

Because of the convergence in the opportunities available to men and women, the gains from marriage have been reduced for some adults. Still, many adults want to be parents and a long-term commitment to a marriage is important in increasing their welfare and the welfare of their children. The commonly available no-fault grounds for divorce produce perverse incentives encouraging adults to focus more closely on their own self-interest and less on the interests of their family. Their incentives would be improved if the normal ground for divorce were mutual consent.

## NOTES

1. Victor R. Fuchs, *How We Live: An Economic Perspective on Americans from Birth to Death* (Cambridge: Harvard University Press, 1983).
2. For a discussion of the evolution and effects of no-fault divorce, see Allen M. Parkman, *Good Intentions Gone Awry: No-Fault Divorce and the American Family* (Lanham, MD: Rowman & Littlefield, 2000).
3. The standard economic discussion of the gains from specialization within a relationship, assumed to be marriage, is contained in Gary S. Becker, *A Treatise on the Family,* enl. ed. (Cambridge: Harvard University Press, 1991), 30–53.
4. For a more detailed discussion of the reform package discussed here, see Allen M. Parkman, "Reforming Divorce Reform," *Santa Clara Law Review* (forthcoming).
5. Under no-fault divorce, many divorces occur when there has only been a minor discord between the spouses. See Paul R. Amato and Alan Booth, *A Generation at Risk* (Cambridge: Harvard University Press, 1997), 220.

# 7

# *Strengthening Couples and Marriage in Low-Income Communities*

## Theodora Ooms

## INTRODUCTION

As a policy analyst I serve as a broker between the worlds of research, practice, and policy. For more than twenty years I have been working in family policy. Within this broad area, marriage—the cornerstone of the family—has been viewed as the "m-word," too sensitive an issue to address directly and publicly.[1] Thus I welcome the signs that marriage is beginning to emerge on the public agenda and that conferences are being held to discuss how to strengthen marriage.

However, the evolving marriage "movement" is, for the most part, inadvertently ignoring the needs and circumstances of low-income couples, even though the poor are the population group most in need of help. Most of the legal reforms and program initiatives currently being proposed to revitalize and strengthen marriage are not likely, in my view, to have any significant impact on marital stability and quality, or on nonmarital childbearing among the poor. There is a major exception. The new federal welfare reform program has the potential to help stabilize and strengthen couple unions among the poor. The 1996 Personal Responsibility and Work Opportunities Reform Act (PRWORA) established four purposes, of which three address promoting marriage, reducing out-of-wedlock childbearing, and strengthening two-parent families. (See Appendix A for background on the law and a preliminary list of activities that would constitute allowable expenditures.)

In this chapter I address four questions. First, why is it important to focus on the state of marriage in low-income communities? Second, what do we know and what more do we need to know about couple unions and marriage among the poor and near-poor? Third, what special barriers exist and what opportunities are there to build on within these groups? Fourth, what can we do, if anything, to help strengthen two-parent families and marriage in these communities? Much of my discussion focuses on the situation in African-American, urban, low-income communities largely because there is some relevant research to draw on, which is not the case with other racial/ethnic groups.

### Reasons to Focus on Low-Income Populations

It is important to focus on couples and marriage among the poor because they are at greater risk of single parenthood and the consequences for their children are more serious. A second reason is the issue of public costs. The rise in single parenthood among the poor has driven up the costs of welfare, Medicaid, and many other public assistance programs. Third, the decline in marriage among the poor and near-poor is influenced by a more complex array of factors and assumes different shapes and patterns than in the rest of the population. Thus efforts to strengthen marriage for the population as a whole are not likely to be successful unless a deliberate effort is made to develop policies and services tailored to the needs and circumstances of poor families.

The decline in marriage (and the related increase in nonmarital childbearing) cuts across nations, class, religion, and race; however, it is most marked among the poor. Low-income individuals are at higher risk of out-of-wedlock childbearing and of cohabitation, are less likely to marry, and when they do marry are more likely to separate and divorce than middle- or high- income couples.[2]

The proportion of children who live with only one parent has more than doubled since 1970, from 12 percent to 28 percent in 1996. Although the proportion is highest for black children, the rise has been steepest for whites.[3] Almost half (49 percent) of children in female-headed households were poor in 1998.[4] Single-parent households are five times more likely to be poor than two-parent households. This development is causing growing concern among policy makers and the public.

The proportion of all American children who are poor has been increasing—from 15 percent in 1970 to 20 percent in 1996, "but virtually all of this increase is associated with the growth of single-parent families."[5] (It is not possible to disentangle the direction of causation, since poverty is both a cause and an effect of single-parenthood.) Sawhill points out that the composition of this group of single parents has changed also. In the 1960s and 1970s, most of the growth of single-parent families was caused by increases in divorce, but in the next two decades all the increase was driven by out-of-wedlock childbearing. Currently, 32 percent of all children are born outside of marriage and these children are more likely to be long-term welfare dependents. (However, 40 percent of these nonmarital births are to cohabiting couples.) Currently, more than half of parents receiving welfare are not married to their child's other parent, nearly 20 percent are divorced or separated, and 11 percent are married.[6]

Studies document that children raised in single-parent homes are at greater risk of poverty, and other negative outcomes such as school drop-out, juvenile delinquency, and teen pregnancy, and are themselves more likely to become divorced.[7] As noted, the increased number of single parents has led to an increase in costs of welfare, medical assistance, food stamps, and many other assistance programs for the poor, as well as programs to deal with the issues of teen pregnancy and parenthood and troubled, poorly educated youth. In summary, there is substantial public interest in reversing the current trends in family formation among low-income populations.

## COUPLE RELATIONSHIPS AND MARRIAGE AMONG THE POOR AND NEAR-POOR

Strategies to strengthen marriage in low-income populations need to be based on a sound understanding of their demographic trends, particular patterns of couple union, and the contexts, causes, and consequences of these patterns. Unfortunately, although some information is available, there are many limitations and gaps in our knowledge of these patterns.

The demographic data that monitor trends in fertility, marriage, and out-of-wedlock pregnancy for the U.S. population as a whole are rarely presented by income or poverty status, as explained by Christine Bachrach. She says that the alternative strategy typically adopted is "to examine trend data according to relatively enduring characteristics that are associated with, but not identical to, poverty."[8] Race is one such characteristic, but it is a poor proxy for income or poverty. Level of education is often preferred.

Another problem is that while analysis of census data can provide a fairly good portrait of the association between poverty and single-parent status, these measures underestimate the presence of men or other adults in single-parent households. The use of the term *female-headed households* gives the false impression that these women are living without other adults in the household. In fact, a substantial minority live with others, both relatives and nonrelatives. Analysis of the 1990 Survey of Income and Program Participation found that 62 percent of single parents lived independently, 16 percent (mostly the younger, unmarried mothers) lived with their parents, 12 percent cohabited with unrelated men, and 11 percent shared with other adults.[9] White and Hispanic mothers are roughly twice as likely to cohabit as black mothers, but black mothers are substantially more likely to live with parents. Moreover, many of the women who report they are living independently have men in their lives as frequent visitors.

Researchers have had a great deal of interest in cohabitation in recent years; however, there remain major gaps in our understanding of patterns of cohabitation in the general population and in low-income populations in particular. We know that cohabitation has been increasing dramatically: there was a sevenfold increase between 1970 and 1996. More than half of all first marriages are now preceded by cohabitation. We also know that cohabitation is somewhat more common among low-income couples.[10] Cohabiting couples have high rates of breakup and their children are exposed to more instability than children of married couples.[11] Yet most cross-sectional surveys do not capture the complex cohabitation histories and visiting relationships of unwed parents. The constant instability of these relationships may be a more serious disadvantage to the children than if they were being raised in a stable, one-parent household.[12] We also don't know about the prevalence or characteristics of long-term cohabiting couples among poor blacks or Latinos, and whether these unions resemble what we used to term "common-law" marriages.

Although there is a growing body of literature about couple relationships and marriage among blacks, there is little data about poor whites, Native Americans, or Latinos, or about the differences between urban and rural poor families. This is a serious gap in research. For example, there is evidence that there are considerable racial-ethnic differences in patterns of and attitudes toward cohabitation and marriage, but these have been essentially ignored in the literature and public discussions about marriage.[13] A growing proportion of the poor in the United States comprises Latino and Asian immigrant families. Strong marriage and family ties and traditional family values are major strengths and resources for many immigrant groups. Apparently the process of assimilation does damage to these "family values." A new wave of studies using census and other data "consistently indicate patterns of low rates of divorce and of single-parent families in the first (immigrant) generation but striking increases in the prevalence of marital disruption over time in the United States and particularly in succeeding generations, for some (immigrant) groups more than for others."[14]

Within the substantial body of literature on African-American families, there are a growing number of qualitative studies on marriage and male/female relationships, especially among the urban black poor. (I gratefully acknowledge the help of Dr. Robert Hill, noted African-American sociologist, for steering me to several invaluable sources of information on this subject.) This research focus has a long and controversial history.

The publication in 1965 of the Moynihan report, *The Negro Family: A Call to Action,* placed a spotlight on the growth in black, female-headed households, and called them "broken" families. The report generated protest from many quarters. Several African-American scholars pointed out the biased nature of much of that research and commentary on black families and recognize that it continues today. They objected to the singular focus on one type of lower-class black family, to the persistent confusion of race and class, and to a preoccupation with pathologies rather than also examining the diversity and strengths within the black community that have enabled so many to survive and others to do well despite the odds.[15]

For example, Hill notes that in the 1990 census, married couples constituted the majority of black family households, yet there is a virtual absence of research on African-American married couples. Hill also laments the failure to study the two-parent, two-earner, low-income black families who reside in the urban "underclass" areas, defined as neighborhoods in which 40 percent or more of the people are poor. He points out that in these areas, half of the families are two-parent, are not poor, and not on welfare, and three out of five families have income from earnings.[16]

Yet while it is important to avoid stereotyping, to present a balanced view of black families, and to focus on their strengths, Hill believes we should not commit the opposite error of avoiding the facts. Researchers must seek to understand the causes of the dramatic decline in marriage among African Americans that has taken place since the 1960s. This decline is all the more dramatic when seen in historical context. Around the turn of the century, black young women were more likely to be married than white.[17] Indeed, in 1940, for every age and sex group, whites exceeded blacks in percentages never-married; but by the 1980s, just the opposite was true. Currently only 70 to 75 percent of African-American women can expect to marry during their lifetimes, as compared with 91 percent of white women.[18]

Black women are much more likely to give birth out-of-wedlock than white or Hispanic women. In 1999, 22 percent of births to non-Hispanic white women, 42 percent of births to Hispanic women, and 69 percent of births to black women were nonmarital.[19] When blacks marry, they are twice as likely to divorce as white or Hispanic women.[20] And yet while the levels of out-of-wedlock childbearing are higher for blacks, the trends have been steadily declining since the early 1990s, whereas they have been rising for whites and Hispanics.[21]

The combined effect of the decrease in black marriage rates, high black divorce rates, and the high (although declining) rates of nonmarital childbearing among blacks is that the majority of African-American children are now living in single-parent homes.

## Explanations for the Decline in Marriage

Four principal explanations are often put forward to account for the nationwide decline in marriage. Most agree that a major factor is the changing economic status of women. Their entry into the labor force and increased earnings have created a so-called "independence effect" by diminishing the economic need for women to marry or stay married. The empirical evidence to support this intuitively appealing argument is slim, however.[22] It also has less salience for African-American populations since black women have historically had high employment rates.

A second explanation given for the decline in marriage, especially among low-income African Americans, is the shortage of "marriageable" black men due to an imbalance in the sex ratio between adult black men and women. This proposed imbalance is caused in part by high rates of male homicide and suicide; high rates of unemployment among low-skilled men, especially young black men in urban areas; and high rates of black male incarceration and drug addiction. This theory was originally put forward by noted African-American scholar William Julius Wilson, based on his extensive studies of the effects of deindustrialization in the Chicago inner-city neighborhoods.[23] It was reinforced by the findings of an edited volume of papers by Tucker and Mitchell-Kernan[24] and has since gained wide currency. Although some empirical evidence has been found to support this thesis, the increasing black male unemployment rates have been found to account for only about 20 percent of the changes in marriage rates for black men from 1960 to 1980.[25]

A third factor most often cited by conservatives as a major cause of the retreat from marriage among the poor is the expansion of welfare programs that occurred in the late 1960s and 1970s. Since these programs were targeted on giving assistance to single-parent families, it is argued that the government was stepping in to take the place of fathers, undermining their responsibility to provide for their families and creating financial incentives to break up or discourage marriage, on the theory that "you get more of what you subsidize."

There has been a vigorous debate among economists about whether research supports the view that welfare programs discourage marriage and encourage divorce. The evidence is mixed and often conflicting. However, on balance, the new consensus is that the welfare programs undoubtedly played some contributory role to the rise in nonmarital childbearing and divorce, but the magnitude of the effects was not large and certainly not large enough to account for the dramatic decline in marriage that has occurred over the past twenty years, and in all classes of society, not only the poor.[26] Some analysts have taken the position that there are substantial financial disincentives for many couples embedded within the various low-income assistance programs, including a high marriage penalty within the Earned Income Tax Credit.[27] Others, however, are not so sure. A recent paper suggests that the calculations of marriage penalties/bonuses are complicated, and when cohabitation is introduced as an option, "two-parent families fare better than single parent families regardless of whether they marry if the calculation takes into account child support payments and the additional costs of maintaining two separate households."[28]

The understanding and effect of financial incentives/disincentives on young people's decisions to marry are unknown. Middle-income couples are not likely to be deterred from marrying by the fact that if both are earners they will be taxed at a higher rate than if they stayed single. However, the potential loss of several thousand dollars in benefits and refundable tax credits may deter young, low-income working couples from marriage and encourage cohabitation, since they are already living at the financial margin.

Fourth, the revolution in cultural and sexual values and gender roles of the past half-century has played a strong role in the changes in reproductive and marital behavior across income levels. William Julius Wilson, in his most recent book, states, "the weaker the norms against premarital sex, out-of-wedlock pregnancy and non-marital parenthood, the more that economic considerations affect the decision to marry."[29] Shifts in attitudes about gender roles may also play a part in relationship difficulties among low-income families. As noted recently by ethnographer Kathryn Edin, "There is certainly evidence that among lower-income adults, women's views (about gender roles) have changed far more dramatically than men's, and the result is a mismatch in sex role expectations of poor men and women."[30]

All four of these factors undoubtedly play some part in the decline of marriage, and in communities with high concentrations of poverty, the economic, cultural, and social forces appear to reinforce each other in a downward, amplifying spiral across generations.

Kathryn Edin and her colleagues have recently conducted in-depth interviews with 130 low-income black, white, and Puerto Rican single mothers in nine neighborhoods in the Philadelphia metropolitan area.[31] These interviews confirm some of the previously mentioned theories; when added to earlier studies conducted by Robin Jarrett, they create some powerful insights.[32] The women revealed four major motives that explained why they are not married to the men in their lives:

- Economic pressures (the men's erratic employment and earnings).
- Belief in male untrustworthiness (women spoke about the inevitability of male infidelity and their inability to handle money wisely or care for children responsibly).
- Yearning for respectability and upward mobility (many of the women associated marriage with home ownership, big weddings, and other markers of financial stability and upward mobility—and none of these seemed possible to achieve by marrying their current partners or boyfriends).
- Maintaining control and independence (these women expressed a strong desire to avoid economic dependence on men, which had often

occurred during their early childbearing years, and envisaged marriage, a status they idealized and desired, as a partnership between equals—they assumed marriage would probably not happen until their children were in school or had left home).

Edin concludes, "These low-income single mothers believe that marriage will probably make their lives more difficult and do not, by and large, perceive any special stigma to remaining single."[33] In a small number of interviews with low-income fathers, Edin and her colleagues confirmed the strong role economics plays as their responses make clear "that the role of the father is inextricably bound to a man's ability to provide for his children—to 'be there' financially and emotionally."[34]

These sociological, demographic, and economic explanations of the decline in marriage leave out an important part of the story. Marital interaction researchers, who are generally clinical psychologists, believe the reasons for high levels of marital instability derive primarily from the nature of the relationship between the couple. They assume that relational qualities and patterns of interaction take on a much greater importance in contemporary marriages than in former times. Most of the traditional economic, legal, social, and cultural constraints that used to keep marriages together (even unhappy ones) have fallen away. In addition, couples now have higher expectations for marital happiness—having all one's needs met by one's marital partner—and are readier to dissolve the union if they are not satisfied. The result is that there is much more pressure on young couples to communicate well, negotiate and resolve conflict, accept each other's differences, and stay committed to working on the relationship. In their carefully controlled clinical studies these marital researchers have been able to identify characteristic patterns of relating that are highly predictive of divorce.[35]

Each of these explanations suggests different approaches to attempting to strengthen and revitalize the institution of marriage. Before discussing these, however, I will highlight a few additional points that need to guide policy and program development for low-income couples. The first group fall into the category of barriers to overcome, the second are more in the nature of opportunities to build on.

### Barriers to Overcome

#### The "M-word"

One of the major barriers to putting marriage on the public agenda is that many of our nation's leaders are reluctant to talk openly about what is happening to marriage today. There are a number of reasons why people want to avoid the subject or believe it is not a legitimate topic for government intervention.[36] Marriage is a personal and sensitive subject and brings with it many different kinds of personal and political "baggage." Some fear that pro-marriage advocates want to restore patriarchy or deny the existence of domestic violence. There is also the real concern that promoting marriage is seen as stigmatizing and blaming single parents—many of whom are doing a good job under difficult circumstances—and that by imposing middle-class values on the vulnerable poor we may be acting coercively.

Progressive leaders are especially concerned that since single-parent households are more prevalent in low-income African-American communities, a pro-marriage agenda may seem especially insensitive to black concerns and realities. These fears and sensitivities about the "m-word," however real, should not be permitted to stifle study and debate on a topic of such importance to low-, middle-, and high-income Americans alike.

## Decoupling of Childbearing and Marriage

Ironically, while Americans persist in highly valuing marriage, they are becoming much less certain that marriage and childbearing need to be linked. Polls reflect a much greater tolerance and destigmatization of unwed childbearing. But when it comes to their own families, Americans in general still disapprove of unwed childbearing and there is a general recognition that it is better to wait until marriage to have a child. A recent report points out that only about 14 percent of U.S. women in 1989 said that they would consider it acceptable for their daughter to bear a child without being married.[37] While black adults are somewhat more accepting, only 28.5 percent say they would consider it acceptable for their own daughter to have a child while unmarried. Surveys of younger people, however, reveal that their attitudes are considerably more permissive about unwed childbearing. And in those African-American communities in which half to three-quarters of the children are born outside of marriage, there is probably less stigma attached to this status and less support for the belief that children are better off if they are born and raised by two married parents.

It is an enormously difficult challenge to think of effective ways of reversing this widespread, growing cultural acceptance of out-of-wedlock childbearing. It will require a marked change in the cultural messages that young people hear and see around them every day.

## Complexity of Couple and Family Relationships

Initiatives to strengthen marriage in low- income communities will need to take into account the complexity of the couple's family relationships. Many low-income couples—whether black, white, or Hispanic—do not move through the traditional stages of courtship (cohabitation), marriage, childbearing, and then perhaps divorce and remarriage that are the familiar sequence in middle-income populations. Family formation nowadays often begins not with marriage, but with the (typically unplanned) birth of a child. Often the baby's parents do not stay together but move on to new partners. Thus from the beginning many cohabiting couple households and first marriages may include a child of one of the partners. Families formed in this way face many ambiguities and tensions about who makes decisions, who the child has to obey, which partner pays what bills, and so forth. In addition, the relationships between the couple and the child's nonresidential parent (often referred to in black communities as "my baby's daddy" or "my baby's mother") are delicate and fraught with difficulty. In some respects these families encounter some of the same tensions and challenges as "blended" stepfamilies.

### External Stressors

Low-income families, especially those who reside in poverty neighborhoods, are daily exposed to a variety of experiences that place extraordinary stress on the couple and family relationships. In addition to the constant stress of making ends meet financially, and of working in unstable, low-paying jobs, they have the frustrations of living in substandard housing in poorly serviced neighborhoods, without adequate transportation, and they and their children are continually in fear of crime and violence. Members of their immediate or extended families may be struggling with depression, alcoholism or drug abuse, HIV/AIDS, or may be in and out of jail, or some combination of those problems. Domestic violence is more prevalent in low-income households. In addition, black and other minority individuals are constantly exposed in the workplace or on the streets to incidents of racism and discrimination. Service providers who work with these couples note how often these accumulated stresses spill over into the home, and anger and frustration too often poison the relationship between couples and between parents and children.

### Opportunities to Build On

#### Persistent High Valuation of Marriage

Although many skeptics assert that the high rates of out-of-wedlock childbearing and divorce indicate that marriage has virtually disappeared as a value among blacks, study after study proves the contrary. Just as in the population as a whole, marriage remains highly valued by African Americans across income levels, and married couples, especially married men, report high levels of satisfaction with their lives.[38]

In the National Survey of Black Americans conducted in 1979–1980 at the University of Michigan (the first nationally representative sample survey of black adults in the nation), respondents identified six major functions for which marriage is considered important: raising children, companionship, having a sustained love life (sex), safety (for women), help with housework, and financial security.[39]

The continuing high value placed on the importance of marriage suggests that initiatives designed to strengthen marriage would be welcomed by many in the African-American community. (This is also certainly true in the Mexican-American community, where there is an even higher cultural value placed on being married.) Indeed, increasing numbers of African-American scholars and community leaders are talking to each other about the status of male–female relations in the African-American community. Many black churches are setting up programs to enrich and restore marriage.[40] And the black popular magazines and journals, such as *Ebony,* frequently feature articles on this subject just as their counterparts do for white readers. Today, male–female relations are the most widely discussed topic in the black media.

### Gender-Role Flexibility

One of the major cultural strengths of African Americans is the flexibility of family roles in general, and specifically between men and women.[41] Two-earner families have long been the norm. Black mothers typically work outside the home and perform other traditional roles of fathers, and fathers often care for the children and carry out traditional women's household chores. This flexibility has enabled many black families to survive economically. To the extent that this egalitarian model is practiced in African-American communities it suggests that a major source of tension for many white couples may be less of a problem for blacks.

### "Magic Moments"

Several recent studies report that there are moments and stages in the development of many low-income couples' relationships that, at least briefly, hold the promise of a better and longer-lasting future together. For example, in Kathryn Edin's study, many mothers report that prior to the pregnancy, their relationships with their children's fathers were warm, romantic, and loving, and a good number said they had even planned to marry, but then the relationship began to fall apart as the boyfriends began to panic at the prospect of having to assume responsibilities and commitments for which they felt unprepared.

Other mothers described a golden period in their relationship with the child's father after their child was born. Often the father came to the hospital during or after the birth, and the couple renewed their desire to stay together and perhaps marry.[42] This finding is echoed by the preliminary results from interviews conducted with young unwed parents in two cities (Austin, Texas, and Oakland, California), part of a twenty-city survey of so-called fragile families. In these couples, more than half of the parents were living together when the child was born, 80 percent were "romantically involved," and 70 percent said their chances of marriage were 50–50 or better. In addition, 86 percent of the mothers were planning to put the father's name on the birth certificate and 90 percent of the mothers want the father to be involved in raising their child.[43] These findings led the researchers to identify the time of the birth of the child to an unmarried urban couple as a "magic moment" that could potentially be built upon. Other studies have shown that this magic moment does not last. The vast majority of these young men have limited skills, low literacy, do not work, or have a poor work history. Within a few years, the couple is likely to drift apart, and many of the fathers will disengage entirely from the relationship with their children.

These findings suggest that if the right kinds of help were offered to poor married or unmarried couples at these "magic moments," perhaps some of the relationships could be stabilized and the deterioration prevented.

### Black Churches as Resources

Religious orientation is one of the greatest strengths of black families. And black churches have played a uniquely important role in the history and spiritual and social life of African Americans. Increasingly, churches with large congregations (in the thousands) and considerable resources carry out a wide range of charitable activities and reform ministries to assist the members of the congregation and address many of the problems and needs of the community at large.[44] Some of these churches have developed strong family and marriage ministries, offering enrichment programs for married couples, workshops for single parents, and male responsibility programs for young male youth.[45] These congregations, which include large numbers of married as well as single individuals, could be a resource for the smaller, less well-endowed churches in low-income communities. One promising program model is to train volunteer married couples as mentors to befriend ("adopt") and support young, low-income parents as they traverse the inevitable ups and downs of their lives together. The need for marriage mentors is acute. Few young people today, especially those growing up in disadvantaged communities, have known examples of strong, healthy, egalitarian marriages that last.

## STRENGTHENING COUPLE RELATIONSHIPS AND MARRIAGE IN LOW-INCOME POPULATIONS

In light of the multiple factors that contribute to the decline in marriage in low-income populations, and the complex circumstances in and pressures on the lives of poor families, it seems clear that the major legal reforms currently being proposed—covenant marriage, divorce law reform, required premarital education—are not likely to have much effect on the status of marriage in low-income communities. They simply do not respond to the complex problems and circumstances low-income couples face. In this section, however, I will suggest that there are a number of economic, cultural, educational, and community-support strategies that are being tried, or are being proposed, that may be relevant and useful to the poor and near-poor. Some of these strategies stand a good chance of having positive effects, although others may be questionable. Any single strategy by itself is unlikely to have much effect. But if they were all tried at once in a community or state—the "saturation" approach—one could reasonably expect to see some changes in family formation behavior. (I do not discuss reforms in state marriage and divorce law, which are the subject of several other chapters in this volume).

*Resources for strategies to aid low-income couples.* All of these strategies will require a serious investment of resources—resources of funding, leadership, and the commitment and time of volunteers. What makes this discussion so timely and compelling is that the 1996 welfare reform law replacing the old AFDC program with the Temporary Assistance for Needy Families program (TANF) can provide states and communities with the funds right now to "promote marriage . . . and to encourage the formation and maintenance of two-parent families." TANF funds should be targeted primarily, though not exclusively, to low-income families. As of late 2001, only four states had made plans to use substantial TANF monies for these purposes. For instance, Oklahoma has made a commitment to use $10 million of unspent TANF funds to help support the governor's multisector initiative to reduce divorce and strengthen marriage. The Arizona legislature enacted legislation that allocates $1.65 million of TANF funds to be spent on prevention-oriented, marriage-related activities.[46]

A second possible source of future federal funding is the Fathers Count Act of 1999, which passed the U.S. House of Representatives with an overwhelming bipartisan majority. Many advocates hope that in the near future it will pass the U.S. Senate, where it has also drawn broad support. This act would provide grants to private and public organizations who will work with poor and low-income fathers to achieve three purposes: help fathers increase their incomes, promote successful parenting, and "promote marriage through counseling, mentoring and other activities." (For more information, see the National Fatherhood Initiative website, www.fatherhood.org.)

*Economic strategies.* Federal and state policy officials readily turn to fiscal incentives as instruments to achieve their policy goals. Thus there has already been some discussion about the need to remove current financial provisions in the tax, welfare, and other programs that may presently serve to deter marriage. States are now free to set their eligibility and other rules for receiving welfare assistance. Thus, they could change policies that currently discriminate against two-parent families and levy penalties on couples who marry. A few states are beginning to do so in small ways. West Virginia is giving married couples a 10 percent higher welfare grant than single parents. Several states are eliminating differential treatment of two-parent and one-parent families in determining eligibility for assistance. Taking this approach one step further, an analyst at a prominent conservative think tank is proposing to experiment with giving large cash bonuses to poor unwed young mothers who marry and stay married.[47]

Another strategy to remove economic barriers to marriage for low-income couples is to offer noncustodial father job training and employment assistance on the same basis as agencies offer this assistance to welfare mothers. The TANF law allows assistance to noncustodial parents, as do the Welfare-to-Work grants funded under the Labor Department. Some advocates point out that this kind of assistance to low-income noncustodial fathers should also be available to low-income married fathers, and this is now possible in the TANF program.

A few advocates note that if men believed they would be held financially responsible for their children, they would be less likely to risk becoming a father or to walk away from marriage. Thus recent policies to encourage and require paternity establishment and the numerous reforms to strengthen child support enforcement can also be viewed as a strategy designed to prevent out-of-wedlock childbearing and reduce divorce.

*Public education/changing the culture.* State authorities and community leaders can use a wide variety of vehicles to provide basic education about marriage, such as the benefits of marriage to children, the rights and responsibilities of marriage, the typical stages of marriage, and resources to get information and help with relationship and marriage problems. Some communities are beginning such public education campaigns to reduce out-of-wedlock childbearing and divorce and to promote marriage. For example, the Virginia Health Department is spending state and federal TANF funds to support community coalitions dedicated to preventing out-of-wedlock pregnancy among young adults, ages 20–29, and promote the message that "marriage is the right place for a child to be born." The Greater Grand Rapids Community Marriage Policy Initiative has developed billboards, posters, full-page newspaper ads, television shows, and brochures to explain the reasons for their initiative, tell stories of successful marriages, and share the "secrets" of strong, healthy relationships. The Florida Bar Association developed a handbook on marriage to give to all couples who applied for a marriage license. The State of Oklahoma has held several well-publicized events to promote their governor's ambitious Strengthening Marriage Initiative.

Developing a pro-marriage culture within the black or Latino communities, however, will require that black and Latino pastors, sports and media stars, singers, professionals, and others speak out in favor of marriage and show by their own example that they value it. In addition, African Americans and Latinos need to become involved in developing educational and promotional materials that will have resonance in their communities.

*Information, education, and community supports for couples.* Many marriage advocates believe that information and education about marriage should be as commonly available and accepted by the public as is information and education about parenting. They believe that every community needs a spectrum of information, education, and community supports to meet the needs of couples at different stages in their relationships. Low-income couples should be able to have the same access to these kinds of services that middle-income couples are beginning to have through their schools, churches, or marriage education programs offered under private auspices.

This spectrum should include courses in high school to develop relationship skills, preventative relationship and marriage workshops and classes for young couples, intensive encounter weekends for troubled marriages, and mentor couples to offer ongoing support. The problem is that the growing field of marriage education—which teaches skills in communication, conflict resolution, acceptance, and commitment, among other topics—offers programs largely designed for middle-income, white couples. However, a couple of the best-known program models have been adapted and used for less-well-off couples, such as enlisted personnel in the military, and for couples of minority ethnic and racial groups (e.g., the University of Denver–based Prevention and Relationship Enhancement Program, PREP, and the Family Wellness model in California).

Since these kinds of programs currently do not exist in low-income communities, advocates should think carefully about adapting them or creating new programs. TANF funds could be used to enhance and extend existing programs to offer ongoing skills-based relationship training. In Oklahoma, as part of a proposal for using unspent TANF funds, an ambitious capacity-building plan has been drafted that will train cooperative extension family life educators, health department child-guidance staff, pastors, laypersons, and others to offer these educational workshops to low-income and other couples on a sliding-scale, fee-for-service basis, or in exchange for vouchers.

Couples should be able to find out about these programs and be motivated to participate in them. Again, Oklahoma plans to invest in training "gatekeepers"—such as nurse home visitors and welfare workers—who in the course of their daily work interact with young couples around the birth of a child or at other critical life stages, such as moving from welfare to work. The training will help the gatekeepers have conversations with the young parents about their relationship and its potential for stability and marriage, and explore their interest in participating in relationship skills–building workshops. This training may also include assessing for the presence of domestic violence, or whether other kinds of services are needed to help stabilize and support the relationship, such as jobs training, alcohol treatment, or legal services.

Couples and marriage education is not a silver bullet. Participation in a one-time course of educational workshops will not be sufficient help for many low-income couples over the long haul. Booster sessions and ongoing supports will typically be needed as well. Couple peer support groups, marriage celebrations and seminars sponsored by churches or other organizations, marriage mentors, and other resources and interventions may also need to be put into place. These resources may be created by working with the religious and nonprofit voluntary sectors.

In my view, any and all of these strategies will be successful only if they obtain a broad consensus of support from the state and community leadership and the public at large. They must be based soundly in research and be inclusive and sensitive to the "hot-button" concerns. I suggest that strengthening marriage strategies for low-income populations, indeed for all populations, should be guided by the following general principles:

- Public promotion of marriage must be careful not to stigmatize single individuals or single parents, must acknowledge the realities of domestic violence, and point out that some marriages should never begin and others are better ended.
- Coercive and punitive policies should never be used to promote marriage.
- Information along with educational services and supports should be available to strengthen relationships between parents whether they are married or not married.
- Community-level initiatives should invite low-income couples, representing the racial and ethnic backgrounds prevalent in the community, to help design and shape the activities and ensure that they are adapted to the needs and circumstances of the populations they are intended to help.
- While it is appropriate to remove existing financial disincentives to marriage, offering substantial monetary incentives to individuals to marry would be unwise policy, since immediate financial gain should not be the sole or even principal reason for marriage.
- Initiatives to strengthen marriage should target couples at highest risk and at especially vulnerable or magic moments when they are most ready and willing to get help.
- Strategies should focus on improving the quality of the marriage or the couple's relationship, not solely on preserving its stability.

## CONCLUSION

There is a strong public interest in reversing the decline in marriage in the nation generally and among the poor and near-poor in particular. The research basis for action, however, is slim. In the past, researchers generally have not disentangled differences by race/ethnicity and income and have largely failed to study low-income couple relationships specifically, whether the couples are married or unmarried. We do know that the decline in marriage among the poor and near-poor is influenced by a more complex array of factors, and assumes different shapes and patterns, than the decline in marriage among middle-class couples. Hence, any reversal of this decline poses a different and more complex set of challenges for low-income couples.

This chapter has suggested that we do know enough to begin to try a number of different strategies tailored to low-income populations and see what works and what seems most acceptable. There are a few hopeful signs that state policy officials are beginning to address the issue. The mission and resources of the TANF program offer an unusual and timely opportunity to plan and implement strategies to strengthen couple relationships and marriage in low-income populations.

## APPENDIX: TEMPORARY ASSISTANCE FOR NEEDY FAMILIES (TANF) PROGRAM AND HOW IT RELATES TO MARRIAGE

In the 1996 law establishing the Temporary Assistance for Needy Families program (TANF), three "family formation" goals are spelled out in the four purposes of the Act (emphasis supplied):

1. "to provide assistance to needy families. . . .
2. "to *end dependence of needy parents* on government benefits *by promoting* job preparation, work and *marriage*. . . .
3. "to prevent and reduce the *incidence of out-of-wedlock pregnancies* and establish annual numerical goals for preventing and reducing the incidence of these pregnancies"
4. " to *encourage the formation and maintenance of two-parent families.*"

Only the first of these family formation goals requires spending TANF funds on "needy" families (as defined by the state). However, our general sense is that for political reasons any activities using TANF funds would need to be targeted primarily in low-income communities. Moreover, state MOE (Maintenance-of-Effort) funds must be targeted on needy families.

The TANF law includes a "charitable choice" provision that allows contracts, vouchers, or other funding for charitable, religious, or private organizations. Thus churches and faith-based organizations can receive funding on the same basis as any other nongovernmental provider. However, in order to avoid entanglement in possible First Amendment issues, some have advised creating a partial "wall" between the government and the religiously sponsored services, such as setting up a separate "religiously affiliated" nonprofit to administer the government-funded programs, provide social services without a religious message, and keep distinct accounting records.

The federal government has given some guidance to states on how to pursue these family formation goals.[48] This guidance document clarifies that states have considerable flexibility in deciding how to spend their block grant funds to achieve the broad purposes of TANF. The guide offered a few suggestions of policy changes or activities that could be engaged in to promote marriage and encourage two-parent families:

1. Provide premarital and marriage counseling and mediation services;
2. Change TANF eligibility rules to provide incentives for single parents to marry or for two-parent families to stay together;
3. Encourage the formation and maintenance of two-parent families (married or unmarried) by using TANF to fund services—such as job placement and training for noncustodial parents—designed to promote responsible fatherhood and increase the capacity of fathers to provide emotional and financial support for their children.

For examples of activities to strengthen two-parent families and marriage that could be funded through TANF, visit the website of the Center for Legal and Social Policy: www.clasp.org.

## NOTES

For a comprehensive review of recent research, see David Popenoe and Barbara Dafoe Whitehead, *Should We Live Together? What Young Adults Need to Know about Cohabitation before Marriage* (New Brunswick, N.J.: The National Marriage Project, 1999).

1. Theodora Ooms, *Toward More Perfect Unions: Putting Marriage on the Public Agenda* (Washington, D.C.: Family Impact Seminar, 1998). Available online: tooms@clasp.org.

2. Christine A. Bachrach, "Changing Circumstances of Marriage and Fertility in the United States." chapt. 2 in *Welfare, the Family, and Reproductive Behavior: Research Perspective,* ed. Robert Moffitt (Washington, D.C.: National Academy Press, 1998); Linda J. Waite, ed., *The Ties That Bind: Perspectives on Marriage and Cohabitation* (New York: Aldine de Gruyter, 2000).

3. Ooms, *Toward More Perfect Unions.*

4. T. A. Lugaila, *Marital Status and Living Arrangements: March 1998 (Update).* Current Populations Reports Series P20-514.

5. I. V. Sawhill, "Welfare Reform and Reducing Teen Pregnancy," *The Public Interest* 138 (Winter 2000): 40–51.

6. Department of Health and Human Services, Administration for Children and Families, *TANF Program: Second Annual Report to Congress* (Washington, D.C.: Office of Policy Research and Evaluation, August 1999).

7. S. McLanahan and G. Sanderfur, *Growing Up with a Single Parent: What Hurts, What Helps* (Cambridge: Harvard University Press, 1994).

8. Bachrach, "Changing Circumstances of Marriage and Fertility in the United States," 26.

9. R. A. London, "The Interaction Between Single Mothers' Living Arrangements and Welfare Participation," *Journal of Policy Analysis and Management* 19 (1): 93–117 (2000).

10. P. J. Smock, "Cohabitation in the United States: An Appraisal of Research Themes, Findings, and Implications." *Annual Review of Sociology* 26 (2000).

11. L. Bumpass and H. Lu, *Trends in Cohabitation and Implications for Children's Family Contexts in the U.S.* NSFH Working Paper No. 83 (Madison: Center for Demography and Ecology, University of Wisconsin–Madison, 1999).

12. See I. Garfinkle and S. McLanahan, "Fragile Families and Child Well-being: A Survey of New Parents," *Focus* 21 (1) (Spring 2000): 9–11.

13. P. N. Cohen, *Racial-Ethnic and Gender Differences in Returns to Cohabitation and Marriage: Evidence from the Current Population Survey.* Population Division Working Paper No.35; W. D. Manning and Nancy S. Landale, "Racial and Ethnic Differences in the Role of Cohabitation in Premarital Childbearing," *Journal of Marriage and the Family* 58:63–77 (February, 1996); R. S. Orepesa, "Normative Beliefs About Marriage and Cohabitation: A Comparison of Non-Latino Whites, Mexican Americans, and Puerto Ricans," *Journal of Marriage and the Family* 58 (February 1996): 49–62.

14. R. G. Rumbaut, "Ties that Bind: Immigration and Immigrant Families in the United States," chap. 1 in *Immigration and the Family: Research and Policy on U.S. Immigrants,* ed. Alan Booth, Ann C. Crouter, and Nancy S. Landale (Mahwah, N.J.: Lawrence Erlbaum Associates, 1997), 27.

15. Robert B. Hill, *The Strengths of African American Families: Twenty-Five Years Later* (Washington, D.C.: R and B Publishers, 1997); A. Billingsley, *Climbing Jacob's Ladder: The Enduring Legacy of African American Families* (New York: Simon and Schuster/Touchstone, 1992).

16. Hill, *The Strengths of African American Families,* 76.

17. R. D. Mare and C. Winship, "Socioeconomic Change and the Decline in Marriage for Blacks and Whites," in *The Urban Underclass,* ed. C. Jencks and Paul E. R. Peterson (Washington, D.C.: Brookings Institution, 1991), 175–202.

18. A. J. Cherlin, *Marriage, Divorce, Remarriage* (Cambridge: Harvard University Press, 1992).

19. S. J. Ventura and Christine A. Bachrach, *Nonmarital Childbearing in the United States, 1940–1999.* National Vital Statistics Reports. (Washington, D.C.: U.S. Department of Health and Human Services, Centers for Disease Control and Prevention, National Center for Health Statistics, October 2000).

20. M. B. Tucker and C. Mitchell-Kernan, ed., *The Decline in Marriage Among African Americans: Causes, Consequences, and Policy Implications* (New York: Russell Sage Foundation, 1995).

21. Ventura and Bachrach, *Nonmarital Childbearing in the United States, 1940–1999.*

22. D. Lichter, "The Retreat from Marriage and the Rise in Nonmarital Fertility," in *Report to Congress on Out-of-Wedlock Childbearing* (Washington, D.C.:

U.S. Government Printing Office: Department of Health and Human Services, 1995), 137–146.

23. William Julius Wilson, *The Truly Disadvantaged: The Inner City, The Underclass, and Public Policy* (Chicago: University of Chicago Press, 1987); William Julius Wilson, *When Work Disappears: The World of New Urban Poverty* (New York: Alfred Knopf, 1996).

24. Tucker and Mitchell-Kernan, *The Decline in Marriage Among African Americans*.

25. Mare and Winship, "Socioeconomic Change."

26. R. A. Moffitt, ed., *Welfare, The Family, and Reproductive Behavior* (Washington, D.C.: National Academy Press, 1998).

27. E. Steuerle, "The Effects of Tax and Welfare Policies on Family Formation" in Family Impact Seminar, *Strategies to Strengthen Marriage: What Do We Know? What Do We Need to Know?* (Washington, D.C.: Family Impact Seminar, 1998). Available from tooms@clasp.org.

28. W. Primus and J. Beeson, *Safety Net Programs, Marriage and Cohabitation*, paper presented at "Just Living Together: Implications of Cohabitation for Children, Families, and Social Policy," The Pennsylvania State University, October 30, 2000. Papers available from www.pop.psu.edu/events.

29. Wilson, *When Work Disappears*, 27.

30. Kathryn Edin, "Few Good Men: Why Poor Mothers Don't Marry or Remarry," *The American Prospect* 26–31, 28 (January 3, 2000).

31. Ibid.

32. Robin L. Jarrett, "Living Poor: Family Life Among Single Parent, African American Women," *Social Problems* 41 (1) (February 1994).

33. Edin, "Few Good Men," 30.

34. Kathryn Edin, L. Lein, T. Nelson, S. Clampet-Lundquist, "Talking With Low-Income Fathers," *Poverty Research News* 4 (2), 10–12 (March/April 2000).

35. See chapters by Stanley and Bradbury in Family Impact Seminar, *Strategies for Strengthening Marriage: What Do We Know? What Do We Need to Know?* (Washington, D.C.: Family Impact Seminar, 1998). Available online: tooms@clasp.org.

36. Ooms, *Toward More Perfect Unions*.

37. Maggie Gallagher, *The Age of Unwed Mothers: Is Teen Pregnancy the Problem?* (New York: Institute for American Values, 1999).

38. Tucker and Mitchell-Kernan, *The Decline in Marriage Among African Americans*; Billingsley, *Climbing Jacob's Ladder*; R. Staples and L. B. Johnson, *Black Families at the Crossroads: Challenges and Prospects* (San Francisco: Jossey Bass,1993); Edin, "Few Good Men."

39. Billingsley, *Climbing Jacob's Ladder*.

40. W. Richardson, *Reclaiming the Urban Family: How to Mobilize the Church as a Family Training Center* (Grand Rapids, Mich.: Zondervan, 1996).

41. Hill, *Strengths of African American Families*.

42. Edin, "Few Good Men."

43. Garfinkle and McLanahan, "Fragile Families and Child Well-Being."

44. Billingsley, *Climbing Jacob's Ladder,* chap. 7.

45. Richardson, *Reclaiming the Urban Family*.

46. Theodora Ooms, *Tapping TANF to Promote Marriage and Strengthen Two-Parent Families.* Testimony before the Sub-committee on Ways and Means Hearing on Marriage and Welfare Issues, May 22, 2001. See http:// waysandmeans.house.gov/humres.htm.

47. R. Rector, "Welfare: Broadening the Reform," in *Issues 2000: The Candidates Briefing Book,* ed. Stuart M. Butler and Kim R. Holmes (Washington, D.C.: The Heritage Foundation, 2000).

48. Department of Health and Human Services, Administration for Children and Families, Office of Family Assistance, *Helping Families Achieve Self-Sufficiency: A Guide on Funding Services for Children and Families through the TANF Program* (December 1999). Available online: www.acf.dhhs.gov/programs/ofa/funds2.htm.

# 8

# Promoting Marriage as a Means for Promoting Fatherhood

## Wade F. Horn

## INTRODUCTION

The most disturbing and consequential social trend of our time is the dramatic increase over the past four decades in the number of children living in father-absent households. In 1960, the total number of children living absent their biological fathers was less than 10 million. Today, that number stands at nearly 25 million, more than one-third of all children in the United States.[1]

The situation is getting worse, not better. By some estimates, 60 percent of children born in the 1990s will spend a significant portion of their childhoods in a father-absent home.[2] For the first time in our nation's history, the average expectable experience of childhood now includes time spent living without one's own father.

This is not good news, especially for children. Almost 75 percent of American children living in single-parent families will experience poverty before they turn 11 years old, compared to only 20 percent of children in two-parent families.[3] Moreover, violent criminals are overwhelmingly males who grew up without fathers, including up to 60 percent of rapists,[4] 75 percent of adolescents charged with murder,[5] and 70 percent of juveniles in state reform institutions.[6]

Children living in a father-absent home are also more likely to be suspended or expelled from school,[7] or to drop out,[8] develop an emotional or behavioral problem requiring psychiatric treatment,[9] engage in early and promiscuous sexual activity,[10] develop drug and alcohol problems,[11] commit suicide as an adolescent,[12] and be a victim of child abuse or neglect.[13]

On almost any measure one can imagine, children who grow up absent their fathers do worse compared to those who live with their two, married parents.[14] In the realm of social science, there are few statements one can make with certitude, but here is one: When fatherhood falters, children suffer.

Fortunately, America seems to be awakening from its three-decade denial about the importance of fathers to families and children. A recent Gallup poll indicates that nearly 80 percent of Americans agree, "The most significant family or social problem facing America is the physical absence of the father from the home."[15] The question is no longer whether fatherlessness matters. The new question is, what can be done about it?

### Child Support Enforcement

The historic answer to the problem of fatherlessness has been child support enforcement. This, of course, is not without merit. Any man who fathers a child ought to be held financially responsible for that child. But as important as child support enforcement may be, it is unlikely by itself to substantially improve the well-being of children for several reasons.

First, having a child support order in place is no guarantee that child support will actually be paid. Some men—the true "deadbeat dads"—can pay, but don't. Others, however, are undereducated and underemployed and have little ability to pay child support. Indeed, 20 percent of all nonresident fathers earn less than $6,000 annually.[16] These fathers are not so much "deadbeat" as "dead broke." Trying to extract child support from such men has been likened to the proverbial attempt to get blood from a turnip.

Second, while receipt of child support has consistently been found to be associated with improvements in child outcomes, the magnitude of the effects tend to be small. That's because the average level of child support paid to custodial mothers is quite modest, only about $2,500 per year.[17] Such a modest amount of additional income, although certainly helpful, is unlikely to substantially improve the life trajectory of most children.

Third, an exclusive emphasis on child support enforcement may drive many low-income, nonresident fathers farther away from their children. As word circulates within low-income communities that cooperating with paternity establishment, but failing to comply with subsequent child support orders, may result in imprisonment or revocation of one's driver's license, many marginally employed fathers may choose to disappear rather than face the possibility of such harsh consequences. Hence, the unintended consequence of tough child support enforcement policies may be to decrease, not increase, the number of children growing up with an actively involved father, proving once again that no good deed goes unpunished.

Finally, an exclusive focus on child support enforcement ignores the many non-economic contributions that fathers make to the well-being of their children. If, however, we want fathers to be more than cash machines for their children, we will need to encourage their work as nurturers, disciplinarians, mentors, moral instructors, and skill coaches, and not just as economic providers. To do otherwise is to effectively downgrade fathers to, in the words of social historian Barbara Dafoe Whitehead, "paper dads."

### Visitation

Some people, dissatisfied with the results of using child support enforcement as the primary strategy for dealing with today's crisis of fatherlessness, advocate enhanced visitation as the mechanism for improving the well-being of children. Indeed, there is evidence that positive involvement by noncustodial fathers enhances child well-being. For example, a recent meta-analysis of sixty-three studies by Paul Amato and Joan Gilbreth found that children who reported feeling close to their noncustodial fathers and had fathers who engaged in authoritative parenting—that is, they listened to their children's problems, gave them advice, provided explanations for rules, monitored their academic performance, helped with their homework, engaged in mutual projects, and disciplined them—were significantly more likely to do well at school and show greater psychological health compared to children whose noncustodial fathers mostly engaged them in recreational activities, such as going out to dinner, taking them on vacations, and buying them things.[18] Hence, positive father involvement by nonresident fathers does count.

Unfortunately, other research has found that nonresident fathers are far less likely than in-the-home dads either to have a close relationship with their children or to engage in authoritative parenting.[19] One reason for this, as Amato and Gilbreth point out, is the constraints inherent in traditional visitation arrangements. Because their time with their children is often severely limited, many nonresident fathers strive to make sure their children enjoy themselves when they are with them. As a result, nonresident fathers tend to spend less time than in-the-home fathers helping their children with their homework, monitoring their activities, and setting appropriate limits, and more time taking them to restaurants or the movies, activities that are not associated with enhanced child outcomes. In essence, many nonresident, but visiting, fathers transform into "treat dads." As such, while visitation by nonresident fathers is certainly to be encouraged, the context of visitation reduces the likelihood that nonresident fathers will engage in behavior most associated with enhanced child well being.

### Cohabitation

If, some argue, enhanced visitation is not the answer, perhaps cohabitation is. In fact, cohabitation is one of the fastest growing family forms in the United States today. In 1997, 4.13 million couples were cohabiting outside of wedlock, compared to fewer than a half million in 1960.[20] Of these cohabiting couples, 1.47 million, or about 36 percent, have children younger than 18 residing with them, up from 21 percent in 1987. For unmarried couples in the 25–34 age group, almost half have children living with them.[21] Indeed, it is estimated that nearly half of all children today will spend some time in a cohabiting family before the age of 16.[22]

Strengthening cohabitation as a means of strengthening fatherhood has found new impetus in recent research by Sara McLanahan and Irwin Garfinkel, who studied "fragile families"—low-income, nonmarried couples who have had a child out-of-wedlock. Preliminary analysis of data from two cities, Oakland, California, and Austin, Texas, suggests that at the time a child is born out-of-wedlock, more than half of these couples are cohabiting.[23] Consequently, the argument goes, interventions should be aimed at strengthening this "fragile family" (so named to emphasize that these families are at greater risk of breaking up and living in poverty compared to more traditional families) and encouraging "team parenting."

Other research, however, suggests that cohabitation is unlikely to produce lifetime dads for children. First of all, cohabitation is a weak family form. Cohabiting couples break up at much higher rates than married couples.[24] Furthermore, only four out of ten couples who have a child while cohabiting ever go on to get married, and those that do are more likely to divorce than couples who wait until after marriage to have children.[25] Overall, three-quarters of children born to cohabiting parents will see their parents split up before they reach age 16, compared to only about one-third of children born to married parents.[26]

The fact that children born to cohabiting couples are likely to see their dads eventually transform into occasional visitors is worrisome for several reasons. First, research on disruptions in early attachment figures suggests children may fare worse when their father is involved early in their life only to disappear than they would fare if they never established a relationship with their father in the first place. If so, encouraging cohabitation may actually be making a bad situation worse.

Second, many men in cohabiting relationships are not the biological father of the children in the household, or at least are not the biological father of all the children in the household. By one estimate, 63 percent of children in cohabiting households are born not to the cohabiting couple, but to a previous union of one of the adult partners, most often the mother.[27] This is problematic in that cohabitation involving biologically unrelated children substantially increases the risk of physical and sexual child abuse.[28] Thus, not only is cohabitation unlikely to deliver a lifetime father to a child, it also brings with it an increased risk for child abuse.

Neither child support enforcement, increased visitation, nor cohabitation is the answer—but that doesn't mean there is no answer.

## The "M"-Word

While it is becoming increasingly popular to speak of the importance of fathers to the well-being of children, it is still out of fashion to speak of the importance of marriage to the well-being of fatherhood. Yet research has consistently found that, over time, nonmarried fathers tend to become disconnected, both financially and psychologically, from their children.[29] Robert Lerman and Theodora Ooms, for example, found that whereas six of ten unwed fathers were visiting their children at least once a week during the first two years of their children's lives, by the time the children were 7.5 years old, that number dropped to only two of ten.[30] Overall, 40 percent of children living absent their fathers have not seen their fathers in more than a year. Of the remaining 60 percent, only one in five sleeps even one night per month in the father's home. Remarriage, or, in cases of unwed fatherhood, marriage to someone other than the child's mother, makes it especially unlikely that a noncustodial father will remain in contact with his children.[31]

Marriage, on the other hand, is a much more effective glue for binding fathers to their children. Indeed, an analysis of a national probability sample of over thirteen thousand households found the most important determinant of whether a father lived with his children was marital status at the time of the child's birth. Fully 80 percent of fathers who were married to the mother at the time of the child's birth were living with all their biological children, compared to only 23 percent of unwed fathers.[32] Given that about 40 percent of all first marriages end in divorce, marriage is not a certain route to a lifetime father. It is, however, a more certain route than any other.

Nevertheless, discussing marriage as the ideal or even preferred family structure is difficult for several reasons. First, marriage is a deeply personal issue. One can safely assume that at least 40 percent of adults in any given audience are divorced. Many others will either have parents who are divorced, a spouse who is from a divorced family, or children who are divorced. When adults touched by divorce hear others suggest that marriage is the "best" or "ideal" situation, they often interpret this as a personal rebuke. No one likes to be told that his or her situation is somehow "second best."

Second, some have bought into the notion of "family relativism": the idea that all family structures are inherently equal, with no differential consequences for children (or adults) except for the greater propensity of single parent families to be poor. Indeed, this argument goes, if we solve the economic disadvantage of single-parent households, there will be no ill effects of growing up in a home without two married parents.

Third, some simply don't like marriage. They either see marriage promotion as a thinly veiled strategy for withdrawing support from single mothers or as a means for reasserting male privilege and dominance over women. To such folks, marriage promotion is not just foolish, but downright dangerous.

The empirical literature is quite clear, however, that children do best when they grow up in an intact, two-parent, married household. We know, for example, that children who grow up in a continuously married household do better at school, have fewer emotional problems, are more likely to attend college, and are less likely to commit crime or develop alcohol or illicit drug problems.[33] That these results are not simply due to differences in income is attested to by the fact that children reared in stepfamilies, which have household incomes nearly equivalent to continuously married households, do not fare any better than children reared in single-parent households. On some measures they may even do worse.[34]

The empirical evidence also is quite clear that adults—women as well as men—are happier, healthier, and wealthier than their single counterparts. Moreover, married adults report having more satisfying sex than nonmarried adults, and married men show an earnings boost that is not evident in cohabiting relationships.[35] In regards to fatherhood, married fathers are, on average, more likely to be actively engaged in their children's lives and, perhaps just as important, are more accessible to them.

Of course, some married households, especially those in which domestic violence and child abuse are present, are horrible places for both children and adults. But contrary to the stereotypes perpetuated by the media and some advocacy groups, the reality is that domestic violence and child abuse are substantially less likely to occur in intact, married households than in any other family arrangement. The truth is the most dangerous place for women and children is a household in which mom is cohabiting with a man who isn't biologically related to the children.[36]

Given that marriage is so important to the well-being of children, adults, and communities, how do we overcome our reluctance to talk about it? Syndicated columnist William Raspberry suggests the answer: Put children back at the center of things.

Adults have spent far too much time arguing among themselves about the virtues of marriage and far too little time helping our children understand why marriage is important and how to form and sustain healthy marriages. Yet national surveys consistently show that young people, far from rejecting marriage as an ideal, desperately want to avoid the serial marriages and high divorce rates of their elders.[37] It is time for us to give our children what they want.

Accomplishing this is not as simple as pointing young couples to the altar and insisting they marry. We do not need more bad marriages. What we need is more healthy, mutually satisfying, equal-regard marriages. To attain that, young couples will need help in acquiring the knowledge and skills necessary to form and sustain healthy marriages. That requires a new commitment of both public and private resources aimed at providing meaningful premarital education to couples contemplating marriage, marital enrichment to those couples who are already married, and outreach to couples in troubled marriages.

It is not, however, just children and young adults in the middle class who want stable marriages. Data from the Fragile Families Initiative suggests that at the time of the child's birth, two-thirds of low-income, unwed couples want—and expect—to get married.[38] The problem is that many, if not most, of these low-income couples do not go on to get married. That, however, may be as much our fault as theirs, for our reluctance even to bring up the topic sends the not-so-subtle message that marriage is neither expected nor valued. When we are afraid even to say the "m"-word, the wonder is not that so few ever get married, but that some actually do.

## CONCLUSION

Marriage cannot be the only answer to strengthening father–child relationships. Not all marriages are made in heaven. Some nonresident fathers are terrific dads. Some male cohabiting partners provide children with valuable economic and social resources. And when nonresident fathers are capable of providing financial support for their children but do not, laws and policies should seek to right this wrong. Nevertheless, if what we really care about is the well-being of children, rather than the desires of adults, the inescapable conclusion is this: Children want and need their fathers as well as their mothers, and fathers are most likely to be positively involved in their children's lives if they are married to the mother. Saying so may not give much comfort to those adults who worship at the altar of self-fulfillment, but it surely gives a greater measure of hope to children who hunger for their dads.

The views expressed in this chapter do not necessarily represent the views of the Administration for Children and Families, the United States Department of Health and Human Services, or the United States government.

## NOTES

1. Wade F. Horn, *Father Facts,* 3rd ed. (Gaithersburg, Md.: The National Fatherhood Initiative, 1998).

2. Frank F. Furstenberg, Jr., and Andrew J. Cherlin, *Divided Families: What Happens to Children When Parents Part* (Cambridge: Harvard University Press, 1991).

3. National Commission on Children, *Just the Facts: A Summary of Recent Information on America's Children and Their Families* (Washington, D.C., 1993).

4. Karl Zinsmeister, "Crime Is Terrorizing Our Nation's Kids," *Citizen* (August 20, 1990): 2.

5. Dewey Cornell et al., "Characteristics of Adolescents Charged with Homicide," *Behavioral Sciences and the Law* 5 (1987): 11–23.

6. M. Eileen Matlock et al., "Family Correlates of Social Skills Deficits in Incarcerated and Nonincarcerated Adolescents," *Adolescence* 29 (1994): 119–130.

7. Deborah Dawson, "Family Structure and Children's Well-Being: Data from the 1988 National Health Survey," *Journal of Marriage and Family* 53 (August 1991): 573–584.

8. Sara McLanahan and Gary Sandefur, *Growing Up with a Single Parent: What Hurts, What Helps* (Cambridge: Harvard University Press, 1994), 58–59.

9. Ronald J. Angel and Jacqueline L. Angel, "Physical Comorbidity and Medical Care Use in Children with Emotional Problems," *Public Health Reports* 111 (1996): 140–145.

10. Christina Lammers et al., "Influences on Adolescents' Decision to Postpone Onset of Sexual Intercourse: A Survival Analysis of Virginity Among Youths Aged 13 to 18 Years," *Journal of Adolescent Health* 26 (2000): 42–48.

11. John P. Hoffman and Robert A. Johnson, "A National Portrait of Family Structure and Adolescent Drug Use," *Journal of Marriage and the Family* 60 (August 1998): 633–645.

12. Judith Rubenstein et al., "Suicidal Behavior in Adolescents: Stress and Protection in Different Family Contexts," *American Journal of Orthopsychiatry* 68 (1998): 274–284.

13. Catherine M. Malkin and Michael E. Lamb, "Child Maltreatment: A Test of Sociobiological Theory," *Journal of Comparative Family Studies* 25 (1994): 121–130.

14. For a complete review of this literature see Horn, *Father Facts*.

15. George Gallup, "Report on Status of Fatherhood in the United States," *Emerging Trends* 20 (September 1998): 3–5.

16. Irwin Garfinkel, Sara S. McLanahan, Daniel R. Meyer, and Judith A. Seltzer, *Fathers Under Fire: The Revolution in Child Support Enforcement* (New York: Russell Sage Foundation, 1998).

17. U.S. Bureau of the Census, *Child Support for Custodial Mothers and Fathers: 1997* (Washington, D.C., 2000).

18. Paul R. Amato and Joan G. Gilbreth, "Nonresident Fathers and Children's Well-Being: A Meta-Analysis," *Journal of Marriage and the Family* 61 (August 1999): 557–573.

19. Susan D. Steward, "Disneyland Dads, Disneyland Moms? How Nonresident Parents Spend Time with Absent Children," *Journal of Family Issues* 20 (July 1999): 539–556.

20. Lynne Casper and Ken Bryson, *Household and Family Characteristics: March 1997* (Washington, D.C.: U.S. Bureau of the Census).

21. Wendy Manning and Daniel T. Lichter, "Parental Cohabitation and Children's Economic Well-Being." *Journal of Marriage and the Family* 58 (November 1996): 998–1010.

22. Larry Bumpass and Hsien-Hen Lu, *Trends in Cohabitation and Implications for Children's Family Contexts in the U.S.*, CDE Working Paper No. 98-15 (Center for Demography Ecology, University of Wisconsin-Madison, 1999).

23. *Dispelling Myths About Unmarried Fathers*, Fragile Families Research Brief, Number 1 (Bendhelm-Thoman Center For Research and Child Well-Being Princeton University and Social Indicators Survey Center, Columbia University, May 2000).

24. Bumpass and Lu, *Trends in Cohabitation.*

25. Kristin A. Moore, "Nonmarital Childbearing in the United States," in *Report to Congress on Out-of-Wedlock Childbearing* (Washington, D.C.: U.S. Department of Health and Human Services, September, 1995), vii.

26. David Popenoe and Barbara Dafoe Whitehead, *Should We Live Together? What Young Adults Need to Know About Cohabitation Before Marriage* (New Brunswick, NJ: The National Marriage Project, 1999), 7.

27. Deborah R. Graefe and Daniel T. Lichter, "Life Course Transitions of American Children: Parental Cohabitation, Marriage, and Single Motherhood," *Demography* 36 (May 1999).

28. Robert Whelan, *Broken Homes and Battered Children: A Study of the Relationship Between Child Abuse and Family Type* (London, England: Family Education Trust, 1993), 29, table 12; see also Martin Daly and Margo Wilson, "Evolutionary Psychology and Marital Conflict: The Relevance of Stepchildren," in David M. Buss and Neil Malamuth, ed., *Sex, Power, Conflict: Evolutionary and Feminist Perspectives* (New York: Oxford University Press, 1996), 9–28; Leslie Margolin, "Child Abuse by Mothers' Boyfriends: Why the Over-Representation?" *Child Abuse and Neglect* 16 (1992): 541–551.

29. E. G. Cooksey and P. H. Craig, "Parenting From a Distance: The Effects of Paternal Characteristics on Contact Between Nonresidential Fathers and Their Children," *Demography* 35 (1998): 187–200.

30. Robert Lerman and Theodora Ooms, *Young Unwed Fathers: Changing Roles and Emerging Policies* (Philadelphia: Temple, 1993), 45.

31. Linda S. Stephens, "Will Johnny See Daddy This Week?" *Journal of Family Issues* 17 (July 1996): 466–494.

32. L. Clarke, E.C. Cooksey, and G. Verropoulou, "Fathers and Absent Fathers: Sociodemographic Similarities in Britain and the United States," *Demography* 35 (1998): 217–228.

33. Linda J. Waite and Maggie Gallagher, *The Case for Marriage: Why Married People Are Happier, Healthier and Better Off Financially* (New York: Doubleday, 2000).

34. Nicholas Zill, Donna Ruane Morrison, and Mary Jo Coiro, "Long-Term Effects of Parental Divorce on Parent–Child Relationships, Adjustment, and Achievement in Young Adulthood," *Journal of Family Psychology* 7 (1993): 91–103.

35. Steven Stack and J. Ross Eshleman, "Marital Status and Happiness: A 17-Nation Study," *Journal of Marriage and the Family* 60 (May 1998): 527–536; see also Maggie Gallagher, *The Abolition of Marriage* (Washington, D.C.: Regnery, 1996); Linda J. Waite, "Does Marriage Matter?" *Demography* 32 (1995): 483–501.

36. Waite and Gallagher, *The Case for Marriage*, 150–160.

37. David Popenoe and Barbara Dafoe Whitehead, *The State of Our Unions, 1999* (New Brunswick, NJ: National Marriage Project, 1999).

38. *Dispelling Myths About Unmarried Fathers.*

# 9

# *Reflections on the Nature of Marriage*

## *Brian Bix*

## INTRODUCTION

American society faces a growing number of claims that marriage rules should be changed, and these claims are coming from disparate directions. Some people are seeking ways to make marriage more binding, and while such proposals often involve counseling and vows, the most significant and most controversial part of these proposals involves making divorce more difficult.[1] Other people want the state to extend marriage (or some institution comparable to marriage) to same-sex couples. As debate swirls around how best to defend, strengthen, or expand marriage, the most basic points can be deceptively complex. This complexity may counsel caution in the face of proposals for both change and resistance to change.

### Recourse to Dictionaries

In *Jones v. Hallahan*,[2] a female same-sex couple sought review of the decision to deny them a license to marry. They argued that the refusal to grant them a marriage license was contrary to their federal constitutional rights. The Kentucky Court of Appeals disagreed, but based its decision primarily on grounds far removed from the Constitution. The court looked at *Webster's New International Dictionary* and *The Century Dictionary and Encyclopedia*, and there learned that marriage was a relationship between people of opposite sex.[3] The court concluded: "It appears to us that appellants are prevented from marrying, not by the statutes of Kentucky or the refusal of the County Court Clerk of Jefferson County to issue them a license, but rather by their own incapability of entering into a marriage as that term is defined."[4]

In *Baehr v. Lewin*,[5] on the other hand, the Hawaii Supreme Court concluded that Hawaii's restriction of marriage to opposite-sex couples presumptively violated the equal protection clause of Hawaii's state constitution.[6] In the course of that opinion, the court denigrated the definition-based arguments raised in *Jones v. Hallahan* and elsewhere as "tautological and circular" and as an "exercise in tortured and conclusory sophistry."[7]

One can understand, at some level, the derision of the Hawaii court when it considered some of the earlier decisions: reference to dictionary entries seems strange at best and dubious at worst as a way to decide important and controversial social issues. At the same time, one might ask the *Baehr* court and its many sympathizers: "If we are not to get our ideas of what marriage is from dictionaries, or any similar source of conventional understanding, where are we to get them?"[8]

Once we unhook the idea of marriage even in part from conventional notions, something else must be found to give the concept shape and structure. We may choose among the attributes usually associated with marriage, but may not be able to justify our selection. Advocates of same-sex marriage seem to believe (or at least put forward as their public position) that "opposite-sex" is not crucial to the institution, but (among other things) two people, rather than a greater number, is crucial. While it may be strategically wise for these advocates to argue that allowing same-sex marriage would not simultaneously justify polygamous marriages,[9] the argument has never been particularly persuasive.

I do not want to be misunderstood. The previous argument is not intended as a defense of a traditional view of marriage or of who should be able to marry. Rather, it is a caution to *both* sides of the same-sex marriage debate, who tend to put forward conceptions of marriage without much analysis or argument. As the next section will show, the institution of marriage has changed significantly since the first historical records. It is therefore suspect for those arguing either for or against change to claim that they are advancing the true nature of marriage. Both sides should be forced to make their arguments on the field of policy and morality, not on that of metaphysics.

## Marriage as a (Changing) Social Good

Marriage is an existing social institution. One might also helpfully speak of it as an existing "social good." The complication in the analysis is that one cannot fully distinguish the *terms* on which the good is available from the *nature* of the good. As Joseph Raz wrote regarding same-sex marriage, "When people demand recognition of gay marriages, they usually mean to demand access to an existing good. In fact they also ask for the transformation of that good. For there can be no doubt that the recognition of gay marriage will effect as great a transformation in the nature of marriage as that from polygamous to monogamous or from arranged to unarranged marriage."[10]

Social goods take their shape through the interacting forces of biology, culture, and history. They change over time. Sometimes the change is conscious, the product of social or political reform movements. At other times, social goods may change as the by-product of other changes in society, with the alteration of the social good seen only in retrospect.

The conventional understanding of marriage is not something we can change at will, though we can make changes in the terms of marriage, which may result in a long-term change in conventional understanding. Perhaps more often than not, changes in terms reflect, rather than cause, a change in the popular perception of the nature and role of the institution. Changes in society (among which changes in the law are frequently both the least and the last) affect how we look at social practices and social institutions, including marriage. Some ways of thinking about marriage and talking about marriage no longer make any sense. The idea of pure fault-based divorce now strikes most Americans as strange. One can always get laughs from students in an American Family Law course by reading the following lines, which come from a case that exemplifies the fault defense of "recrimination": "The fact that married people do not get along well together does not justify a divorce. Testimony which proves merely an unhappy union, the parties being high strung temperamentally and unsuited to each other . . . is insufficient to sustain a decree."[11]

Few of us can get back into the mind-set in which the societal stake in marriage was thought so large, and the importance of individual happiness so small, that the partners' incompatibility and unhappiness could be considered all but irrelevant to the question of divorce.[12]

Equally significant are the changing social realities against which marriage occurs. For example, the common-law doctrine of coverture once meant that women lost most or all of their property rights (along with their rights to contract and to sue and be sued in their own names) on marriage; the Married Women's Property Acts changed that. If one takes a long historical view of marriage, the changes have been quite radical. There was a time when one's family fortune (if one was from the wealthier sector of society)[13] or the future viability of one's farm or business (if from a lower class) depended crucially on whom one married and on the marriage lasting. Therefore, it was not surprising that parents, relatives, and even close friends were understood to have a significant say in the selection of a marriage partner.[14] As one commentator summarized the cause and effect of the change: "With capitalism, marriage stopped being the main way that the rich exchanged their life's property, and that the rest of us found our life's main co-worker."[15]

More recently, social changes have included greater equality for women in job opportunities and pay. The ability of women to maintain and control the property with which they enter marriage and the income they earn while married, along with the ability to support themselves on their own if need be, makes living alone after or instead of marriage a more viable option than it once was. This changes the role, and thus the nature, of marriage.

What of the express changes to the terms of marriage? Going back centuries, there was the change from polygamous to monogamous marriage (with polygamous marriage still accepted in some foreign cultures)[16]; there were prohibitions about marriage within a certain range of consanguinity (though, again, there are some contemporary cultures in which marriages are common between, say, first cousins, though they would be forbidden in many American states)[17]; and there has been a move from private to public (and publicly regulated) marriage.[18] Since colonial times, to give only a partial list, America has seen the growing availability of divorce, and most recently the option of no-fault divorce; the general (but not complete) eradication of causes of action for breach of promise to marry, criminal conversation, and alienation of affections; the demise of coverture disabilities; the removal of gender-based legal obligations (husbands to support, wives to obey, etc.); the removal of the marital exemption from rape law; a growing willingness to enforce marital and premarital agreements; the rise and fall of anti-miscegenation laws; and the decline of intraspousal tort immunities and some marital evidentiary privileges.[19]

The basic point is that those who would like to "keep marriage the way it always has been" should see that this is not an option. Marriage, like most cultural institutions and most social goods, is ever changing. Nevertheless, we can have preferences about the direction in which marriage changes and we can act, sometimes effectively, on those preferences.

### Marriages and Domestic Partnerships

Even putting to one side people's complicated reactions to homosexuals and homosexuality, the high level of opposition to authorizing same-sex marriage should not be surprising. When one asks people about express and public changes to the institution of marriage, there is usually strong opposition, even when there are no conceivable or legitimate reasons for that opposition. The best example may be the recent South Carolina referendum to remove that state's outdated law against interracial marriage. This law had been of no legal effect since 1967, when the Supreme Court declared all such laws invalid because contrary to the Fourteenth Amendment to the United States Constitution.[20] Despite that fact, in November 1998, 40 percent of South Carolina's population voted against getting rid of the law.[21]

Many people who are sympathetic to the idea of equal rights for homosexuals nonetheless oppose same-sex marriage.[22] At the same time, the popular opposition to same-sex marriage seems to dissipate (or at least to diminish significantly) when it is suggested as an alternative that same-sex couples be allowed to register for a "domestic partnership" or similar legal status, where this alternative arrangement would give such couples many and perhaps all of the rights and benefits now linked to conventional marriage.[23] In other words, the perception seems to be that it is okay for same-sex couples to marry, as long as it is not called *marriage*. To the extent that this view reflects current popular perception, it only underlines the more-symbolic-than-real grounding of the opposition to same-sex marriage. If we are granting the same social good to two groups, and merely giving different names for the good, then little of substance can be at stake in denying the same name to the same good.

## The Purpose of Marriage

When *Baehr v. Lewin*, the Hawaii same-sex marriage case, was remanded by the Hawaii Supreme Court to allow the State of Hawaii to try to show that its restriction of marriage to opposite-sex couples was narrowly tailored to meet a compelling state purpose, the testimony the state presented appeared to be exclusively on the relative merits of opposite-sex couples and same-sex couples as parents.[24] This exemplifies the extent to which, these days, thinking about the importance of marriage as an institution tends to focus on its value as a structure within which children can be reared.[25] However, focusing on various ways of parenting as the justification for regulating marriage seems faulty in an era when significant numbers of children are, for better or for worse, being brought up by unmarried parents and a significant number of marriages do not result in children.[26]

In the current social and legal context, it is not easy to discern the specific purpose or value of marriage. If we are going to talk about revitalizing marriage, then an obvious, if often ignored, first step is to offer some judgment as to what we think its purposes or benefits are. There was a time when one could speak more confidently that marriage was about rearing children, or (in a different historical period) was about the transmission of property across generations, or (at yet a different period) was about the channeling and control of sex. Currently, marriage seems not to be about any of these things, or at least not unambiguously or solely about any of these. (Additionally, many people today would want to add love and public commitment to the list of candidates.)

Still, the reformers (who want to make divorce harder) and opponents of reform (who oppose extending marriage to same-sex couples) return insistently to the topic of children. The value of marriage as a stable structure in which to bring up children seems to be strongly supported by the evidence.[27] At the same time, if the primary purpose of marriage is to create a stable and supportive context within which to rear children, this may only offer an additional reason for extending marriage to same-sex couples.[28] Whatever we might think about such practices, a growing number of children are being raised by same-sex couples. According to a recent report, 40,000 children are living with same-sex couples, and another 100,000 are living with homosexual single parents.[29] As the District of Columbia Court of Appeals pointed out (when considering the analogous question of whether both members of a same-sex couple would be allowed to adopt a particular child), a child's having two legal parents, rather than only one, creates substantial benefits for the child.[30] One can achieve that result the hard way, through adoption by both parents,[31] or one can achieve the result an easier way, by allowing same-sex marriage (or some comparable legal analogue).

It seems equally difficult either to equate marriage with the raising of children or to separate the two completely. The problem is that while we have the same institution for couples who have children as for those that do not, many people think quite differently about the two kinds of marriages. Much of the concern about strengthening marriage has been connected to the short-term and long-term damage that divorce seems to cause children. Thus, at least as regards marriages in which there are minor children, we want parents to try harder, to hold on longer, to feel a stronger sense of duty and commitment, for the sake of the children. It is less clear that we would offer an equally strong call to duty and sacrifice to couples where no minor children are involved.[32] This suggests that different legal treatment may be appropriate. Although we might in the abstract prefer that people hold to their commitments, many perceive a rough balance of pain and equity, between what can happen if someone is allowed to leave too easily, and if someone is forced to stay against his or her (or their) strong preferences.

## CONCLUSION

To wonder whether we want to keep the institution of marriage as it has been for centuries is to ask the wrong question. Wherever we might go from here, marriage is a radically different institution than it was centuries ago, or even decades ago. We need to be modest about the extent to which we can legislate changes either in the way people think about marriage, or in how they act within it. At the same time, there are likely actions that can and will add to the "greatest good of the greatest number." However, we need to start by thinking about the role marriage currently plays within this society before reflecting on the role we might want it to play.

## NOTES

I am grateful to Naomi R. Cahn, Erin O'Hara, Warren F. Schwartz, Lynn D. Wardle, and Robin West, and to those present at the March 2000 Conference, "Revitalizing the Institution of Marriage for the 21st Century," for their comments.

1. These proposals are well summarized in Lynn D. Wardle, *Divorce Reform at the Turn of the Millennium: Certainties and Possibilities,* 33 Fam. L.Q. 783, 783–93 (1999).

2. 501 S.W.2d 588 (Ky. 1973).

3. Id. at 589.

4. Id. See also *Singer v. Hara,* 522 P.2d 1187, 1192 (Wash. App. 1974) ["appellants are not being denied entry into the marriage relationship because of their sex; rather they are being denied entry into the marriage relationship because of the recognized definition of that relationship as one which may be entered into only by two persons who are members of the opposite sex." (footnote omitted)].

5. 852 P.2d 44 (Haw. 1993).

6. A subsequent referendum changed the state constitution to authorize legislation confining marriage to opposite-sex couples. The Hawaii Supreme Court then declared the issue to be moot. *Baehr v. Miike,* 994 P.2d 566 (Haw. 1999).

The Vermont Supreme Court recently followed the lead of the Hawaii court in *Baehr* by deciding that the exclusion of same-sex couples from Vermont's marriage statute violates the Vermont state constitution, by depriving such couples of the legal benefits available to married couples. *Baker v. Vermont,* 744 A.2d 864 (Vt. 1999). In response to that judgment, the Vermont Legislature passed, and the governor signed, a bill creating "civil unions," which gives same-sex couples all the state-law benefits and obligations of opposite-sex marriage. 2000 Vt. Laws 91.

7. *Baehr v. Lewin,* 852 P.2d at 63.

8. The *Baehr v. Lewin* court offered the following definition or description of *marriage:* "[M]arriage is a state-conferred legal partnership status, the existence of which gives rise to a multiplicity of rights and benefits reserved exclusively for that relation." *Baehr,* 852 P.2d at 58. However, no source is given for that understanding.

9. See, e.g., William N. Eskridge, Jr., *The Case for Same-Sex Marriage: From Sexual Liberty to Civilized Commitment* (New York: The Free Press, 1996) 148–149; Maura I. Strassberg, *Distinctions of Form or Substance: Monogamy, Polygamy, and Same-Sex Marriage,* 75 N.C. L. Rev. 1501 (1997).

10. Joseph Raz, *Ethics in the Public Domain* (Oxford: Clarendon Press, 1994), 23.

11. *Rankin v. Rankin,* 124 A.2d 639, 644 (Penn. 1956) (citations omitted).

12. Student resistance to the notion that one must morally merit a divorce for it to be granted (basically the official line in most states prior to no-fault) is also noted in Carl Schneider, *Marriage, Morals, and the Law: No-Fault Divorce and Moral Discourse,* 1994 B.Y.U. L. Rev. 503, 508–518.

13. See, e.g., John Habakkuk, *Marriage, Debt, and the Estates System: English Landownership 1650–1950* (Oxford: Clarendon Press, 1994), 146 ("To a greater extent than among other social groups, marriage [of members of landed families]

was a family rather than an individual matter and it was closely linked with decisions about property").

14. "[O]ne defender of traditional behavior [marriage arranged by parents] tried in 1663 to base filial obedience on the sanctity of private property: 'Children are so much the goods, the possessions of their parent, that they cannot, without a kind of theft, give away themselves without the allowance of those that have the right in them.'" Lawrence Stone, *The Family, Sex and Marriage in England 1500–1800* (New York: Harper & Row, 1977), 128.

15. E. J. Graff, *What Is Marriage For?* (Boston: Beacon Press, 1999), xiii.

16. See Ira Mark Ellman, Paul Kurtz, and Elizabeth S. Scott, *Family Law* (Charlottesville: Lexis Law Publishing, 3rd ed. 1998), 117.

17. See Gibbons, *The Risks of Inbreeding Among Humans,* 259 *Science* 1252 (1993), quoted in Ellman, Kurtz, and Scott *Family Law,* 113. ("In regions of Asia and Africa, consanguineous marriages account for between 20% and 50% of all unions.").

18. See Graff, *What Is Marriage For?* 193–209.

19. The list could be significantly lengthened, especially if one included changes in the legal relationship between marriage and parental rights: e.g., the changing standards in custody decisions (in some places, from paternal preference to maternal preference to the facially neutral "primary caretaker"), and the changing legal rights of illegitimate children and unwed fathers. For an overview of how marriage laws have changed just since 1960, see Milton C. Regan, Jr., *Marriage at the Millennium,* 33 Fam. L.Q. 647 (1999).

20. *Loving v. Virginia,* 388 U.S. 1 (1967).

21. Ellen Goodman, "For Gays Seeking Marriage, A Long Wait Before 'I Do,'" *Boston Globe,* January 3, 1999, at E7. Of course, some portion of that vote reflects unapologetic racism, but it seems hard to believe that this is the explanation for the full 40 percent.

22. National opinion polls cited in a December 8, 1999, press release by the National Gay and Lesbian Task Force show support for equal rights for homosexuals in employment as high as 83 percent; the same press release conceded that support for same-sex marriage is only around 30 percent. National Gay and Lesbian Task Force, "Press Release: Support for Gay and Lesbian Equality on the Rise, NGLTF Policy Institute Study Shows," December 8, 1999, available online: www.ngltf.org/press/120899.html.

23. See, e.g., Mike Yuen, "Same-Sex Marriage Debate Rages On, Now Over Domestic Partnership Bill," *Honolulu Star-Bulletin,* November 6, 1998 ("[S]tatewide surveys . . . pointed to wider acceptance of domestic partnerships than same-sex marriages").

24. *Baehr v. Miike,* 1996 W.L. 694235 (Hawaii Cir. Ct., 1st Cir. 1996), aff'd without opinion, 950 P.2d 1234 (Haw. 1997), rev'd on mootness grounds, *Baehr v. Miike,* 994 P.2d 566 (Haw. 1999). An extended excerpt of the circuit court opinion appears in Judith Areen, *Family Law: Cases and Materials* (Westbury, NY: Foundation Press, 4th ed., 1999), 28–39.

25. The State of Vermont, defending its opposite-sex marriage law, raised the question of children for a different purpose: its argument was that sanctifying same-sex unions would undermine the connection between marriage and child-raising. *Baker v. Vermont,* 744 A.2d at 881–882. This justification was accepted by the

trial court against a state constitutional challenge, id. at 868, but not considered sufficient by the Vermont Supreme Court. Id. at 881–84.

26. See, e.g., *Baker v. Vermont*, 744 A.2d at 881-82 (noting the growing lack of equation between childrearing and opposite-sex marriage). Milton Regan has recently made a heroic, if not entirely successful, effort to investigate the meaning of marriage detached from considerations of parenthood. Milton C. Regan, Jr., *Alone Together: Law and the Meanings of Marriage* (New York: Oxford University Press, 1999).

27. And the evidence is not only from this country: according to a report from Britain's Office for National Statistics, "More than half of all cohabiting couples who have children will split up by the time their first child is five years old, compared to just 8 per cent of married parents." Alexandra Frean, "Marriage Still Best Way to Bring Up Children," *The Times* (London), December 8, 1999, on-line version www.the-times.co.uk.

28. As the Vermont Supreme Court noted: "[T]o the extent that the State's purpose in licensing civil marriage was, and is, to legitimize children and provide for their security . . . the exclusion of same-sex couples from the legal protections incident to marriage exposes their children to the precise risks that the State argues that marriage laws are designed to secure against." *Baker v. Vermont*, 744 A.2d at 882.

29. Associated Press, "Ban on Gay Marriages May Hurt Kids," *New York Times* December 16, 1999, on-line version www.nytimes.com.

30. *In re M.M.D.*, 662 A.2d 837, 857–859 and nn. 43–48 (D.C. Ct. App. 1995).

31. This is in the case of a male same-sex couple, as in *In re M.M.D.* In the case of the female same-sex couple, one woman will often be a biological parent, but the other woman will likely need to adopt to gain parental status. See, e.g., *Matter of Petition of L.S. & V.L.*, 119 Daily Wash. L. Rptr. (D.C. Super. Ct., October 21, 1991).

32. William Galston reaches a similar conclusion. William A. Galston, *Liberal Purposes: Goods, Virtues, and Diversity in a Liberal State* (New York: Cambridge University Press, 1991) 286.

# 10

# Adoption by Unmarried Cohabitants, Same-Sex Couples, and Single Persons in Europe

## Rainer Frank

### INTRODUCTION

Adoption has a tradition dating back hundreds of years in the European countries that have been influenced by Roman law. This is the case especially in France, Italy, Spain, and Germany. Other European countries, such as those in Scandinavia (Denmark, Norway, Sweden, Finland), along with Great Britain and the Netherlands, only introduced the concept of adoption into their legal systems in the twentieth century. But it is a common factor in all countries that the institution of adoption is no more than an attempt to imitate nature.

The principle that adoption is an imitation of nature manifests itself in many legal systems, for example, through statutory regulation of both a minimum and maximum age for the adoptive parent and a minimum and maximum age difference between adoptive parent and child. German law, for instance, stipulates that one of the adoptive parents be at least 25 and the other 21 years of age.[1] In Great Britain it is sufficient that both adoptive parents be 21 years old,[2] while in Sweden and Denmark an adoption is in exceptional circumstances possible at age 18.[3] As regards the maximum age limit, most countries with no express statutory regulation tend toward a maximum age limit of 45, while Portugal allows in exceptional circumstances adoption until the age of 60.[4]

The minimum age difference between the adoptive parent and child varies from 18 years in Austria,[5] Italy,[6] and the Netherlands,[7] to 16 years in Switzerland,[8] and 14 years in Spain,[9] while the prescribed maximum age difference is 40 years in Italy[10] and 50 years in Portugal.[11]

German law serves as a convincing illustration that artificial family relations have historically focused on natural processes: before 1900, German law was not only familiar with the idea of acceptance of a child as one's own but also with acceptance of a biologically unrelated child as a grandchild. It was thus possible to create artificial relations between people with the age difference between grandparent and grandchild. If we go back even further into German history, we come across so-called blood brotherhood, a legal institution by which legal relations identical to those between siblings could be created between two people in a formal ceremony.[12]

In Europe adoption is, with few exceptions, only open to married couples, since all European legal systems not only recognize but also actively promote families within marriage. The German Constitution, for instance, stipulates (art. 6 sec. 1 Bill of Rights) that marriage and family be particularly protected by the legal order.

The attempt to create artificial family relations without reference to nature is a product of the modern age. We all know that there are numerous children who grow up with people to whom they feel closely attached, and from whom they receive love and protection, although the relationship has not been, or cannot be, blessed with the formality of adoption. I am thinking of children who grow up with their grandparents, of stepchildren for whom an adoption by the stepparent is not possible because their father or mother is still alive, of orphans who live in a family in one of the famous Swiss SOS children's villages founded by Steiner, of foster children whose natural parents do not adequately care for them, or of children in a commune who have developed ties with various people of either the same or opposite sexes, and so on. When considering the institution of adoption, we must take pains to free ourselves from the perception that adoption is the only appropriate means of guaranteeing the untroubled rearing of children outside the parental home. We must likewise abandon the notion that the legal order must in all cases lend its approval by way of adoption to those affiliations that display the signs—in whatever manner—of a functioning family. Life proves too diverse for there to be one legal concept, rooted in nature, which could furnish an ideal solution in all cases. Likewise, it must also be remembered that adoption is an institution that is intended to serve exclusively the interests of the child and to be for its protection; it does not consider the interests of the adoptive parents, even when they may have the understandable human desire to make a public statement that the child is theirs.

It must be emphasized from the start that when discussing adoption by single or unmarried people of the same or different sex, one need not make any qualitative statements about these relationships. A lot has already been written on that subject.[13] While discussion on this topic is necessary and interesting, it does not take us any further, as it is not pursued in an objective and unbiased manner, and there are differences of opinion even among experts. This chapter is based on the presumption that there can be wonderful relationships between children and single individuals, between children and stepparents, between children and married or unmarried parents, and also between children and gay or lesbian parents. This discussion, however, is restricted exclusively to legal and policy considerations and attempts to define the problem with reference to the legal situation in Europe.

## Adoption by Single Persons

In Europe, adoptions by single people tend to be exceptions. Adoption by single people is rarely prohibited explicitly. An example of this is to be found in Italy, where Article 6 of the law on adoption from 1983 provides that only married couples, and not single people, may adopt a foreign child. The reason why a single person may adopt in exceptional cases in almost all European countries is the increasing prevalence of relationships analogous to those between father and child or mother and child, in which cases it seems suitable to later reinforce the relationship by way of a legal adoption. These cases exclusively concern relationships in which adoption was not initially contemplated, and the father/child or mother/child relationship had already been in existence long before they eventually decided to go for an adoption.

If those wanting to adopt are married, then the couple must as a general rule adopt jointly. Marriage therefore in principle excludes the possibility of an adoption by only one spouse. National laws on adoption, however, often contain provisions allowing exceptions: in Switzerland[14] for example, adoption is permitted for one spouse if the other spouse's whereabouts have been unknown for two years. In Great Britain,[15] adoption by one spouse is possible if the other spouse is deemed unfit to adopt on the grounds of physical or mental illness. Other countries allow adoption by one spouse when he or she has been living separately from their spouse for a number of years.[16] Nonetheless, the crucial point is that most European legal systems regulate in detail those exceptional cases in which one marriage partner may adopt a child on his or her own.

As a starting point for the following reflections it may be assumed that adoption in Europe by single people, although possible, is rare and that married couples must in principle adopt jointly. The adoption by only one spouse, even when the other supports the adoption, is not allowed, other than in exceptional cases.

In recent times this position has been regarded as common ground for further discussion. As in the United States, many European legal systems are concerned with the question whether same-sex couples should be allowed to marry or enter into registered partnerships and, if so, whether they ought to be able to adopt a child in the same way as a traditional married couple. A further question concerns the issue whether it should be possible for unmarried cohabitants of different sexes to make a joint adoption. Both issues are reviewed here. In any case, it is interesting that the discussions on reform concern only adoption by couples of the same or different sex and couples married or cohabiting. Nobody is seriously contemplating the possibility of an adoption with the aim of legally giving the child three parents, which would by no means appear to be theoretically excluded. One need only consider the situation in which a child has developed close emotional ties with its natural parents as well as a stepparent. Here nature's example that a child should not have more than two parents appears to be accepted. By the same token, it is not regarded as desirable that adoption by single persons be encouraged to a greater extent than is the case at present.

In this context, new Dutch legislation effective April 1, 1998,[17] came as a surprise. Until then Dutch law had, without exception, not allowed adoption by single people; since then it has been possible. Compared to other European legal systems this is extraordinary. Even more striking is that, both in the reasons officially given for the law and in a range of subsequent publications, it is repeatedly emphasized that in the Netherlands it is no longer of any relevance whether the adoptive parent is married or not, or alternatively lives with a partner of the same sex or not. Before the Dutch law was passed, it was generally regarded as desirable throughout Europe that an adoption by a married couple necessitated the joint adoption of the child by both spouses and that this should apply to other kinds of partnership, if the possibility of adoption by nonmarried cohabitants were to be considered at all. Yet it seems questionable whether the number of adoptions in the Netherlands by single people will actually increase: At present the possibility of adoption by a single person, in particular by homosexuals and lesbians, is a political issue in the Netherlands. There is a draft bill that would enable joint adoptions by lesbian and homosexual couples, but it has not been enacted.[18] The possibility of an adoption by only one of the partners should, for the time being, solve the problem because, to avoid discrimination, there is a desire to treat single adoptions by a same-sex partner no differently from those by one member of a married or unmarried couple. It is disappointing, however, that discussion of the possibility of adoption by same-sex couples in the Netherlands has led to a situation in which a person in a long-term relationship, whether with a partner of the same sex or not, would be able to adopt a child without taking the partner into consideration. It seems to me that the interests of the adoptive parent have been given priority over those of the child.

In countries where adoption by a single person is not permissible under current law, single women occasionally opt for artificial insemination in an attempt to fulfill their desire to have a child without a father. The case of "virgin of Birmingham"[19] was a cause of sensation in Great Britain in this regard. Although the issue of artificial insemination raises unique ethical, moral, and religious problems, the resemblance of this practice to adoption should not be disregarded. When a legal system values giving an adopted child both a father and a mother, it should, in those cases in which it allows medical intervention and the use of sperm banks, correspondingly withhold its support for a woman who wishes to bear a child without a father. The Human Fertilisations Acts of the various European States do not unfortunately reveal a uniform stance. In Great Britain[20] artificial insemination is possible even for single women. In Switzerland,[21] artificial insemination requires that the woman be married and that the husband agree to the procedure. France[22] allows artificial insemination when the woman has been living in a relationship corresponding to marriage for at least two years, while the Austrian Human Fertilisation Act[23] deems it sufficient that the woman either be married or living in a relationship equal to marriage, but with no requirement as to the duration of cohabitation. Cohabitation is difficult to determine and so is its duration. Further, a woman who does not satisfy the requirements for artificial insemination in her own country would be able to find a doctor abroad who was prepared to meet her demands. If, however, a legal system regards it as paramount that both adopted children and those conceived by artificial insemination have both a mother and a father, it should enforce this principle through legal measures—that is, by placing sanctions on the nonobservance of those regulations.

### Adoption by Unmarried Cohabitants

Only two European countries permit adoption by unmarried cohabitants: Spain and the Netherlands. In Spain,[24] the possibility of adoption by unmarried cohabitants was introduced in 1997, with the Netherlands doing likewise in 1998.[25] For those who followed the heated debate on adoption by same-sex couples, it will surely be a surprise that the issue of adoptions by unmarried cohabitants has not yet been the subject of serious discussion in Europe. This has proved to be unusual since (1) the discussion of the legal recognition of unmarried cohabitants has been going on substantially longer than the discussion of the recognition of same-sex couples, (2) the number of heterosexual couples is significantly and proportionally greater than same-sex couples, and (3) the prevalence of the former is constantly increasing. If one imagines a futuristic vision of society—which I hope will not come to pass—in which the overwhelming majority of the population cohabit without marriage, the legislature would have little choice but to provide for the possibility of adoption by those who are not married. But we have not yet reached this point. A large number of those who currently cohabit without marriage are young people who later get married as soon as they want to start a family, or divorced people who already have a failed relationship behind them and do not want to marry a second time. But these people in general are not interested in adoption. This may explain why the political pressure to allow adoption by unmarried cohabitants is not particularly strong.

Furthermore, today it is realistically justifiable to give preference to married couples as adoptive parents over unmarried cohabitants. The marriage partner assumes not only moral but also legal obligations toward his or her partner. One is in particular obliged to pay maintenance, which in the instance of an adoption is of interest to the child, since the parent with custody cannot be deprived of all means of financial support. Similar considerations apply to divorces: the divorced spouse who is not able to support herself enjoys the right to claim maintenance and certain pension benefits from the former marriage partner. Furthermore, any property acquired during the course of the marriage must be divided equally if there is a divorce, which constitutes a form of financial security. The reciprocal obligations assumed on marriage, however, represent not only a form of economic security for the adopted child; marriage is also an external manifestation of the desire of the partners to have a family. If—and this is the crucial point—the status of the institution of marriage is increasingly undermined, then indeed one should consider whether the ability to adopt should be reserved for married couples only. I would like to illustrate this point with an example: it has become common in Germany to enter prenuptial agreements providing that the marriage partners would not owe each other anything if they divorced. The courts have recognized such contracts as valid despite the fact that when the couple reached the agreement, they could not have known how many (if any) children they would have, how long the marriage would last, and what sort of financial or personal sacrifices they would make for one another.[26]

Such marriages are essentially marriages without legal consequences, which are from the start intended for a limited period only. It would be hard for me to accept that couples who have married on such a basis (and hence whose marriage only really exists on paper) should be allowed to adopt just the same as traditionally married couples.

## Adoption by Homosexual Couples

### The Legal Position in Europe

Adoption by homosexual and lesbian couples has become a topic of public interest in Europe. To my knowledge, the Spanish province of Navarra is the only European legal system that so far has allowed same-sex partners to jointly adopt a child.[27] Although a draft law, which provides for the possibility of adoption by lesbian or homosexual couples, has already been around for some time in the Netherlands, the proposal for adoption by same-sex couples only passed the Upper House on December 19, 2000, and took effect in spring of 2001, so the effects are unknown.[28] In Denmark, a bill came into force on July 1, 1999, that, although not permitting homosexual couples to adopt, grants homosexuals and lesbians the possibility of adopting their partner's child.[29] The adoption of a stepchild by the homosexual partner is therefore permitted.

Europe is far from accepting the possibility of adoption by same-sex couples. Discussion in the media of the issue bears no relation to the legal reality. The present heated debate in Europe centers around the question whether homosexuals or lesbians should be able to marry or enter some other formalized relationship, which is either comparable to marriage or at least creates legal consequences that could somehow elevate the relationship to something more than mere informal cohabitation.

Marriage or registered partnerships between homosexuals do not at present exist in the vast majority of European countries. Scandinavian states, including Denmark,[30] Norway,[31] Sweden,[32] and (Greenland) Island,[33] along with the Netherlands[34] and the Spanish province of Navarra,[35] have gone furthest; in these places it is possible for homosexual and lesbian couples to formalize registered partnerships, the effects of which come close to those of a marriage. But other than in Navarra, the possibility of an adoption is expressly excluded. There are in other states, like France,[36] Belgium,[37] and the Spanish regions of Aragon and Catalonia,[38] alternative ways of formalizing same-sex relationships, though their effects have little in common with those of marriage. One gets the impression that in Europe many states, including Germany, are currently in search of a compromise between giving in to political pressure on the one hand and not having to open the institution of marriage to same-sex couples on the other.

## The Danish Statute from June 2, 1999

Denmark was in 1989 the first country in the world to introduce the concept of a registered partnership for same-sex couples. In principle, the registered partnership has the same legal effects as marriage, with the exception of those implications of marriage that are gender-specific, as well as the possibility of joint custody and joint adoption. The subsequent amendment of June 2, 1999,[39] opened up for the first time the possibility of one of the registered partners adopting the child of the other. Justification for the amendment was drawn from the fact that over the ten-year existence of the institution of the registered partnership it had been shown that "numerous" children were growing up in the context of such a relationship, an eventuality not foreseen by the earlier legislators. The legal position of these children had been, so it was said, seriously compromised: were the parent with sole custody of the child to die, there would be no legally secure means to enable the child to remain living with the surviving registered partner with whom it may possibly have developed close emotional ties. Furthermore, such children would be unable to claim maintenance if the couple were to break up, nor could they claim inheritance if bereaved of the nonparent partner.

Since the justification for the legislation refers to "numerous" children growing up in same-sex registered partnerships, it would be appropriate to consider the statistics: each year in Denmark only about two hundred same-sex partnerships are registered, while roughly thirty-five thousand marriages are celebrated. This means that considerably fewer than 1 percent of all registered couples involve partners of the same sex. To date—some ten years later—there are less than two thousand same-sex couples in registered partnerships in Denmark. A 1997 statistical investigation reached the surprising result that only 128 Danish children were growing up with a parent living in a registered partnership. If we further consider that of these 128, only a small number are eligible for adoption because, for example, both biological parents are still alive, or because an adoption is excluded on other grounds, one wonders whether the law was perhaps passed as a means of appeasing certain interest groups. Also, where the justification for the law refers to the child having no right to maintenance against the surviving partner following the death of the natural parent, one might ask why the same partner who wanted to adopt the child would not be prepared to maintain the child or make it an heir outside the context of adoption.

Particularly embarrassing is the amendment's additional proviso that, in contrast to Danish children, foreign stepchildren will not be eligible for adoption by the registered partner. Behind this rule is the concern that Third World countries might no longer be willing to send children to Denmark for adoption if they knew that these children would later grow up as adopted children in a homosexual or lesbian partnership. Therefore that which the Danish legislator regards as appropriate for Danish children does not count for children from abroad.

### Personal Commentary

When discussing "adoption by same-sex couples," we must distinguish between two issues: (1) whether same-sex couples should, like married couples, be able to adopt children unrelated to either of them, and (2) whether one of the partners may adopt the natural child of the other, thus creating a parent–child-relationship between the child and both of the partners.

I personally consider untenable the position that advocates the adoption by same-sex couples of children who are completely external to the relationship. I do not reject the possibility of homosexual or lesbian couples being good parents to a child. But that does not mean to suggest that a legal system should allow such couples to adopt in the same way as married couples. Homosexual and lesbian relationships by their nature do not aspire to procreation and so cannot invoke the maxim "adoption imitates nature" as regards the creation of a parent-child relationship. Therefore any claim of discrimination against same-sex couples is without foundation. It is not subject to dispute that the homosexual orientation of a couple is not in itself a valid argument to demand that the legislator consent to the possibility of adoption. Same-sex couples repeatedly emphasize that sexual orientation is totally irrelevant. But if neither marriage nor heterosexual orientation are deemed to be a prerequisite for adoption, then one would accordingly have to acknowledge the feasibility of absolutely any couple adopting, so long as it could be established that both partners were ready and able to successfully assume the mantle of parenthood. Were the maxim "adoption imitates nature" not decisive, then one would also have to ask whether it necessarily had to be two people who took on the role of parents. After all, given the appropriate circumstances, a child can be raised properly by a single person, or even by three people.

The issue is slightly different regarding the adoption of stepchildren in a same-sex relationship. Here one is not concerned with establishing a parent–child-relationship, but rather with the consolidation by legal means of a relationship that already exists. In contrast to adoption of a nonnatural child, in the cases in which a stepchild is adopted there is already some natural mother–child or father–child relationship between one of the parents and the child. Nevertheless, I am of the opinion that even the adoption of a stepchild by a same-sex partner should not in law be possible. Children who grow up in a same-sex relationship have a natural father and mother just the same. Even when the child may have a troubled relationship with its natural, noncustodial father or mother, or indeed if the biological father or mother has died, this does not change the fact that the child has a natural father or mother who remains a part of the child's life. To me it makes a world of difference whether in particular cases the natural father is replaced by a stepfather or whether in a same-sex relationship a woman legally assumes the role of the natural father. Considerations apply here similar to those used in a number of jurisdictions regarding the adoption by relatives. In order to avoid things being complicated by natural blood ties, a number of legal systems prohibit the adoption by siblings or grandparents.[40] Therefore the adoption as a stepchild by the same-sex partner should only be considered when the identity of the child's natural father or mother is not known, when the child has been conceived by artificial insemination, or when it is not possible to determine who the father or mother is. But even under these circumstances I see no need for an adoption by the homosexual partner. No court would hamper close emotional ties between the child and its mother's or father's partner after the death of the natural parent. Under German law, the deceased's partner could in such cases raise the child as a legal guardian, voluntarily undertaking the responsibility of maintaining the child and, if the person wishes, nominate the child as his or her legal heir; there would be no need for an adoption. However, I do concede that this argument could be employed against adoption by the new spouse of the noncustodial, heterosexual natural parent. As a matter of fact, I regard the adoption of stepchildren with a certain skepticism:[41] relations between stepchildren and stepparents are a part of our social fabric and should be the subject of suitable legislation, but they should not be altered unnecessarily by adoption. A stepparent is as much part of the stepchild's life as both the parent who has been awarded custody and the other natural parent. As a rule, there is no legal necessity to elevate a stepparent to the status of an adoptive parent, as the family equilibrium of the natural parent and the stepparent is not under threat. After more detailed scrutiny, it appears that adoptions of stepchildren are often founded on the selfish motives of the adopting parent, who may want to exclude the natural parent or by some symbolic act make someone else's child his or her own. However none of this would actually make any difference to the child's life.

## CONCLUSION

In assessing proposals to open adoption to single individuals, unmarried couples, and same-sex couples that are being considered in many countries in Europe, the interests and welfare of children must be the paramount concern. The principle that adoption is an imitation of nature has functioned well to protect the interests of children. That principle is challenged by claims for adoption by single persons, and by unmarried and same-sex couples. Because adoption is not the only way to provide for the interests of children outside of the natural family, and since the legal order need not lend its approval by way of adoption to all affiliations that display signs of familial relations, I do not agree with adoptions by homosexual couples. Similarly, adoptions by single people should be limited to exceptional cases. I agree with legislation that requires heterosexual couples who wish to adopt jointly to be already married, because the act of marriage signifies an acceptance of the legal responsibility for one another, which can only be beneficial to the adopted child.

## NOTES

1. § 1743 BGB (Civil Code, Germany).
2. Adoption Act, 1976, § 14 (England).
3. Children and Parents Code, Ch. 4 § 1 (Sweden); Adoption Act § 4 (Denmark).
4. Civil Code, Art. 1979 (Portugal).
5. § 180 Abs 1 ABGB (Civil Code, Austria).
6. Adoption Act, Art. 6, Codice civile (Civil Code, Italy).
7. Civil Code, Art. 228 (Netherlands).
8. Schweizerisches Zivigesetzbuch, Art. 265 (Civil Code, Switzerland).
9. Código Civil, Art. 175 (Civil Code, Spain).

10. Adoption Act, Art. 6, Codice civile (Civil Code, Italy).

11. Civil Code, Art. 1979 (Portugal).

12. Cf. Rainer Frank, *Grenzen der Adoption* (Frankfurt am Main: Metzner, 1978), 220.

13. Frederick Bozett, ed., *Gay and Lesbian Parents* (New York: Praeger, 1987); Patterson, "Children of Lesbian and Gay Parents," *Child Development* 63, 1025–1042 (1992); *This Child Does Have Two Mothers,* 78 Georgetown Law Journal 459–575 (1990); Niemeyer, *"Kinder homosexueller Eltern: Kein Ende der Diskussion über die Reform des Familienrechts?"* Familie und Recht 141–142 (1997); Jörg Risse, *Der verfassungsrechtliche Schutz der Homosexualität* (1997), 337–341.

14. Schweizerisches Zivigesetzbuch, Art. 264b (Civil Code, Switzerland).

15. Adoption Act, 1976, § 15 (England).

16. § 179 Abs 1 ABGB (Civil Code, Austria) (a minimum period of three years in separation); Schweizerisches Zivigesetzbuch, Art. 264b (Civil Code, Switzerland) (a minimum period of three years after a decree of separation has been passed).

17. Act of 24.12.1997 (Netherlands).

18. Tweede Kamer 1998–99, No. 26672; cf. Pintens, *Partnerschaft im belgischen und niederländischen Recht,* FamRZ 69–77 (2000). Nine months after this paper was presented, the Dutch Parliament Upper House completed passage of such a bill on December 19, 2000. See note 28.

19. Cf. Derek Morgan and Robert G. Lee, *Blackstone's Guide to the Human Fertilisation and Embryology Act 1990* (London: Blackstone Press, 1991), 147.

20. Cf. Human Fertilisation and Embryology Act 1990 § 13 (5) (England); Gillian Douglas, *Law, Fertility and Reproduction* (London: Sweet & Maxwell, 1991), 121–122.

21. Fortpflanzungsmedizingesetz (Human Fertilisation and Embryology Act) 1998, Art. 3 (Switzerland).

22. Code de la Santé Publique, Art. L. 152-2 (France, 1994).

23. § 2 Fortpflanzungsmedizingesetz (Human Fertilisation and Embryology Act) 1992 (Austria).

24. Código Civil, Art. 175, of the Act 21/1987 as amended in 11.11.1987 (Civil Code, Spain).

25. Civil Code, Art. 227 (Netherlands). (The Act of 24.12.1997, took effect on 1.4.1998.)

26. In detail, Rainer Frank, *Jahre BGB-Familienrecht zwischen Rechtspolitik, Verfassung und Dogmatik,* 100 Archiv fuer die civilistische Praxis 401–425, 410 (2000); in comparison also, Büttner, FamRZ (1998), 1–8.

27. Act of 3.7.2000, Art. 28 (Boletin Oficial del Parlamento de Navarra, 5.7.2000, No. 58).

28. Tweede Kamer 1998–99, No. 26672 and 26673; cf. Pintens, *Partnerschaft im belgischen und niederländischen Recht,* FamRZ, 69–77, 76 (2000). Nine months after this paper was presented, the Dutch Parliament Upper House completed passage of such a bill on December 19, 2000. See note 18. Isabelle Wesselingh, *Dutch Senate Approves Landmark Gay Marriage, Right to Adopt Law*, Agence France-Presse, Tuesday, December 19, 2000.

29. Lov om aendring af lov om registreret partnerskab from 2.6.1999 (Denmark).

30. Lov om registreret partnerskab (Denmark, 1989); cf. Nielsen, *Legislation on*

*Assisted Reproduction, Reports on Adoption, The Family Principle and Blessing Registered Partnerships,* International Survey of Family Law (1996), 135–145.

31. Lov om registreret partnerskap (Norway, 1993); cf. Lodrup, *Registered Partnership in Norway,* International Survey of Family Law (1994), 387–394.

32. Lag om registrerat partnerskap (Sweden, 1994); cf. Saldeen, *The Rights of Children to Speak for Themselves and Obtain Access to Information Concerning Their Biological Origins, Etc.,* International Survey of Family Law (1994), 441–448.

33. Log um stadfesta samvist (Greenland, 1996).

34. Gesetz über die registrierte Partnerschaft (Act on Registered Partnerships) from 5.7. 1997 (Netherlands, 1.1. 1998); cf. Forder, *An Untouchable Family Law: Partnerships, Parenthood, Social Parenthood, Names and Some Article 8 ECHR Case Law,* International Survey of Family Law (1997), 259–307.

35. Act of 3.7.2000 (Boletin Oficial del Parlamento de Navarra, 5.7.2000, No. 58).

36. Pacte Civil de Solidarité (PACS), Act No. 99–944 from 15 November 1999 (France); cf. Hauser, *Deutsches und Europäisches FamilienRecht (DEu FamR)* (2000), 1–3.

37. Loi instaurant la cohabitation légale from 23.11.1998 (Belgium); cf. Pintens, *Partnerschaft im belgischen und niederländischen Recht,* FamRZ (2000), 69–77.

38. Ley 6/1999 relativa a parejas estables no casadas (Aragon); Ley 10/1998 de uniones estables de pareja (Catalonia).

39. In detail, on the act and to the following, Jens M. Scherpe, *Zehn Jahre registrierte Partnerschaft in Dänemark, Deutsches und Europäisches FamilienRecht* (2000), 32–37.

40. The adoption by grandparents and siblings is prohibited, for instance, in Spain (Civil Code, Art. 175), in Serbia (Family Code, Art. 158), and Croatia (Family Code, Art. 140). The Netherlands only prohibits the adoption by grandparents (Civil Code, Art. 228 No.1b).

41. Cf. Rainer Frank, *Grenzen der Adoption* (Frankfurt am Main, 1978), 68 ff.

# 11

# Assisted Reproductive Technology (ART) and the Family: Risk or Revival?

## Ruth Deech

**INTRODUCTION: MIXED CONSEQUENCES**

The availability of assisted reproduction technology (ART) affects assumptions that we bring to the understanding of family life. It goes to the heart of our beliefs about the family, marriage, and humanity. Every announcement of a new development in the techniques of assisted reproduction is accompanied by an element of publicly expressed fear, as well as elation. That fear relates to the maintenance of the family as we know it. For example, enabling an otherwise childless couple to give birth represents the creation of a traditional nuclear family; while enabling lesbians and single women to give birth leads to the creation of family forms that are widely disapproved, and a feeling that acceptance is being imposed.

Freedom to reproduce as one wills has never been a universal principle of civilized societies. There have always been restraints designed to achieve fundamental purposes. In democratic societies, law has regulated reproductive practices, so as ART becomes a major factor in human reproduction, its regulation is expected.

The perceived threat of ART to the traditional family unit rests on a complex argument. For some decades now there has been increasing tolerance of a high divorce rate, nonmarital cohabitation, homosexuality, single parenting, abortion, adultery, underage sex and pregnancy, births out of wedlock, and diverse lifestyles. Yet the regulation of ART is largely premised in its ability to help the traditional nuclear family, which lacked only children to make it complete. Its original success lay in "completing" those families. However, once ART was extended to unconventional families there were complaints that family life was being undermined, even though natural fertility is leading to far more unusual families than ART ever could. This debate about why there should be regulation of ART has not come to a conclusion.[1]

The complex interaction between ART, marriage, and contemporary notions of the family may be summarized as follows: traditional notions about marriage gave rise to great pressure to have children, and infertility was seen as bad from many perspectives. This attitude encouraged investment in and acceptability of ART, which in turn contributed to the growing rejection of marriage as the only valid union. The newer-style unions have sought legal and social validation by recourse to ART to give them children.

The interrelationship of ART and attitudes about marriage and the family is circular. It is tritely observed that new family forms such as one-parent families, cohabitation, stepfamilies, and same-sex couples have become more common, as have later marriage and age of childbirth, a decline in marriages, and a rise in divorces and remarriages. Yet these factors have driven reproductive technologies forward, as much as the other way round. ART has contributed to an atmosphere in which legal and biological parenthood do not necessarily coincide and has provided the facility for the nontraditional to mimic the traditional.

The law and practice of ART in Britain were established following the report of the Warnock Committee in 1984,[2] which leaned toward the traditional: "As a general rule it is better for children to be born into a two-parent family, with both father and mother."[3] In the debate on the bill that became the Human Fertilization and Embryology Act 1990, attempts to limit ART to the married or to two-parent families narrowly failed. In practice, techniques have spread beyond service to infertile married couples; for example, ART can facilitate procreation by a woman who has no partner, a widow or widower, homosexuals and lesbians, and others in need of reproductive assistance. These have thrown into sharp focus the use made of section 13(5) of the act, the requirement that the clinician considering treating a woman must consider, among other things, the baby's "need for a father" before deciding that she is a suitable case for treatment. In Britain, most ART treatment is offered to married couples and many clinics are known to reject single patients automatically. By contrast, the rising rate of natural conception outside marriage, which has given a rate of 36 percent births out of wedlock in Britain, has led to increased questioning of regulation in the selection of patients for ART when there is no regulation applied to the naturally fertile.

*Childlessness.*   Douglas has described the ancient historical, religious, and cultural growth of the pressure to bear children.[4] It has almost always been viewed as the woman's failing if she does not give birth, even though in nearly 50 percent of cases the fault can now be attributed more accurately to the man. In societies in which women have no other role, or children are the only possible form of support for aged parents, or the dominant religion demands childbearing, the pressure to be fertile is overwhelming and adds to the natural sense of loss felt by any woman concerned about her infertility. Even in modern Western societies, societal and parental pressures put on (possibly voluntarily) childless couples to have children are well known. ART, and its depiction in the media as much more successful than it actually is, deprives the infertile of any excuse for accepting their fate and getting on with their lives without children. Every media story about "miracle babies" must drive the infertile and their friends and family to the belief that by trying harder and spending more, they too could become parents. ART reinforces the underlying assumption of society that all married couples, especially women, want a baby. This child-centered approach may reinforce the false notion that a woman cannot be valid without children, which is detrimental to women's health and status.

*Procreation for respectability.* The deployment of ART happened to coincide with the period in which marriage ceased to be the only forum for childbearing and rearing. As marriage rates dropped, the separation of marriage and sex, sex and babies, became acceptable. It was also the period in which homosexuals commenced intense lobbying to be accepted as normal and equal, which included campaigning to be allowed to marry and have babies. Procreation became the hallmark of acceptability and respectability for all these nontraditional groupings, and they sought to take advantage of the newly developed and more successful ART to achieve social approval.

In Europe, their ability to access ART was extended by European Community law, which gave the right to seek medical services in any country. The European Convention on Human Rights also increased access to ART by its grant of remedies for discrimination and rights to private and family life.[5] These treaties have made it almost impossible to deny access to ART to single women and homosexuals and have opened the way for social use of ART techniques and for sex selection. Now there is little value in asking whether the use of ART has undermined marriage; this is conceded, and one can only look at whether ART is undermining the two-parent family.

The new emphasis on the "family," as distinct from marriage, has turned away from the traditional two parents and children and focused instead on the presence of children and the intention to have them. Now it is said that children make a family, rather than the other way around. Hence it must seem to nontraditional units such as cohabitants, same-sex partners, and single people that the presence of children will make them into a family. An example is the recent account of two British homosexual men who fathered twins by an American surrogate mother from mixed sperm. This led to public debate about whether this was achieved out of desire for the children, or desire for the hallmark of a "real family"—just another step in the campaign by homosexuals for "equivalence" to heterosexual families.

Thus, children have replaced the marriage contract, the wedding ring, and the certificate as the seal of a "family." These attitudes are bolstered by studies claiming that the traditional two-parent family is not the only satisfactory structure for rearing children.[6]

*Infertility.* It is said that one-sixth of couples are infertile, based on the number who seek medical assistance. The rate is probably higher if one were to count all individuals. This may be because of higher rates of abortion, sexually transmitted diseases, and environmental factors in society: as they rise so will recourse to ART. This has come as a surprise to the 1960s generation of women, who were the first to believe that they could control their fertility (because of legalized abortion and access to modern contraception), and choose fertility or infertility at almost any stage of life. As more of them and later generations of women entered higher education and sought careers, they postponed childbirth. Divorce and remarriage have also led to older childbearing. Fertility drops quite dramatically at age 38,[7] and much infertility is now due not to pathology but simply to aging. Because there is also a shortage of babies available for adoption, there is no alternative to ART. Providing more information to young people about the prevalence and causes of infertility might reduce recourse to ART.

Infertility may be treated with traditional surgery and pharmacology as well as with modern ART techniques. While ART techniques such as gamete donation, IVF, and cryopreservation tend to be regulated, more traditional treatments are usually not regulated.

### Artificial Insemination, Surrogacy, and Cloning Issues

Donor insemination (DI) by an anonymous donor, surrogacy, and cloning pose different threats to our traditional notions of marriage and the family. DI is used by single women and couples when the husband or male partner is infertile, has a low sperm count or a genetic disease, has had a vasectomy, or has been treated by radiotherapy or chemotherapy. Since self-insemination is an alternative to treatment in clinics, DI is hard to control and the law must accommodate it to encourage resort to the safer practices offered by clinics, in preference to resorting to self-insemination with possibly unsafe sperm.

The result of DI is to create a family where otherwise there might have been none and to give the appearance of normality. However, new developments in genetics and conclusions about psychology are forcing a change in our attitudes about DI and family normality. There is growing support for the "right to know one's father" as genetic knowledge and preimplantation genetic diagnosis become more widespread and important. The analogy is also being drawn with adoption, where the best practice is considered to be openness and where, by British law, an adult adoptee may seek knowledge of his or her biological parents.[8] Section 31 of the Human Fertilization and Embryology Act goes no farther than to allow collection of non-identifying information about the sperm donor. The Warnock Report favored donor anonymity in the interests of the infertile couple's privacy and desire to appear like any other family. Genetic paternity is further disguised by provisions of the Act that the husband (or partner) of the woman receiving treatment is to be treated as the father, unless he objects.[9] The 1990 Act guarantees, insofar as primary legislation can, the anonymity of sperm donors donating under this law. Section 31(5) of the HFE Act states, in effect, that the law will not be changed retrospectively to remove anonymity, an important factor in persuading volunteer donors to come forward. Under section 31(4), the HFEA may impose a requirement through regulations that one must give information to those who have discovered that they are IVF children. No regulations specifying the detail of information to be collected have yet been made.

There are heavy practical and social difficulties in disclosure, highlighting the clash between social and genetic notions of the family and parenthood. Donors are kept anonymous not only for their own sakes and to achieve detachment, but also for the sake of the infertile husband who is rearing the child. The relationship with the social father may be jeopardized if the law is changed, or it may survive intact as apparently most relationships between adoptive parents and their children have. It would be difficult to ensure disclosure of the donor's identity. Since it is reported that most successfully treated infertile couples do not tell the child of his or her origins, a disclosure rule might well encourage more social parents to withhold information from their child. Reluctant couples might go abroad to seek treatment in a country where anonymity was ensured. Removal of anonymity may limit the supply of sperm donors, as potential donors would fear not only disclosure years later but also further law reform affixing them with some financial responsibility for their children.

A child needs to know the identity of his or her father not only for medical and genetic purposes, but also, it is said, in order to understand his or her background as currently constructed, and for inheritance purposes. If these reasons are compelling, then there is logic in allowing all children, born of ART or not, to seek the truth about their origins, perhaps by DNA testing. There are doubtless children in stepfamilies and other reconstructed families who are under a misapprehension about their parenthood. Commercial DNA testing laboratories in Britain report that 30 percent of the tests submitted to them reveal that the father has been misidentified. It is likely that the completion of the Human Genome Project and its consequences will add to the forces that will weaken the traditional family in favor of biological openness.

Surrogacy also illustrates how the new ART goes beyond the two-parent presumption. Surrogacy is now accepted as a device of last resort.[10] When successful, it enables the commissioning couple to become a real family and the wife to become a mother. It is used to avoid inheritance of genetic diseases and overcome physical inability to give birth, and it has the potential to be used for convenience, as to give children to gay and lesbian couples and single men. Against its use is the grave danger of the birth mother changing her mind, the commercialism inherent in the arrangement, and the Catch-22 situation whereby if the birth mother gives up the baby as promised, she is regarded as unnatural, and if she does not, she is regarded as selfish. Surrogacy presents some of the most complex problems concerning truth about genetic origins versus the happiness and "normality" of infertile couples. Under the Surrogacy Arrangements Act of 1985, there is a presumption in favor of the surrogate mother as the legal mother, entitled to security of status, even though she may not be the genetic mother of the child.[11] The surrogate mother cannot be required by the commissioning parents under any contractual arrangements to hand over the child. Thus, the welfare of the baby is rated more highly than any family appearances. Again, the origins of the child may be kept from him or her because surrogacy is perfectly possible on a do-it-yourself basis, and no information may ever be available to the child about paternity or maternity. Surrogacy clearly raises basic questions about what constitutes parentage. Five adults may be directly involved in a surrogacy: the commissioning couple, the carrying mother, and two gamete donors.

Cloning represents perhaps the ultimate threat to marriage and the family. It involves taking the nucleus from an adult cell and inserting it into an enucleated egg, and then fusing the two into fertilization by the administration of an electric shock. The resulting embryo is then transferred into a surrogate mother, or into the egg donor as in usual IVF. Cloning could eliminate the role of the father completely, and could undermine core concepts connected with traditional family life. Through cloning, lesbians could bear children not only without contact with a man, but also without even having to resort to the sperm bank for donor insemination. In both Britain and the United States human reproductive cloning has been almost universally rejected, even as a last-resort treatment for infertility.

Apart from the almost automatic aversion and fear expressed by even well-informed members of the public, the arguments against human cloning are the risks to health; the distortion of the order of the generations by, in effect, creating a twin of a parent in a later generation; the fact that children might be born with a genetic inheritance from only one person, that is, with no father at all in any sense of the word, excluding men completely from the reproduction process. There would also be social problems arising from novel family structures and relationships, which would in all likelihood be changed by the dominating influence of the parent responsible for the entire genetic makeup of the child. There is aversion to the thought of deliberate engineering of the genes of an individual, in place of the random combination of the genes of two parents, as has always been the case. Yet one might argue that there has always been some manipulation of the genetic makeup of a future child by the choice of adults in combining together,[12] and there is nothing more traditional in this context than matchmaking of one sort or another in an attempt to marry two well-suited individuals.

Under the Human Fertilization and Embryology Act, the clinician considering giving infertility treatment to a particular patient is required to consider the welfare of the potential child,[13] which militates against permitting cloning. Cloned children might be discriminated against or exploited. What would be their place within the family, whose generations would have been so abruptly disordered, and what would happen to general notions of the family and its hierarchy? Would a cloned child be subject to excessive control from its parents or one parent, who already would have demonstrated an excessive tendency to control by having resorted to cloning for personal replacement purposes? Would the parent reject the child if, despite cloning, he or she turned out to have a personality other than expected? Who would be identified as the legal and social mother, given that the social grandparents would in fact have been the providers of the genes of the mother and therefore the cloned child? Would this affect responsibility for the child? If the adults rearing the child knew that its genetic makeup was predetermined, and assumed that certain traits were inborn, would they strive to ensure that the expected traits were encouraged in a child, or would the adults feel free to abandon the child to its (they believe) predetermined fate? Our concepts of the family, upbringing, and relationships would have to be reconsidered, and in the meantime there might be damaging effects on cloned children.[14]

### Singles Procreating

Much controversy has arisen in connection with the extension of ART to single people. Marriage seems scarcely to be given preference in reproduction and its consequences.[15] Respect for the married family is preserved in British law by the welfare test. The Code of Practice developed by the HFEA,[16] which practitioners are expected to observe under penalty of losing their licenses, governs the details of its application. The clinician has to make inquiries concerning the age and health of the patients, their commitment to rearing the child in a stable environment, and whether there is anything in their medical or legal histories that would render them unfit to be parents. Single status seems to be considered here. Nevertheless, many clinicians do not treat these requirements as seriously as they should, either because their main objective is simply to treat the patient or possibly because they do not believe in restrictions on access to ART, given how totally unsuitable people may freely become parents if they are able to conceive naturally.

### Motherhood and Fatherhood

It may be asked how these new developments affect the concepts of being a "father" and a "mother" within the marriage and family context. The birth mother still seems to be given more legal recognition than any other type (e.g., the egg donor). So the surrogate mother is the legal mother,[17] but once the commissioning woman has secured a parental responsibility order under section 30 of the HFE Act, she will be the legal mother of the child. The effects of ART on women, especially mothers, are more social than legal. Because of the pressure to avail oneself of the new techniques, there is a danger of stereotyping women as fulfilled only if they have children.

Women have long been able to prolong their fertile years by freezing embryos, which may be left over after IVF, for use in the future. Now it is possible for women to freeze their unfertilized eggs so that in theory a young woman could freeze her eggs while they were still at their healthiest (say in her twenties) for use at a time that suited her and her professional advancement. This has proved controversial, but it gives women the right to postpone fertility in the way that a man can by freezing his sperm, and the freezing of eggs is more acceptable than the freezing of embryos to those who believe that life begins at conception.

The effects of ART on fathers have not been the same. ART has demonstrated the many ways in which women can have children without men and can imply devaluation of fatherhood. For example, the essence of cloning is that there is no father at all; and posthumous conception by artificial insemination is perfectly feasible when a man has stored his sperm during his lifetime and consented to its use by his widow, or by anyone else, after his death. Indeed, there have even been cases in which women have demanded that sperm be removed from dying and dead men by electro-ejaculation for the women's use.[18] (This latter practice is contrary to British common and statute law and to conventions on human rights,[19] for it is a breach of human rights to remove gametes or perform medical operations on a person who is unconscious and unable to consent unless it is to save his or her life.)

The threat that modern ART may make men dispensable is indeed a threat to men and to marriage. The treatment of the man as a mere collection of spare parts is also disturbing. It is dehumanizing to remove from an unconscious man the reproductive parts, so that he may be reproduced without his knowledge or consent, rendering him a step toward someone else's goal. Likewise the practice of donor insemination of single women could be said to devalue the role of men in the birth and rearing of children, and deprives the children of the benefit of a father. The social commentator Melanie Phillips described the situation as follows: "Thanks to the wonders of reproductive technology, women can now do without a male presence altogether. Fatherhood has been reduced to an emission in a test-tube. Donor insemination liberates families from fathers."[20]

ART practice and law have emphasized acceptance of a child and intention to have it as the key to recognition of the legal status of father. Under the HFE Act, the man treated with the woman is the parent,[21] and so is the commissioning father with a legal order after surrogacy.[22] Likewise, the complexities of ART fatherhood and the delayed use of frozen sperm and embryos are not recognized in inheritance law,[23] but clearly our traditional notions of inheritance within the family must be reconsidered.

### Equality

Future developments are likely to move still further away from marriage and the family. Equality between the sexes leads women to believe that they should be fertile into old age just as men are, so there will be more pressure to have babies post-menopause and late in second marriages. Human rights law will inevitably give rights to nontraditional families and single persons to seek access to ART on equal footing with the married and heterosexual. Article 14 of the European Convention on Human Rights prohibits discrimination on grounds of personal status. It applies to the rights and freedoms of the Convention, which include the right to marry and found a family,[24] and rights to private and family life.[25] Much will depend on the interpretation given to those substantive rights. Any differences in treatment would have to be reasonably justified. So far in European law, marriage has been held to be different from nonmarriage[26] and lesbians not permitted to enjoy family life,[27] but this may well change.

Depending on whether access to insemination in circumstances in which there can be no father amounts to private or family life, and whether the desire by all persons for insemination by any donor is included, Article 8 of the Convention on Human Rights[28] might support a claim by a widow seeking insemination with her late husband's sperm, regardless of how it was procured. The other aspect of Article 8 is interference with "family life." Is an attempt by a single person to become a parent equivalent to family life? These questions await interpretation. The Treaty of Amsterdam will add a new article to the EC Treaty empowering the community legislature to take action to combat discrimination on the ground of sexual orientation. This provision could strengthen the claim of homosexuals to ART assistance.

## CONCLUSION

There is no ready answer to the question whether ART undermines or strengthens marriage and the family, except that ART is both affected by and contributes to social attitudes toward these questions. It is possible that genetic engineering and preimplantation genetic diagnosis may reinforce marriage in the sense that there will be an understanding of the contribution of father and mother and a special obligation may be felt to produce healthy children and avoid diseases carried by one parent. There is an equal danger that children will be treated as a product, with disposal of "undesirable" embryos, or embryos born to order if sex selection is allowed. There is, therefore, much to be said for the British model of regulation of the practice of ART. In this way, it is possible to keep the practice of ART imbued with public notions of acceptability and welfare of the child by control over movements in ART.

## NOTES

This chapter was written in my personal capacity and not as chair of the Human Fertilisation and Embryology Authority.

1. M. H. Johnson, "Should the Use of ART be Deregulated?" 13 *Hum. Reprod.* 1769–1776 (1998).

2. Warnock Committee, *Report of the Committee of Inquiry into Human Fertilization and Embryology,* 1984, Cmnd. 9314.

3. Ibid., ¶ 2.11.

4. Gillian Douglas, *Law, Family and Reproduction* (London: Sweet & Maxwell, 1991), ch.6.

5. *European Convention on Human Rights,* arts. 14, 8.

6. S. Golombok, "Lesbian Mother Families," in *What Is a Parent?* ed. Andrew Bainum, Shelley Day Sclater, and Martin Richards (Portland, Or.: Hart Publishers, 1999).

7. Human Fertilization and Embryology 8th Annual Report (1999), tables 4.5, 4.10 and fig. 4.2.

8. Adoption Act 1976 § 50 (England).

9. Human Fertilization and Embryology Act 1990 §§ 28 (2) and (3) (England).

10. M. Brazier, A. Campbell and S. Golombok, *Surrogacy* (London: City University of London, 1998), Cm. 4068.

11. Human Fertilization and Embryology Act 1990 § 27 (England).

12. Harris, "Clones, Genes and Human Rights," in *The Genetic Revolution and Human Rights,* ed. Justine Burley (Oxford: Oxford University Press, 1999).

13. Human Fertilization and Embryology Act 1990 § 13(5) (England).

14. Ruth Deech, *Family Law and Genetics,* 61 M.L. Rev. 697 (1998).

15. Morgan and Lee, "Regulating Artificial Reproductive Technology," presented at the International Society of Family Law Conference on Biomedicine, the Family and Human Rights (1999).

16. *Code of Practice,* 4th ed. (1998), part 3.

17. Human Fertilization and Embryology Act 1990 § 27 (England).

18. *R. v. Human Fertilization and Embryology Authority ex parte Blood*, 2 All E.R 687 (1997).

19. S. McLean, *Review of the Common Law Provisions Relating to the Removal of Gametes and of the Consent Provisions in the Human Fertilization and Embryology Act 1990* (1998); *European Convention on Biomedicine and Human Rights* (Council of Europe, 1997), art. 6.

20. *The Sex-Change Society* (1999), 139.

21. Human Fertilization and Embryology Act 1990 § 28 (England).

22. Id. § 30.

23. Id. § 29.

24. *European Convention on Human Rights*, art. 12.

25. Id., art. 8.

26. *Lindsay v. UK*, 49 D.R. 181 (1986).

27. *S v. UK*, 47 D.R. 274 (1986).

28. *European Convention on Human Rights*, art. 8, "Respect for private and family life."

# 12

# *Marriage and Belonging:* *Reflections on* Baker v. Vermont

## David Orgon Coolidge

## INTRODUCTION

Must one be able to marry a person of the same sex to truly belong to the community? This is the central issue presented by the landmark case of *Baker v. Vermont.*[1] If we treat the case as merely another *Baehr,*[2] *Brause,*[3] or *Tanner,*[4] we miss the point entirely. There is something different about *Baker* that invites us to deeper reflection and response. *Baker* is the first communitarian marriage decision from a high court in America. This is good news or bad news, depending on what you think the term *communitarian* means.

In this brief essay, I will do three things. First, I will explore what is different about the *Baker* decision. Then I will explore some of the implications of that difference. Finally, I will offer a critical assessment of *Baker*'s vision of what it means to belong to the community.

## WHAT IS DIFFERENT ABOUT *BAKER*?

*Baker* is a breathtaking decision. There is nothing like it. It is simultaneously a blunt philosophical manifesto, a sweeping historical interpretation, and a bold exercise in practical constitutional adjudication. This is true of both the majority opinion and the concurring and dissenting opinions. The latter, however, chose to follow trails that had already been blazed earlier in Oregon and Hawaii.[5] Chief Justice Amestoy's majority opinion breaks new ground. These words from the chief justice's opinion have been quoted almost everywhere:

> The extension of the Common Benefits Clause to acknowledge plaintiffs as Vermonters who seek nothing more, nor less, than legal protection and security for their avowed commitment to an intimate and lasting human relationship is simply, when all is said and done, a recognition of our common humanity.[6]

The phrase most often repeated is "our common humanity." It has a great ring to it. But I would argue that the most important phrase is "legal protection and security for their avowed commitment to an intimate and lasting human relationship." In other words, the court defines the plaintiffs' challenge to the marriage statute in a particular way: As the seeking of "legal protection and security" by three couples with an "avowed commitment to an intimate and lasting human relationship." By holding that the Vermont Constitution requires that same-sex couples be offered the rights, duties, and benefits of marriage (if not the name itself), the court seems to believe it has found a way to "acknowledge" that the plaintiffs are not only fully "Vermonters," but also persons with whom the justices share a "common humanity."

The plaintiffs themselves did not approach their challenge in this manner. They launched an equal protection/due process lawsuit similar to previous challenges. They made the standard liberty and equality arguments, albeit dressed up in Vermont constitutional garb. As far as they were concerned, the Vermont Supreme Court should simply guarantee their right to marry.[7]

### Constitution as Community

However, the Vermont Supreme Court did not do what the plaintiffs demanded. Instead, it rejected the analysis offered by both sides and rested its decision on an interpretation of the Common Benefits Clause found in Chapter I of the Vermont Constitution:

> That government is, or ought to be, instituted for the common benefit, protection, and security of the people, nation, or community, and not for the particular emolument or advantage of any single person, family, or set of persons, who are a part only of that community; and that the community hath an indubitable, unalienable, and indefeasible right, to reform or alter government, in such manner as shall be, by that community, judged most conducive to the public weal.[8]

From this, the court sees the Vermont Constitution as embodying a "principle of inclusion." Indeed, the contention of the chief justice's opinion is that *Baker* is not about marriage, but rather about equal rights for couples under the Common Benefits Clause.

The introduction to the majority opinion claims, "The issue before the Court, moreover, does not turn on the religious or moral debate over intimate same-sex relationships, but rather on the statutory and constitutional basis for the exclusion of same-sex couples from the secular benefits and protections offered married couples."[9] Read that sentence again closely. The court seems to believe that the community itself is made up not only of individuals but also of "couples"—whether same-sex or married. In the body of the opinion, Amestoy argues that the Common Benefits Clause states a "principle of inclusion"[10] that applies to opposite- and same-sex couples alike. This argument is based on giving all citizens their fair share of benefits.[11] The holding of *Baker* is that the denial of marital benefits to same-sex couples violates the Common Benefits Clause.[12] It does not require same-sex "marriage,"[13] but equal benefits,[14] which (instead of marriage status), it turns out, is a sufficient "recognition of our common humanity."[15]

## Marriage as Commitment

Why this bifurcation of marital status and marital benefits? Why did *Baker* conclude that legalizing same-sex marriage was simply unnecessary to address the claims of the plaintiffs? Because once the concept of a "couple" becomes the central feature of one's analysis, marital status is almost beside the point.

*Baker* redefines marriage as a committed relationship in order to arrive at its holding. It does so, however, in a way that is brilliantly opaque. The court reasons that the Vermont Constitution generally forbids "artificial governmental preferments and advantages," and that Vermont's marriage law specifically offers such an "artificial preferment" to some couples and not others.[16] This striking assumption—that marriage is an "artificial preferment"—takes us to the heart of the question.

What does it mean that *Baker* redefines marriage as an "artificial preferment"? It means that Amestoy adopts the idea that marriage is a creation of law to promote social stability. This view of marriage can be summarized in five points, illustrated by passages from his text:

1. *Marriage has nothing to do with sexual difference.* "The laudable governmental goal of promoting a commitment between married couples to promote the security of their children and the community as a whole provides no reasonable basis for denying the legal benefits and protections of marriage to same-sex couples, who are no differently situated with respect to this goal than their opposite-sex counterparts."[17]

2. *Marriage is a wholly malleable institution that exists solely to achieve certain goals.* "In short, the marriage laws transform a private agreement into a source of significant public benefits and protections. While the laws relating to marriage have undergone many changes during the last century, largely toward the goal of equalizing the status of husbands and wives, the benefits of marriage have not diminished in value."[18]

3. *Marriage is a policy device to promote stable relationships.* In rebutting the state's claimed justifications for its marriage law, the court said: "The State's interest in extending official recognition and legal protection to the professed commitment of two individuals to a lasting relationship of mutual affection is predicated on the belief that legal support of a couple's commitment provides stability for the individuals, their family, and the broader community."[19]

4. *Marriage is a policy device to protect children.* This resembles the stability argument: "Therefore, to the extent that the state's purpose in licensing civil marriage was, and is, to legitimize children and provide for their security, the statutes plainly exclude many same-sex couples who are no different from opposite-sex couples with respect to these objectives."[20]

5. *Marital benefits are something to be equally distributed as a matter of basic fairness.* Applying the constitutional standard, the court concludes in the words repeated before: "The extension of the Common Benefits Clause to acknowledge plaintiffs as Vermonters who seek nothing more, nor less, than legal protection and security for their avowed commitment to an intimate and lasting human relationship is simply, when all is said and done, a recognition of our common humanity."[21]

These passages reveal a deeper view at work. Instead of treating marriage as something existing outside the law, the court treats it as created by the law for couples. Marriage can be deconstructed and reassembled according to basic concepts such as "equality" or "inclusion." What matters is "common humanity."[22]

To summarize, *Baker* is different from previous court opinions in two respects: It treats the central question as one of whether or not the community is excluding couples, and it treats benefits for couples as the central issue, defining marriage as a purely legal form.

### Implications of the Communitarian Turn

The chief justice's opinion in *Baker* is "communitarian" in the sense that it emphasizes that we are relational selves, rather than autonomous self-creating beings.[23] Communitarianism is an attempt to transcend individualism and pure "rights talk."[24]

The court's holding in *Baker* analyzes both the state and marriage from the communitarian perspective. First, by conceptualizing the Vermont Constitution according to a "principle of inclusion," the court treats Vermont law as not just a structure, but as the most all-inclusive community. After all, the court argues, "the essential aspect of [the plaintiffs'] claim is simply and fundamentally for inclusion in the family of state-sanctioned human relations."[25] The phrase "the family of state-sanctioned human relations" is itself strikingly communitarian.

Second, the court's emphasis on granting "equal rights" for couples, not merely for individuals, could be said to embody a more relational view of what marriage is all about. It treats "intimate relationships" as the social reality with which marital benefits and protections are concerned, and insists that justice be done to relationships.

This is a new approach to constitutional and marriage law. We previously noted, that it is different from earlier cases based purely on the pursuit of individual rights. It does not assume that the state exists solely to guarantee individual rights, and it does not assume marriage is essentially an individual contract.

However, the court's approach is also different from a traditional approach to the question. On the constitutional side, it has clearly taken upon itself the mantle of guardian of the community, with all the risks and dangers that involves. This community is evidently so all-embracing that its guardians are free to redefine social institutions. Toward the end of the opinion, the chief justice states, "The challenge for future generations will be to define what is most essentially human." These are not words to inspire confidence in the court's commitment to limited government and the rule of law. The court seems to view the state as the embodiment of the community, purely and simply. This is not individualism, but may well be its opposite. On the marriage side, the court has redefined the meaning of marriage. The statutes of every state embody the view that marriage is the union of a man and a woman, equal yet different, who join their lives to form a family.[26] This is a specific kind of relationship—not merely a relationship, or an "intimate" or "committed" relationship, but a sexual relationship. To be sure, this concept has been under attack during the last fifty years, and alternative models of marriage have been proposed.[27] However, as we have seen, every state that has been challenged by its court to redefine marriage has said no.[28] In the "traditional" view that informs existing law, marriage statutes recognize a unique male–female sexual community, not just "couples."

Taken together, the two dimensions of the court's analysis raise a straightforward question: Who do they think they are? Do the chief justice and his colleagues know more about "couples" and marriage than their legislative colleagues, or Vermonters in general? If there are contending views of marriage in the air among the citizens and public officials, then what grounds does the court have for attempting to end that contention by judicial fiat?

There is also a shadow side to the court's pronouncements about "common humanity." They imply that failure to require equal benefits for same-sex couples would represent a denial of their common humanity. Now that is a serious charge.

Neither the attorney general nor any of the amici defending Vermont's existing marriage law questioned the humanity of the plaintiffs. They did not even question whether they were capable of loving relationships. They only questioned whether the plaintiffs could actually marry each other, given the nature of marriage, and they rejected the notion that the Vermont Constitution could be reasonably read to require that result.

By leveling such a charge, the court divided the community it claimed to represent. This is not to say that members of the community did not agree with the court. Some did—and these persons were given an instant judicial imprimatur. But what of the others? What of the supporters of traditional marriage? They were deemed the enemies of community (and are often called bigots, haters). This is the rhetoric of exclusion. It permeated the legislature's subsequent debates over the proposed Civil Unions Act.[29]

Indeed, by presenting the issue in these terms, the court paints itself into a corner. To hold as it did on "common humanity" it must define those who dissent as "exclusive."

## ANOTHER VIEW OF BELONGING

There are other ways to approach the issue. They also involve attention to community. I will briefly sketch one such approach, which I think is wiser than the one taken by the *Baker* court.

In addition to the libertarian and egalitarian traditions of marriage, there is also a pluralist tradition.[30] The key feature of the pluralist tradition (which is itself plural) is that it recognizes a plurality of communities in society. Marriage is one of those communities. It is based on a sexual bond. Government is another one of those communities. It is based on a political bond. There are others. None is reducible to the others, and the task of the law is to do justice to all of them.[31]

Within this framework, it is not necessary to choose between individual rights and social institutions. The legislative branch is capable of judging whether further individual rights should be granted. If it decides that it needs to extend certain benefits to unmarried persons, it can do so. But it need not redefine marriage in order to address the concerns of unmarried persons. It only needs to balance the different concerns—the well-being of marriage, the needs of individuals, and the concerns of other communities—and arrive at some judgment about how to address the issues.

Put simply, one's "common humanity" does not depend on whether one actually participates in a specific institution. And one's "belonging to the community" does not rest upon having one's point of view affirmed by government, which is after all only one community.

## CONCLUSION

*Baker* is a significant decision because it represents a turn toward community. However, *Baker*'s specific approach has problems, because it makes "couples" the basic social unit and makes marriage a creation of the state.

Nevertheless, *Baker* reaffirms the important social functions played by marriage, rather than treating marriage just as a bundle of benefits to be redistributed on an equal basis. It identifies two major purposes of marriage law—encouraging stable relationships and healthy children—and declares that these are indeed legitimate state purposes, and that marriage has served these purposes well. This is light years away from language suggesting that marriage is based on heterosexism. The court even rejects the interracial marriage analogy. In these respects it evidences genuine concerns that are shared by all. The controversy begins when the court concludes that the Vermont Constitution requires that marital benefits be extended to same-sex couples because these couples are "similarly situated" when it comes to achieving the purposes of the marriage law.

These are tumultuous times, and a cacophony of views is contending for power. As we sort these questions out, I think most policy makers will reject the views that marriage is purely an individual contract (which really ought to be privatized) or that marriage is just a state-created benefits system (which really ought to be universalized). We may even transcend the dialectic between "individual rights" and "state interests." The real debate, as I see it, is going to be between those who believe that "couples" are the foundation of society, and those who believe that marriage requires two sexes. In that debate, may all of us acknowledge the "common humanity" of all those involved.

## NOTES

1. *Baker v. Vermont,* 744 A.2d 864 (Vt. 1999) (ordering the Vermont Legislature to offer the benefits of marriage to same-sex couples based on the Common Benefits Clause of the Vermont Constitution).

2. *Baehr v. Lewin,* 852 P.2d 44 (Haw. 1993) (holding that the Hawaii marriage statute reserving marriage to opposite-sex couples violated the state's constitution, and remanding to the lower court to determine whether the state had a compelling interest in the marriage statute); *Baehr v. Miike,* Civ. No. 91-1394, 1996 WL 694235 (Haw. Cir. Ct. December 3, 1996) (holding that the state had not established a significant justification for its marriage statute); *Baehr v. Miike,* Civ. No. 91-1394-05 (Haw. December 9, 1999) (ordering dismissal of the case due to ratification of a state constitutional marriage amendment); see also David Orgon Coolidge, *The Hawaii Marriage Amendment: Its Origins, Meaning, and Fate,* 20 U. Haw. L. Rev. 19 (2000).

3. *Brause v. Bureau of Vital Statistics,* 1998 WL 88743 (Alaska Super. 1998) (holding that a same-sex couple have a fundamental right to choose a life partner and that a trial should determine if the state has a fundamental interest to justify its current marriage law), overruled by the passage of SJR 42 (approx. November 3, 1998), now Art. I, § 23 of the Alaska Constitution. See also Kevin Clarkson, David Coolidge, and William Duncan, *The Alaska Marriage Amendment: The People's Choice on the Last Frontier,* 16 Alaska L. Rev. 213 (1999).

4. *Tanner v. Oregon Health Sciences Univ.*, 971 P.2d 435 (Or. Ct. App. 1998) (holding that "sexual orientation" is a suspect classification under the Oregon Constitution, that OHSU's policy of offering benefits solely to married couples discriminated on that basis, and that same-sex couples must be offered the same benefits). See also William C. Duncan and David Orgon Coolidge, *Marriage and Democracy in Oregon: The Meaning and Implications of Tanner v. Oregon Health Sciences University"* 36 Willamette L. Rev. 503 (2001).

5. Justice Dooley agreed with the result, but strongly disagreed with the reasoning in two respects. First, as regards the specific issue of the marriage law, Dooley argued that the court should have decided this case via a more traditional "heightened scrutiny" of a "suspect class." 744 A.2d at 892–93 (Dooley, J., concurring and dissenting). Second, he was not persuaded that the court had actually produced clear guidelines for the application of the Common Benefits Clause. Id. at 897.

Justice Johnson joined the court's opinion, but would have issued the marriage licenses. Id. at 898 (Johnson, J., concurring and dissenting). First, Johnson explained that the purpose of a marriage license is to create a record to identify where benefits should be given and that the state had no public health or safety justifications for the existing marriage law. Second, she disagreed with the remedy adopted by the court. Id. at 902. Finally, she alone argued that the marriage statute discriminated on the basis of sex, and that the "heightened scrutiny" applied to sex-based classifications should be applied. Id. at 904–907.

6. *Baker*, 744 A.2d at 889.

7. The preliminary motions, appellate briefs, and oral argument all treated the case as though it were about marriage. These materials are available online at www.vtfreetomarry.org/fs_lawsuit.html. See also Carey Goldberg, "Vermont Supreme Court Takes Up Gay Marriage," *New York Times*, November 19, 1998, at A1.

8. Vt. Const., Ch. I, Art. 7.

9. *Baker*, 744 A.2d at 867.

10. Id. at 875.

11. Id. at 876.

12. Id.

13. The term *same-sex "marriage"* is in quotes to indicate my belief that same-sex unions are not marriages, a belief that I realize some readers will not share. For a discussion of the substantive issues, see David Orgon Coolidge, *Same-Sex Marriage? Baehr v. Miike and the Meaning of Marriage*, 38 S. Tex. L. Rev. 1 (1997).

14. *Baker*, 744 A.2d at 867. Therefore, Amestoy offers other legislative responses that would potentially fulfill the court's command, such as registered partnerships. Id.

15. Id. at 889.

16. Id. at 876.

17. Id. at 884.

18. Id. at 883.

19. Id.

20. Id. at 882.

21. Id. at 889.

22. See David Orgon Coolidge, "What the Vermont Court Has Wrought," *The Weekly Standard*, January 17, 2000, at 21.

23. On this see especially the brilliant work of Milton C. Regan, Jr., *Family Law and the Pursuit of Intimacy* (New York: NYU Press, 1993).

24. See Mary Ann Glendon, *Rights Talk: The Impoverishment of Political Discourse* (New York: Free Press, 1992) for one of the most cogent diagnoses of the problem.

25. *Baker,* 744 A.2d at 889.

26. See David Orgon Coolidge and William C. Duncan, *Definition or Discrimination? State Marriage Recognition Statutes in the "Same-Sex Marriage" Debate* 32 Creighton. L. Rev. 3 (1998).

27. See Coolidge, *Same-Sex Marriage,* 29.

28. See Clarkson, Coolidge, and Duncan, *The Alaska Marriage Amendment*; Coolidge, *The Hawaii Marriage Amendment.* In addition, courts have rejected challenges in other states. On the history of cases prior to Hawaii and Alaska, see William N. Eskridge, Jr., *The Case for Same-Sex Marriage* (New York: Free Press, 1996), 52–59.

29. For a description of the 2000 legislative session, see David Orgon Coolidge and William C. Duncan, "Beyond *Baker.*" A more popular narrative can be found in David Orgon Coolidge, "The Civil Truth about 'Civil Unions,'" *The Weekly Standard* (June 26, 2000), 26–29.

30. Coolidge, *Same-Sex Marriage,* 44 et seq.

31. For an introduction to the varieties of pluralism, see Luis E. Lugo, ed., *Religion, Pluralism, and Public Life: Abraham Kuyper's Legacy for the Twenty-First Century* (Grand Rapids, Mich.: W. B. Eerdman, 2000).

# 13

# Marriage Policy and the Methodology of Research on Homosexual Parenting

## Robert Lerner and Althea K. Nagai

Social science research demonstrates that civil marriages between partners of the same sex . . . would provide the benefits of civil marriage to children of same-sex couples.

The children of gay and lesbian parents are as well adjusted as those of their heterosexual counterparts.
—Amicus Brief on behalf of the Vermont Psychiatric Association and Others, *Baker v. Vermont*

## INTRODUCTION

In 1999, the Vermont Supreme Court ruled that the state must afford same-sex couples the same legal benefits, protections, and rights as married couples. Although many factors played a role in the court's decision, one factor was the court's apparent acceptance as established fact the conclusions in the Vermont Psychiatric Association (VPA) brief regarding childrearing by same-sex couples. The VPA and others argued that what applies to traditional marriage also applies to same-sex unions in an ironic twist on widely applauded efforts to recognize both the negative consequences of single-parent families and the benefits of traditional marriage for children. The VPA brief cited many studies in support of its conclusions. The Vermont Supreme Court accepted some of these studies uncritically and based its ruling in significant part on these claims.

The Vermont court cited at least three social science studies about the lack of harmful effects of childrearing by same-sex couples. [*Baker v. Vermont*, 744 A.2d 864, 881–882 (Vt., 1999)]. After citing these studies for one point (numerical), the court relied without citation on the essential "no difference" claim of these studies and of the Vermont Psychiatric Association amicus brief for its major conclusion.

Therefore, the court reasoned, "to the extent that the state's purpose in licensing civil marriage was, and is, to legitimize children and provide for their security, the statutes plainly exclude many same-sex couples who are no different from opposite-sex couples with respect to these objectives. If anything, the exclusion of same-sex couples from the legal protections incident to marriage exposes their children to the precise risks that the State argues the marriage laws are designed to secure against. In short, the marital exclusion treats persons who are similarly situated for the purposes of law, differently" (*Baker*, 744 A.2d at 882).

The Vermont court recognized the significant benefits of marriage. It ruled that the statutory classification (allowing opposite-sex couples but disallowing same-sex couples to marry) was logically "disjoined" from the state purposes of the law—protecting children and "furthering the link between procreation and child rearing." Therefore, the exclusion of same-sex couples from the rights and benefits of marriage denies them the common benefits and protections of the law guaranteed by the Vermont Constitution. "The laudable governmental goal of promoting a commitment between married couples to promote the security of their children and the community as a whole provides no reasonable basis for denying the legal benefits and protections of marriage to same-sex couples, who are no differently situated with respect to this goal than their opposite-sex counterparts" (*Baker*, 744 A.2d at 884).

A critical purpose of marriage under the law, the state contended, which is also embodied in widely held social norms that surround marriage, is to provide for the security and responsible socialization of children within stable, loving adult unions. The Vermont court appears to have accepted uncritically and erroneously that children's well-being is not adversely affected by being raised in a union of homosexual parents. We believe this claim to be scientifically premature, at best. Research in this area has a long way to go before reliable judgments are possible. Accordingly, we believe that legal policy calling for legalization of same-sex marriage must, at least for now, not rely on the current body of scientific knowledge on this topic as supporting evidence.

To ascertain the likelihood of the claims that there is no difference in child well-being between children reared in homosexual unions and children reared in heterosexual unions, we conducted a large-scale study of the methodology used by these studies. We investigated forty-nine original research studies published in social scientific journals and books that dealt with homosexual parents, their children, or both. (See the end of the chapter for a partial list of studies reviewed.) We excluded dissertations, review articles, and articles in the nonscientific press from consideration. Each study was evaluated according to how well it embodied standard criteria for valid inference in scientific research.

Our general finding is that the methods used in these studies contain serious flaws. We argue that the current maturity of research on homosexual parenting does not meet the standard for use in legislative forums or legal cases to buttress any arguments on the relative merits of same-sex parenting, or relied on to establish marriage policy more generally. This is especially so in a matter so fundamental as changing the legal framework surrounding marriage.

The flaws found in nearly all these studies include: (1) falsely affirming the null hypothesis (the hypothesis that something is due to chance, rather than a systematic cause); (2) inadequate sample size and inadequate statistical power; (3) failure to use comparison groups properly or at all; (4) omission of necessary statistical controls, including inadequate consideration of spurious noncorrelation; (5) unreliable measures; (6) sample selection bias; and (7) misused statistical techniques. This chapter focuses first on one flaw so crucial that it alone calls into question the findings of this literature. All these studies, either implicitly or explicitly, attempt to "prove" the null hypothesis—that is, that there is no relationship between the independent and dependent variables. After explaining why this flaw is so serious, we explore how its problems affect other aspects of research designs and data analyses. Then we explain briefly some of the other serious methodological flaws in these studies. Space does not permit a full explanation of all the flaws.[1]

## The Logic of Scientific Hypothesis Testing

To understand why trying to "prove" the null hypothesis can be a serious problem in research, we need some background in the standard operating procedures in quantitative research. Social science research methods emphasize the importance of testing an explicit, positive research hypothesis. An independent variable is hypothesized to "cause," or influence, a dependent variable.[2] The hypothesis should be stated as a proposition in the form: "The greater the *a*, the greater the *b*," where *a* is the independent variable and *b* is the dependent variable. For the researcher to confirm the hypothesis, a counter, or "null," hypothesis—that there is no relationship between *a* and *b* and that any apparent relationship is due to chance—must be able to be rejected with a degree of statistical reliability.

To study the effects of same-sex unions on children, for example, the researcher could stipulate the following positive hypothesis (among several): that homosexual parents are more likely to raise children who grow up to be anxious and depressed than are heterosexual parents. The null hypothesis, in this case, would be that there is no relationship between parents' sexual orientation and children's anxiety and depression. Only two of the studies we analyzed, Pagelow and Miller, actually state a positive research hypothesis. Twenty-nine fail to state the research problem in any kind of hypothesis-testing format, while eighteen studies seek to find no differences between heterosexual and homosexual parents in child outcomes. This last research design is problematic because of the difficulties inherent in "proving" that outcomes are due to chance; that is, proving the null hypothesis.

### The Problem of Affirming the Null Hypothesis

Two major problems result from testing a hypothesis that "it makes no difference in the size of $b$ (the dependent variable) whether $a^1$ or $a^2$ (two possibly influential independent variables) is present"—a hypothesis of no difference—which is the inversion of the usual social science research procedure. First, failing to reject the null hypothesis, the possibility of chance, necessarily leads to an indeterminate result, since the hypothesis of no difference assumes without testing that any change in $b$ resulted from chance, without causation by either independent variable $a^1$ or $a^2$. In contradictory fashion, the hypothesis of no difference also assumes that if there is a change in $b$ resulting from cause, the change is caused by both independent variables in the same way (so there is no difference between results caused by $a^1$ and results caused by $a^2$).

Second, inverting the standard hypothesis-testing procedure, without making compensating changes, makes it too easy to fail to test the possibility that results were caused by chance. Failing to reject the null hypothesis is the typical outcome in the gay-parenting studies, and this partiality violates both the letter and the spirit of scientific procedure.

Rigorous procedures in quantitative social science require statistical testing of a positive research hypothesis. A simplified example may help to visualize what is involved. For example, suppose a researcher hypothesizes that political liberalism leads to greater support for abortion rights than does political conservatism. One way to test this research hypothesis is to use a national sample survey of the American public. Using this body of data, one would compute the average, or mean, "abortion support score" for those calling themselves "liberal" and the average "abortion support score" for those calling themselves "conservative." Presumably, political liberals have higher abortion support scores than conservatives. The question arises, however, whether any difference between abortion support scores might be due to chance. To answer that question, statisticians have developed tests of statistical significance to differentiate insignificant and significant results. Insignificant differences result from such factors as sampling error, measurement error, or just random fluctuations. These competing claims should be considered as possible explanations for *any* research finding. Chance occurrences of this kind do happen—individuals do win the lottery and draw royal flushes in honest poker games.

To ascertain whether the findings can be explained by random variation, the researcher carries out a statistical hypothesis test. This requires a research hypothesis and a null hypothesis. The research hypothesis is the positive statement previously discussed—"the greater the *a*, the greater the *b*." The null hypothesis is a hypothesis of no effect. In the abortion example, the research hypothesis is that liberals are more pro-choice than conservatives. The null hypothesis is that there is no difference between liberals and conservatives. Both statements cannot be true.

The null hypothesis is the mathematical assumption needed for statistical hypothesis testing. It is needed to create the model from which one calculates the probability that the null hypothesis is true given the data at hand. After the calculations are carried out, the test statistic is calculated, and its associated probability computed. If the test statistic is greater than the critical value (e.g., $t \geq 2.00$), the null hypothesis is rejected at the associated level of statistical significance (e.g., $p \leq 0.05$, meaning that the results are likely the result of chance in only five out of one hundred cases), and the research hypothesis is accepted.

The hypothesis-testing situation is constructed in order to yield a decisive outcome. If the null hypothesis is rejected, then the alternative positive research hypothesis is accepted. The burden of proof is on the investigator to show support for the positive research hypothesis.

A larger problem occurs if the researcher fails to reject the null hypothesis. A researcher may neglect to show that a result is not the product of chance for two reasons. First, if whatever differences the researcher finds are due to chance, no statistical or causal relationship between the independent and dependent variables exists. In that case, the researcher can't reject the null hypothesis because it explains his or her findings. Second, the research hypothesis may be true, but because of a flaw in the study design it cannot be shown with the data at hand. Because every failure to reject the null hypothesis always has these two possible explanations, the null hypothesis cannot simply be "accepted" in the same way that it can be rejected and the positive research hypothesis accepted. Further investigation is always required.

Most same-sex parenting studies make precisely this mistake. They falsely assume that the failure to reject the null hypothesis means that no difference exists between heterosexual and homosexual parents. The only study that showed any awareness of the problem—Chan, Raboy, and Patterson—did nothing to correct for it. The "findings" of no difference between heterosexual and homosexual parents as reported in the literature are inconclusive.

### Error, Sample Size, and Statistical Power

The fallacy of affirming or "proving" the null or the no difference hypothesis also compromises other important parts of these studies' research designs. As mentioned, "statistical significance" is the measurement of the possibility of results occurring by chance. A statistical significance of 0.05 means that even when the null hypothesis is true, "significant" findings may occur 5 percent of the time. So, if we generate twenty test statistics, one out of twenty tests will be statistically significant due to chance alone because there is a 5 percent probability of that result, or $p \leq 0.05$.

Although 100 percent certainty is not possible, reduced insecurity is. Researchers can set the significance level at 0.01, whereby 1 percent of the results are significant even though the null hypothesis is true. A higher standard of certainty may be called for when findings are used to support particularly controversial conclusions. If one falsely believes that failing to reject the possibility of chance results (the null hypothesis) means that the results must have been caused by chance, then it will be tempting to find a way to make it even harder than usual to reject the null hypothesis. The more statistically sophisticated homosexual parenting studies appear to have tried this approach. For example, the study by Tasker and Golombok and that by Chan, Raboy, and Patterson misuse a corrective procedure called the "Bonferroni multiple comparison procedure" to adjust their significance levels. The Bonferroni procedure is legitimately used as a corrective when many different significance (or "probability of chance") tests are calculated using the same data, because some will produce statistically significant results due to chance alone. The procedure makes it more difficult to reject the null hypothesis at a given level of statistical significance. Because the Bonferroni procedure makes it easier to say that research results represent random chance and are not statistically significant, it should not be used in studies that seek to find no effect—the outcome the Bonferroni procedure will help the researcher find. In one study, use of the procedure lowered the needed significance level to reject any given null hypothesis from the standard 0.05 to a highly unusual 0.003 (Chan, Raboy, and Patterson).

Another major defect of the homosexual parenting studies is that their samples are far too small to provide reliable scientific conclusions. This can be understood by looking at the larger, interrelated set of mathematical relationships of which any statistical test is a part. Falsely rejecting the null hypothesis is what statisticians refer to as a Type I error. It describes the situation in which the investigator rejects the no difference hypothesis even though there is no difference. The higher but less strictly the investigator sets the significance level (e.g., $p \leq 0.20$ versus $p \leq 0.01$), the greater will be the likelihood of being able to reject the null hypothesis—but also, the greater will be the likelihood of committing a Type I error. Type I errors are often referred to as "false positives." That is, the test yields a positive result that is in reality false.

Type I error is only one kind of error that the testing situation may produce. The other type of statistical error potentially present is called Type II error. This occurs when one fails to reject the null hypothesis when it should be rejected because the null hypothesis is false and the alternative hypothesis is true. Type II errors are often referred to as "false negatives." That is, the test provides a negative result that is in reality false.[3]

Closely related to the Type II error rate is the "power" of a statistical test. The power of a test is its ability to reject the null hypothesis when it should be rejected—thus avoiding Type II errors. The power of a test is calculated using sample size, significance level, anticipated effect size (the magnitude of the difference), and the statistical test used. Given a particular test, effect size, significance level, and the sample size used, any study can be assessed to see if it had enough power to reasonably be expected to reject the null hypothesis.

The homosexual parenting studies allow for an unacceptably large Type II error rate. The statistical tests used have too little power for researchers to have confidence that their failures to reject the null hypothesis are due to a lack of differences between heterosexual and homosexual parents. The failure to reject the no difference hypothesis could be due to their small sample sizes.

We began our evaluation of the statistical power of these studies by setting the significance level at the conventional 0.05 level.[4] We chose to detect the "small" effect as described by the psychometrician Jacob Cohen.[5] We follow Cohen's suggestion because he and others have found that many important effects in social science research are small, because the data are often unreliable, because experimental controls are lacking, because measurement is imprecise, and because the effects sought after are often subtle. One should also look for small effects when research is new, since new research is more unreliable than old.

An especially important reason to use the small effect size criterion is because of the null hypothesis–confirming nature of same-sex parenting studies. An appropriate means for achieving the research objective of the same-sex parenting studies is to create a statistical test with the power to detect a very small effect size. The smaller the effect size sought and the more consistent the repeated failure to reject the null hypothesis for this small effect size, the more likely it is that the "no-difference" findings are correct. This is what the same-sex parenting studies should have done but did not.[6]

The desired Type II error rate should be set at 0.20, which is four times the size of the standard level of statistical significance (or Type I error rate) of 0.05.[7] Setting the probability of Type II error as 0.20 means setting the level for sufficient power at 0.80 (4 × 0.20). This gives us our success criterion for evaluating sample size. Statistical power values greater than or equal to 0.80 mean that the test has sufficient power to reject the null hypothesis and thereby avoid false negative–inaccurate results that would lead one to believe the results of the test occurred by chance. Statistical power values less than 0.80 indicate that the test lacks sufficient power to reject the null hypothesis.

If a study fails to reject the null hypothesis, and it has insufficient power, the nonsignificant, or "likelihood of chance," results are inconclusive. This is why a power analysis is absolutely necessary for studies that hope to "accept" the null hypothesis. Failure to reject the null hypothesis always allows for multiple interpretations of the findings, unlike rejecting the null hypothesis.[8]

The relevant sample sizes for some common statistical tests are taken from a set of tables provided by Cohen. The smallest sample size for an adequate study requires one of 393 subjects, assuming a Type II error rate of 0.20 and a small effect size.[9] Using the criteria previously described, we determined the number of subjects used for each study we analyzed and the statistical power of each test. The studies all fall grossly short of the minimum power required except for Cameron and Cameron, which achieved a power of 0.75. The next largest sample, in Green et al., had a grossly inadequate power level of 0.13, or an 87 percent chance of failing to reject the null hypothesis.

With the exception of Cameron and Cameron (1996), the power of these studies is on the order of 0.20, meaning an 80 percent chance of failing to reject the null hypothesis. This is about four times too small. Given such lack of power, the no-effect conclusions cannot be accepted; in other words, one cannot conclude that there is no difference between heterosexual and homosexual parenting.

### The Problem of Spurious Noncorrelation

All these studies also contained the possibility of spurious correlation. A relationship between an independent and a dependent variable may be due to the operation of uncontrolled extraneous variables. The correlation may be spurious, or mistaken. A famous example of such a relationship is the correlation between the number of storks sighted (in Swedish counties) and the birth rates of these counties. Since storks do not deliver babies, there is no actual statistical relationship between the large number of storks sighted and the higher birth rates in rural counties as compared to urban counties. The third, mistaken variable—a belief that storks deliver babies—is extraneous, or irrelevant to any relationship between birth rates in urban and rural Swedish counties. No logical condition for interpreting a statistical relationship between two variables—stork sightings and births—exists. Although the correlation between birth rates and stork sighting is real, the relationship between the presence of storks and babies is spurious.

Homosexual parenting studies face a parallel but different problem, because they seek to find no relationship between homosexuals in parenting roles (as opposed to heterosexuals in parenting roles) and aspects of parenting. When this is the case, a finding of no correlation is misleading because a relevant third variable, which is called a suppressor variable, might have been omitted from the analysis. This is the problem of spurious noncorrelation. Although correlation does not necessarily equal causation (i.e., an association between two things does not mean that one caused the other), noncorrelation does not necessarily equal noncausation (i.e., the lack of an association between two things does not mean that one did *not* cause the other). Controlling for a suppressor variable produces a statistically significant partial correlation (or association) between the initial variables even though they have no correlation without controlling for the suppressor variable.

One indication that a variable may be an extraneous suppressor variable is that it is positively correlated with both the independent and dependent variables. Likely suppressor variables are those that are positively associated with one variable and negatively associated with the other variable. Some potential suppressor variables include parental education or IQ, the type of relationship between parents and their significant others, child variables such as gender and age, parent's socioeconomic status, and parent's psychiatric treatment history.

In their study of families created via donor insemination, Chan, Raboy, and Patterson found that homosexual parents have significantly more education than their heterosexual counterparts. Parental education is a potential suppressor variable because many positive child outcomes are positively related to parental education. If lesbian and heterosexual mothers produce the same positive child outcomes when the lesbians are better educated than their heterosexual counterparts, one cannot conclude that there is no difference between lesbian and homosexual mothers as causal factors in positive child outcomes. The extraneous suppressor variable that makes a significant difference between the two groups of mothers—education—must be taken into account. When educational levels are properly equated or controlled for, heterosexual mothers may produce more favorable outcomes, or lesbian mothers may produce better outcomes, or the outcomes may be statistically the same for both groups of mothers. Education, however, is not entered into Chan, Raboy, and Patterson's equations and so their analysis does not account for the extraneous suppressor variable of education.

None of the homosexual parenting studies considered the potential problem of spurious noncorrelation. Just as correlation need not indicate causation, noncorrelation need not imply noncausation. This problem is also evidence of the early state of these studies. Investigating possible spurious correlations, suppressor variables, and controlling for these effects in statistical analyses is a sign that research in an area is maturing, becoming more sophisticated and more reliable.

## CONCLUSION: WHAT WE DON'T KNOW AND WHY IT MATTERS

To ascertain the effect of parents' sexual orientation on their children, studies must follow the logic of scientific procedure. This includes having proper control groups, proper statistical testing and analysis, proper procedures for dealing with problems of contamination and researcher bias, proper sample sizes, and, above all, a research design that does not try to "confirm" the null hypothesis—to "prove" that a relationship is the result of chance.

These studies reviewed here and in more detail in our larger monograph are all seriously flawed in one way or another. They often use procedures that are weak in eliminating possible errors or threats to validity. Many use procedures that "stack the deck" in favor of their favored outcomes. Some misanalyze or misreport their own findings.

The history of social science research on challenging, sensitive issues such as this one indicates that seldom do the findings of the first wave of research studies survive unchallenged when more sophisticated studies are done. Major modifications of these findings and sometimes even outright reversals are common. Confidence in research results is increased to the extent that they survive demanding, ongoing empirical tests of increasing sophistication.

Our findings have serious implications. In order to offer the benefits of marriage or adoption to same-sex couples, some courts, like the Vermont Supreme Court, appear to have relied on the veracity of the research we have reviewed to assure themselves that no adverse consequences for children will occur due to the legalization of same-sex marriage. Our review of the methodology shows this assurance to be scientifically premature at least and possibly unfounded. Although this is not the same as concluding that traditional family arrangements are better, it indicates that current social science research is not yet mature enough to buttress legal or legislative conclusions.

## A PARTIAL LIST OF STUDIES EVALUATED

Bigner, J. J., and R. B. Jacobsen. "Parenting Behaviors of Homosexual and Heterosexual Fathers," *Journal of Homosexuality*, 18 (1/2) (1989), 173–186.
———. "Adult Responses to Child Behavior and Attitudes Toward Fathering: Gay and Nongay Fathers," *Journal of Homosexuality*, 23 (3) (1992): 99–112.
Brewaeys, A., I. Ponjaert, E. V. Van Hail, and S. Golombok. "Donor Insemination: Child Development and Family Functioning in Lesbian Mother Families

with 4 to 8 Year Old Children," *Human Reproduction* 12 (1997): 1349–1359.

Cameron, P, and K. Cameron. "Homosexual Parents," *Adolescence* 31(124) (1996): 757–776.

Chan, R. W., B. Raboy, and C. J. Patterson. "Psychosocial Adjustment among Children Conceived via Donor Insemination by Lesbian and Heterosexual Mothers." *Child Development* 69 (2) (1998): 443–457.

Flaks, D. K., I. Ficher, F. Masterpasqua, and G. Joseph, "Lesbians Choosing Motherhood: A Comparative Study of Lesbians and Heterosexual Parents and Their Children." *Developmental Psychology* 31 (1995): 105–114.

Golombok, S., and F. Tasker, "Do Parents Influence the Homosexual Orientation of Their Children? Findings from a Longitudinal Study of Lesbian Families," *Developmental Psychology* 32 (1996): 3–11.

Golombok, S., A. Spencer, and M. Rutter, "Children in Lesbian and Single-Parent Households: Psychosexual and Psychiatric Appraisal," *Journal of Child Psychology and Psychiatry* 24 (4) (1983): 551–572.

Green, R., J. B. Mandell, M. E. Hotvedt, J. Gray, and L. Sarnith, "Lesbian Mothers and Their Children: A Comparison of Solo Parent Heterosexual Mothers and Their Children," *Archives of Sexual Behavior* 15 (1986): 167–184.

Harris, M., and P. Turner, "Gay and Lesbian Parents." *Journal of Homosexuality* 12 (1986): 101–113.

Hoeffer, B., "Children's Acquisition of Sex-Role Behavior in Lesbian-Mother Families," *American Journal of Orthopsychiatry* 51 (3) (1981): 536–544.

Huggins, S. L., "A Comparative Study of Self-Esteem of Adolescent Children of Divorced Lesbian Mothers and Divorced Heterosexual Mothers," *Journal of Homosexuality* 18 (1–2) (1989): 123–135.

Kweskin, S.L., and A. S. Cook, "Heterosexual and Homosexual Mothers' Self-Described Sex-Role Behavior and Ideal Sex-Role Behavior in Children," *Sex Roles* 8 (1982): 967–975.

McNeill, Kevin F., Beth M. Rienzi, and Augustine Kposowa, "Families and Parenting: A Comparison of Lesbian and Heterosexual Mothers," *Psychological Reports* 82 (1998): 59–62.

Miller, B., "Gay Fathers and Their Children," *The Family Coordinator* 28 (4) (1979): 544–552.

Miller, J. A., R. B. Jacobsen, and J. J. Bigner, "The Child's Home Environment for Lesbian Versus Heterosexual Mothers: A Neglected Area of Research," *Journal of Homosexuality* 7 (1) (1982): 49–56.

Mucklow, B. M., and G. K. Phelan, "Lesbian and Traditional Mothers' Responses to Adult Response to Child Behavior and Self-Concept," *Psychological Reports* 44 (1979): 880–882.

Pagelow, M. D., "Heterosexual and Lesbian Single Mothers: A Comparison of Problems, Coping, and Solutions," *Journal of Homosexuality* 5 (3) 1980: 189–204.

Patterson, C.J., "Children of Lesbian and Gay Parents," *Advances in Clinical Child Psychology,* vol.19, edited by T. H. Ollendick and R. J. Prinz (New York: Plenum, 1997), 235–282.

Tasker, F., and S. Golombok. "Adults Raised as Children in Lesbian Families," *American Journal of Orthopsychiatry* 65 (2) (1995): 203–215.

## NOTES

1. See our monograph, D. O. Coolidge and A. Nagai, *No Basis: What the Same Sex Parenting Studies Don't Tell Us*, (Washington, D.C.: Marriage and Law Project, 2001), for a more detailed discussion of the criteria and findings, as well as a complete list of the forty-nine studies. The focus in the current chapter is on those studies that use statistical tests.

2. T. Cook and D .T. Campbell, *Quasi-Experimentation, Design and Analysis Issues for Field Settings* (New York: Houghton-Mifflin, 1979); J. A. Davis, *The Logic of Causal Order* (Beverly Hills, Ca.: Sage, 1985); T. Hirschi and H. C. Selvin, *Principles of Survey Analysis* (New York: Free Press, 1973); C. F. Nachmias and D. Nachmias, *Research Methods in the Social Sciences* (New York: St. Martin's Press, 1996); M. Rosenberg, *The Logic of Survey Analysis* (New York: Basic Books, 1968); P. Rossi and H. E. Freeman, *Evaluation: A Systematic Approach*, 5th ed. (Newbury Park, Calif.: Sage, 1994).

3. There is an inherent trade-off between Type I and Type II error rates in any test situation. For a given effect size and a given sample size, the smaller size of the Type I error rate, the larger the Type II error rate will be and vice versa. Statistical analysis requires investigators to weigh the possible risks of the two types of error and reach the best available solution.

4. Where relevant, these calculations assume two-sided significance tests (chi-square tests and F-tests are inherently nondirectional). This is because none of these studies reviewed here ever carried out a one-tailed hypothesis test and because the true opposite of the null is the two-sided test. In any event, computing the power using a one-sided hypothesis produces only slight increases from the reported values.

5. Jacob Cohen, *Statistical Power Analysis for the Behavioral Sciences*, 2nd ed. (Hillsdale, N.J: Erlbaum, 1998), 83, 13, 25. Cohen considers a Pearson correlation of 0.10 to be a small effect, one of 0.30 to be a medium effect, and one of 0.50 to be a large effect (79–80). The magnitudes of small, medium, and large effects are arbitrary, but useful.

6. Cohen suggests that an even higher degree of power, such as 0.90, should be used for evaluating studies seeking to "accept" the null hypothesis. Ibid., 104.

7. Cohen states that the Type II error rate should be four times that of Type I error rate because in the social sciences, at least, Type I errors (false positives) are substantially more serious than are Type II errors (false negatives). Failure to find something is not as serious as finding something that is not there. Ibid., 56. The nature of our studies, however, indicates that this might be too generous.

8. Statistically significant results, however, indicate that the power level was adequate.

9. If the power for this t-test is calculated using a one-sided alternative, the required sample size shrinks to 300.

# 14

# Institutionalizing Marriage Reforms Through Federalism

## Lynn D. Wardle

## INTRODUCTION: THE MARRIAGE REVITALIZATION AND LAW REFORM MOVEMENT

There is growing concern in the United States about the institution of marriage, particularly about the instability and reduced importance of marriage in the lives of contemporary Americans. National concerns about family and marriage have galvanized because of a number of social conditions that separately and together signal a social crisis that cannot be ignored. For example, nonmarital cohabitation is at an all-time high in the United States; children born out of wedlock now account for nearly one-third of all births in this country; for three decades the rate of divorce has hovered at high rates rarely seen and never before maintained for so long.[1] Another matter of concern is that a movement to legalize same-sex marriage has persuaded judges in several states to support the redefinition of marriage to include gay and lesbian couples.

Because of such concerns about marriage, there is growing pressure on lawmakers to "do something" to revitalize and protect marriage, and growing debate over proposals for marriage and divorce law reform.[2] Among the most visible manifestations of the growing political influence of this movement have been the recent adoption of covenant marriage proposals by three states (Louisiana, Arizona and Arkansas) and introduction of similar bills in twenty other legislatures,[3] the movement to encourage or require premarital education classes or instruction,[4] and the divorce reform movement that seeks to modify existing unilateral, no-fault divorce laws.[5] Together these various strands constitute a substantial, growing, and diverse marriage revitalization/law reform movement that demonstrates a significant public concern that marriage is in trouble and that our society and lawmakers should "do something" to strengthen and protect marriage.

I support the goals of the marriage revitalization movement and many of the proposed public and private policy initiatives to strengthen marriage and reform divorce law, including better premarital preparation, long-overdue divorce reform to correct the abuses associated with unilateral, no-fault divorce and provide greater protection for the children of divorce, and proposals to rethink the consequences of divorce, particularly the distribution of economic benefits and burdens. Because the concerns that drive this movement are so serious, and the need for marriage and divorce law reform is so great, it is important that appropriate methods and proposals be used to achieve meaningful, effective, lasting reforms. The pursuit of ineffective reform proposals and the use of improper methods to institutionalize reforms could delay or even destroy the present opportunity to remedy a growing crisis and provide needed relief and protection for many vulnerable individuals and families.

This chapter examines one important structural principle that applies to any marriage law reform—federalism. Although federalism impedes the quick enactment of national legal remedies to marriage-related problems, it also increases the likelihood that properly institutionalized marriage reforms will be authentic, effective, and lasting.

### Two Dimensions of Federalism and Family Law

The regulation of domestic relations, including the definition and regulation of marriage and divorce, have long been considered to fall almost entirely to the states. "From the earliest days of the Republic until the recent past, family law has unquestionably belonged to the states."[6] While the national government has power to regulate other areas that collaterally or indirectly influence family law (including marriage law), the federal government has no power to directly regulate marriage or divorce or other family relations and institutions in the United States. The Supreme Court of the United States has observed, not infrequently, that the "[r]egulation of domestic relations [is] an area that has long been regarded as a virtually exclusive province of the states."[7] Thus, the enforcement of family law is left primarily to state courts, and the bulk of the governing rules are state, not federal, laws.[8]

Federalism's deference to state regulation of family relations has two dimensions, substantive and jurisdictional; both have constitutional overtones. Substantively, the powers of the federal government are limited to those specifically enumerated in the Constitution, and since the power to regulate family relations is not so enumerated, that power is deemed reserved to the states.[9] Thus, while federal legislation and regulations dealing with national matters such as commerce, defense, health, social security, taxes, and federal programs often have a definite impact on family relations; the direct regulation of family relations historically has been deemed to be beyond the proper scope of the federal lawmaking authority. In several notable recent decisions (including a significant decision in the year 2000 involving a law arguably related to family regulation, the Violence Against Women Act), the Supreme Court has applied the federalist principle to invalidate as unconstitutional laws enacted by Congress that went beyond the limited powers delegated to Congress.[10] Marriage has been a particular area of deference to state regulation. Just twenty-five years ago the Supreme Court reiterated its declaration made in 1878 that "[t]he State . . . has absolute right to prescribe the conditions upon which the marriage relation between its own citizens shall be created, and the causes for which it may be dissolved."[11] Although the exact contours of constitutional federalism are not clear, "[t]hroughout the debate on federalism, family law emerges as the one clear case in which federal involvement is inappropriate, an uncontested core rendered special precisely because almost everything else has been nationalized and the limits on federal power elsewhere are so murky."[12] Federalism's absence of power to directly regulate marriage is a matter of substantive constitutional law.

Notwithstanding federalism's constitutional prohibition of Congress's direct regulation of family relations, federal laws may profoundly influence family law in two ways. First, in the course of directly regulating subjects that are within the power of Congress to regulate, state family law may be indirectly affected because when federal and state laws conflict, the federal law preempts the countervailing state law. For instance, in *McCarty v. McCarty*,[13] the Supreme Court held that federal law governing military retirement pay, interpreted as vesting ownership in the military member alone, preempted state (California) community property law, which gave the spouse an equal ownership interest in the property that could be awarded to her upon divorce. Thus, federal income tax laws define who may be considered "married" for purposes of filing joint returns, federal immigration laws define who may be considered "married" for purposes of visas and immigration, and under its power to regulate "full faith and credit," Congress has enacted a law protecting the right of states to refuse to recognize same-sex marriages validly created in other states and has defined the term *marriage* as used in federal law as a heterosexual union. The protection of individual liberties by the Constitution is also undeniably within the power of Congress, and expansion of federal constitutional equal protection, substantive and procedural due process doctrines, and federal civil rights laws has created some significant limits on state regulation and enforcement of domestic relations. Federal courts have even invalidated some state marriage restrictions as infringements on federal constitutional liberties.[14] Notwithstanding these pockets of congressional power to influence family law indirectly and to protect individual rights, the substantive limits of federalism on the power of the national government to regulate marriage remain well established.

Second, federal courts historically have declined to exercise diversity jurisdiction (over parties from different states trying to sue each other in federal rather than state court) in suits involving family relations claims, and even in cases involving federal question jurisdiction they have hesitated to resolve domestic disputes.[15] The Supreme Court has also acknowledged a limitation on the power of federal courts to hear state-based claims for divorce, custody, and alimony.[16] This domestic relations exception was first applied nearly 150 years ago when the Court declared: "We disclaim altogether any jurisdiction in the courts of the United States upon the subject of divorce, or for the allowance of alimony."[17] Although the Supreme Court has rejected the argument that the Constitution bars federal courts from hearing at least some cases that involve family law-related issues,[18] constitutional shadows still obscure this jurisdictional limit.

### The Policies Behind Federalism in Family Law

Behind both of these federalism practices are many strong and important policy values. Thus, federalism in family law is not a mere anachronism but is a doctrine based on significant perceptions of the realities associated with the government of a large, heterogeneous nation. These underlying policy values include pluralism, communitarianism, experimentation, and respect for state expertise and sovereignty.

#### Pluralism

Among the values preserved by federalism in family law is a desire to preserve pluralism, especially concerning families. Proposals to create a single, all-sovereign national government and abolish the states or take over their sovereignty (preserving them as mere administrative units of a fully sovereign national government) were rejected by the drafters of the Constitution. The debates of 1787 show that nearly all the Founders believed that preservation of separate sovereign states within the national union was essential to allow to flourish the kinds of healthy differences that we today would call *pluralism*. Then, the differences were linked to regional, religious, cultural, and economic differences. Today social, racial, ethnic, ideological, political, and even sexual diversity might form the basis for differences, but regardless of the kind of differences, Americans today seem to value pluralism as much as the Founders did.

Federalism in family law preserves pluralism by guaranteeing at least fifty different zones for family policy development. Rather than having one government set one ubiquitous national marriage policy, dozens of different governments are able to establish their own marriage laws and pursue their own vision of what is good in their own marriage policies. For reformers advocating innovation and seeking to deviate from established practices and processes, pluralism offers the opportunity to persuade some group of citizens or lawmakers to pursue a different vision.

## Communitarianism

Communitarianism is also protected by federalism. By insisting that marriage be regulated at a local (state) rather than national level, the vitality of small communities—who would be drowned out in policy debates at the national level but who may have some significant voice in state politics—is enhanced. Views about marriage, in particular, reflect the values of small communities, communities of extended families and kinship connections, religious communities, ethnic communities, and communities of persons living in proximity to each other and thus sharing common experiences (from weather to economic conditions). While no state in the twenty-first century is a small community (e.g., of kinship or religion), each state is much smaller than the nation and is much more likely to respect and reflect the interests and concerns of small communities.

Federalism in family law reflects the long-held belief that laws regulating families should reflect local values. Matters involving families are so sensitive and delicate that any attempt to regulate them at the national level would guarantee neglect of the interests of minority communities.[19] Federalism in family law also embodies the classic republican principle that laws should reflect the values—the spirit—of the particular political community that would be subject to the laws. Montesquieu recognized that communities would differ.[20] Thus, federalism facilitates meaningful self-government.

Moreover, because states and regions of the country face problems related to marriage and family in different degrees, federalism allows for more precise policy interventions targeted to specific problems. For example, Western and "Bible-belt" states have significantly higher rates of divorce than states in the Midwest and Northeast. The response to divorce reform in the former states may be more aggressive, while the response in the latter states may be more measured and cautious. Regardless of the issue, federalism allows policy makers and lawmakers to suit their actions to the needs of the people in their state.

## Experimentation

Federalism allows the states to experiment with different policies, rules, and procedures in a way that creates fifty separate laboratories. As Justice Brandeis wrote: "It is one of the happy incidents of the federal system that a single courageous State may, if its citizens choose, serve as a laboratory; and try novel social and economic experiments without risk to the rest of the country."[21] This means that reformers do not have to "risk everything" on a proposed reform; if one state tries a new approach there are forty-nine other states in the "control group," and citizens who are deeply troubled by the laws and policies of one state may largely avoid them by moving to a neighboring state. State independence concerning family law reform also means that the search for solution to national marriage problems need not proceed one-at-a-time, but rather, dozens of different approaches may be tried simultaneously. States can reduce the time it takes to learn what works and what doesn't by studying what happens in other states, without having to repeat the errors of unsuccessful approaches.

### Respect for State Expertise and Shared Sovereignty

Federalism in family law entails respect for the expertise of state lawmakers, who have been enacting and revising family laws since the time of the American colonies. It also embodies respect for the dignity and expertise of state courts, built of centuries of experience deciding domestic relations cases. (It also manifests federal judges' dislike for family disputes, and a belief that the federal government has more important national priorities to regulate.) Federalism in family law embodies the long-valued principles of comity and "shared sovereignty," and concern about overcentralization of governmental power at any one level or unit of government (a core concern of Americans since 1776). For reformers this can be a boon because perceptions of the need for reform are more likely to be recognized at the local level, by local government officials, than by government officials geographically removed from many problems and without accountability for remedying them.

### Federalism: Obstacle or Opportunity for Marriage Revitalization Law Reform?

Some proponents of marriage law reform may view federalism in family law as a significant limitation. One-stop nationwide marriage law reform is not possible. Because federal law is the "supreme law of the land" and trumps state law, there is the constant temptation to institutionalize the desired reforms in federal law, either by legislation or judicial interpretation. Law reform is often thought of in terms of immediacy—as an instant solution, a quick fix. Politicians tend to want to see big results now, certainly no later than their next campaign. Impatient advocates of reform usually prefer to deal with one legislative body (the U.S. Congress) rather than going to fifty different states and persuading fifty different legislatures. Thus, initially, federalism may seem like a heavy burden and obstacle to marriage law reform.

The serious social conditions that make marriage entry or marriage continuation such a discouraging, even frightening prospect for so many, and that cause some to seek alternatives to marriage, did not appear overnight. Remedying those conditions will require long-term commitment, long-term solutions, and the development of widespread social consensus, not the manipulation of political processes. Reform of cultural values must match legal reforms.

The process of developing consensus state-by-state commanded by federalism principles also promises the possibility of institutionalizing of real and lasting social reform. The marriage revitalization movement seeks to accomplish a revolution in the popular understanding of marriage and the elements of a good marriage. The movement desires major reform of the institutional rules, remedies, and processes that support marriage and provide redress for troubled marriages. Real and lasting social revolutions occur over the course of years. Marriage revitalization is not a short-term project. The conditions that create significant social barriers to choosing marriage, to achieving and maintaining successful marriage, and that cause stresses on marriages that weaken and threaten marriage quality and stability are not problems that can be solved overnight. Just as they have developed over several decades, it will take some time to fully achieve the solutions. There will be no quick fix to remedy problems of marital devaluation and instability. The marriage revitalization/reform movement must pervade the "grassroots" of society to be fully effective.

Thus, the "burden" of federalism also is an advantage for proponents of authentic social reform, because it forces grassroots, state-by-state reform. It provides the opportunity to set up "pilot projects" in one state to be a model or experiment to benefit all states. It means defeat in one state is not a final defeat. It means success in one state can be the catalyst for success in other states. In the long run, federalism in family law provides the foundations for effective marriage reform and insures codification of genuine social reforms, not in general federal law but in state laws that more specifically reflect and shape social mores. It reduces the possibility of getting stuck on ineffective, hasty, apparent solutions.

For marriage reformers who advocate a new vision of a revitalized institution of marriage and seek to alter existing marriage and divorce laws that the legal establishment comfortably maintains, the pluralism of federalism offers the opportunity to persuade innovative state governments, some critical mass of influential citizens in one or more of the fifty states, to pursue that new vision and revitalize marriage. The communitarianism of federalism works to the advantage of marriage revitalization and reform because those kinds of reforms are likely to find acceptance in small communities first, especially religious communities, minority communities of immigrants or ethnic minorities with strong traditional family values, and perhaps some localities hard-hit by the devastating consequences of disposable marriage and divorce-on-demand. Experimental federalism offers the chance to learn much quickly about what government programs do and do not work, to avoid "reinventing the wheel," and to expedite discovery and implementation of successful reforms to revitalize marriage.

## CONCLUSION: MARRIAGE REVITALIZATION LAW
## REFORM THROUGH FEDERALISM

Marriage revitalization may be primarily a cultural or social matter, but it must be institutionalized in law if it is to last and be reliable in modern society. Institutionalizing marriage reforms in law must respect the limits of and must be accomplished through the processes of federalism if those reforms are to be authentic, effective, and lasting. Marriage revitalization and institutionalization in law of such reforms involve a great undertaking that can and must be achieved within the parameters of federalism, which provides the only proven structure and process for implementation of genuine and effective family reforms in America.

## NOTES

1. See James Herbie DiFonzo, *Customized Marriage*, 75 Indian L.J. 875, 877, 909–911 (2000) (statistics re: breakdown of family).

2. See generally DiFonzo, *Customized Marriage*; Lynn D. Wardle, *Divorce Reform at the Turn of the Millennium: Certainties and Possibilities*, 33 Fam. L. Q. 783 (1999); Katharine T. Bartlett, *Saving the Family From the Reformers*, 31 U.C. Davis L. Rev. 809 (1998); Katherine Shaw Spaht, *For the Sake of the Children: Recapturing the Meaning of Marriage*, 72 Notre Dame L. Rev. 1547 (1998); Laura Bradford, Note, *The Counterrevolution: A Critique of Recent Proposals to Reform No-Fault Divorce Laws*, 49 Stan. L. Rev. 607 (1997).

3. See, e.g., Amy L. Stewart, *Covenant Marriage: Legislating Family Values*, 32 Ind. L. Rev. 509, 515 (1999) (citing bills).

4. See, e.g., Fla. Stat. Ann. §§ 741.0305 (fee reduction); 741.04 (waiver of waiting period); 61.21 (parent education course); Marriage Preparation and Preservation Act, ch. 98-403 (Fla. H.B. No. 1019) (2d Reg. Sess. 1998) (eff. Jan. 1, 1999); see generally Nicole D. Lindsey, Note, *Marriage and Divorce: Degrees of "I Do," An Analysis of the Ever-Changing Paradigm of Divorce*, 9 U. Fla. J.L. & Pub. Pol'y, 265, 275 (1998).

5. See Wardle, *Divorce Reform at the Turn of the Century*, 786–790 (summary of recent actions taken and proposed).

6. Brian Bix, *State of the Union: The States' Interest in the Marital Status of Their Citizens*, paper originally presented at ISFL conference (in author's possession), citing Anne C. Dailey, *Federalism and Families*, 143 U. Pa. L. Rev. 1787, 1821 (1995).

7. *Sosna v. Iowa*, 419 U.S. 393, 404 (1975); see also *Lehman v. Lycoming County Children's Services Agency*, 458 U.S. 502 (1982); *Moore v. Sims*, 442 U.S. 415 (1979); *Barber v. Barber*, 62 U.S. (21 How.) 582 (1859).

8. Federalism in family law has been the subject of significant discussion and debate in the legal community in recent years. See, e.g., Libby S. Adler, *Federalism and Family*, 8 Colum. J. Gender & L. 1997 (1999); Ann Laquer Estin, *Federalism and Child Support*, 5 Va. J. Soc. Pol'y & L. 541 (1998); Jill Elaine Hasday, *Federalism and the Family Reconstructed*, 45 UCLA L. Rev. 1297 (1998); Anne C. Dailey, *Federalism and Families*, 143 U. Pa. L. Rev. 1787 (1995); Naomi Cahn, *Family*

*Law, Federalism, and Federal Courts*, 94 Iowa L. Rev. 1073 (1994); Naomi R. Cahn, *Family Law, Federalism, and the Federal Courts*, 79 Iowa Law Review 1073 (1994). See also Bix, *State of the Union.*

9. U.S. Const., Amend. X; see *The Federalist* No. 10 (J. Madison); No. 17 (A. Hamilton); No. 45 (J. Madison).

10. See, e.g., *United States v. Morrison*, 529 U.S. 598, 615–616, 620, (2000) (holding that Congress was without constitutional power under either the Commerce Clause or the Fourteenth Amendment to enact a law, 42 U.S.C. § 13981, providing a civil action and remedy for victims of gender-motivated violence); *United States v. Lopez*, 514 U.S. 549 (1995) (Gun-Free School Zone Act goes beyond legitimate congressional power to regulate interstate commerce).

11. *Sosna v. Iowa*, 419 U.S. 393, 404 (1975), quoting *Pennoyer v. Neff*, 95 U.S. 714, 734–735 (1878). See Bix, *State of the Union*, 23–24.

12. Jill Elaine Hasday, *Federalism and the Family Reconstructed*, 45 UCLA L. Rev. 1297, 1297–1298 (1998).

13. 453 U.S. 210 (1981).

14. *Loving v. Virginia*, 388 U.S. 1 (1967) (antimiscegenation law); *Zablocki v. Redhail*, 434 U.S. 374 (1978) (child support marriage restriction); *Turner v. Saffley*, 482 U.S. 78 (1987) (prisoner marriage restrictions).

15. See C. Wright, A. Miller, and E. Cooper, *Federal Practice and Procedure* ¶ 3609 (1984).

16. See generally *Ankenbrandt v. Richards*, 504 U.S. 689 (1992) (tort claim for abusing children is not barred by any constitutional limit on federal court jurisdiction or by domestic relations exception to diversity jurisdiction).

17. *Barber v. Barber*, 62 U.S. (21 How.) 582, 584 (1859). The Court reiterated this limit on the jurisdiction of federal courts in *Ex parte Burrus*, 136 U.S. 586, 593–594 (1890), when it declared: "The whole subject to the domestic relations of husband and wife, parent and child, belongs to the laws of the States and not to the laws of the United States."

18. *Ankenbrandt*, 504 U.S. at 693–695.

19. Charles Louis de Secondat (Baron de Montesquieu), *The Spirit of the Laws*, Book XIX, ch. 14, and at Book XIX, ch. 5 (London: G. Bell & Sons, T. Nugent trans., 1902).

20. Montesquieu wrote: "[T]he government most conformable to nature, is that which best agrees with the humour and disposition of the people in whose favor it is established. . . . [Laws] should be adapted in such a manner to the people for whom they are framed." Ibid., Book I, ch. 3. He further proclaimed that "[i]t is the business of the Legislature to follow the spirit of the nation." Ibid, Book XIX, ch. 5.

21. *New State Ice v. Liebmann*, 285 U.S. 262, 311 (Brandeis, J., dissenting).

# 15

# Fixing the Family: Legal Acts and Cultural Admonitions

## Carl E. Schneider

Of course, this is a somewhat vague conclusion. But in a question of significance, of worth, like this, conclusions can never be precise. The answer of appreciation, of sentiment, is always a more or a less, a balance struck by sympathy, insight, and good will. But it is an answer, all the same, a real conclusion. And in the course of getting it, it seems to me that our eyes have been opened to many important things.
—William James, *What Makes a Life Significant*

## INTRODUCTION

A lawyer invited to participate in a conference on strengthening marriage naturally supposes himself obliged to comment on whether law might be used to achieve that goal. It is common for laypersons and even for lawyers who ought to know better, to suppose that, because law commands flamboyant means of coercion—jail, fines, harassment, and disgrace—law is equipped to salvage decrepit social institutions. I am skeptical. I have already expressed my doubts in the essay, "The Law and the Stability of Marriage," which explored the devices at the law's disposal that might promote marriage. That essay seems to have provoked some disapproval among friends of marriage. Here, then, I want to defend and explain what I said there.[1]

## THE PRIORITY OF CULTURE

Before we can decide whether law can strengthen marriage, we must decide what *strengthening marriage* means. Heaven knows this is an absurdly hard question. Here, it must suffice to say that I will assume that the law's goal should be to make marriage a more solid social institution. By "more solid," I mean an institution with greater power to persuade people who wish to form families to marry and to dissuade the married from behaving faithlessly.[2]

Marriage surely used to be a sturdier institution than it is today, but its strength did not depend on the law. Rather, its authority depended on its cultural prominence and potency. As I wrote in my earlier essay, "'The family' is a social institution, predominantly created, shaped, and sustained by social forces and not primarily by law."[3] Men and women have always entered marriage imbued with cultural precepts about how people generally and spouses particularly should treat each other. They live their married lives surrounded by people who have embraced those cultural precepts, who live by them, and who implicitly and explicitly urge them on others. The social pressure to heed the precepts these forces create is not irresistible—it is often resisted. But it is on these pressures that familial institutions must primarily depend.

### The Limits of Family Law

In principle, law can buttress the social forces that support the institution of marriage. The law should certainly try to do so. But I believe that familial institutions must rest primarily on culture, rather than law, for two reasons. First, family law is interstitial. Second, family law is feeble. To put these two points differently, family law attempts to do relatively little to sustain the institution of marriage, and what it does try to do, it does not do effectively.

Let me explain, briefly. As I wrote in "The Law and the Stability of Marriage," "family law is highly interstitial. That is, there are only a few points in most people's lives when family law directly touches them."[4] The law largely leaves husband and wife free to govern their relationship, and even their children, however they prefer short of a few kinds of outrage. This is because both ends of the political spectrum agree, at least in the abstract, that people should be left to live their own lives. But partly because the interstitiality of family law also grows out of the law's feebleness. Family law, as much as any area of law, persistently encounters what I call "enforcement problems."[5] Law has enough trouble regulating public conduct, as I am reminded every time I drive to work and feel the swoosh of cars going by me at 95 miles an hour and watch people racing through stop signs. Regulating private conduct is much harder, especially conduct that concerns life's most volatile interests and emotions. Thus, even that stern Victorian James Fitzjames Stephen wrote, "You cannot punish anything which public opinion, as expressed in the common practice of society, does not strenuously and unequivocally condemn. . . . Law cannot be better than the nation in which it exists, though it may and can protect an acknowledged moral standard, and may gradually be increased in strictness as the standard rises."

I concluded my essay by noting that the law's means of strengthening marriage were "thin and unsatisfying, that all the proposals are in a useful sense speculative, that some of them probably would not work, that some of them would be too costly, and that some of them are politically impossible."[6] I suggested that any real strengthening of marriage would have to come not from law but from social and cultural reform. The interstitiality of family law continues to strike me as quite a sufficient reason to doubt that family law, in and of itself, can do much to help re-institutionalize marriage.

## Hostile Cultural Forces

However, I am now inclined to think I understated the problems of deploying family law to strengthen marriage, and overstated the hope of re-institutionalizing marriage through cultural crusading. I believe I did not sufficiently emphasize some cultural forces that seem likely to cripple any attempt at such a re-institutionalization. In this chapter, I want to identify one set of surging cultural attitudes that stand in our way.

Persuading people to live together as they want, for as long as they want, is no great trick. Persuading them to build kind and stable lives together is. Yet the latter is presumably the goal of marriage as a social institution. Social institutions strive to induce people to behave against their impulses and even against their short-term interests. As Philip Rieff has observed, "[A] culture survives principally . . . by the power of its institutions to bind and loose men in the conduct of their affairs with reasons which sink so deep into the self that they become commonly and implicitly understood."[7]

### The Fear of Obligation

But bind? *Bind?* There's the rub. The problem for re-institutionalizing marriage, through law or through cultural reform, is that contemporary Americans—particularly the upper-middle-class Americans who most influence cultural attitudes—are skeptical of, distrust, and detest binding forces of all kinds. They are skeptical of law's duties, of moral obligations, of social claims and personal commitments. "Don't tread on me"—such is our declaration. This dislike of all that might bind imperils the whole enterprise of social institutions—not least of which is marriage.

Americans of all political stripes find it easy, even natural, to distrust their government. The right decries "big government" and calls the left the party of big government. But the left is also the party of civil liberties and of dark suspicions about government intrusions on "privacy." When it comes to government regulation of the family, left and right almost unite in distrust. Both sides see merit in government non-intervention. The left can't get enough of *Roe v. Wade*. The right finds more and more to like in parents' rights. Both left and right have at recent moments in our history seen parents' rights as a necessary bulwark against meddlesome government. True, both right and left welcome government's restraining hand when they like the results. But right and left unite at the levels of principle and viscerally espouse "non-intervention."[8]

Of the American allergy to moral obligation I have written much in recent years.[9] The Americans who today most influence our cultural tone—and particularly the well-educated young Americans in whom these attitudes are most readily perceived—find they do not even know what is meant by a moral duty (unless perhaps it be a duty to oneself), and are loath to speak in the outmoded, confining, small-minded, and even dangerous language of morality.[10] These Americans are moral relativists who consider their own moral views just as accidental as other people's. They see in moral obligation a cloak for intolerance. To visit the breach of a moral duty with sanctions is to be "punitive," and they detest the punitive.

The American distrust of social obligation—even social obligation that arises out of personal commitments—is particularly relevant to the prospects of re-institutionalizing marriage. One principal strain of American culture today secretes powerful chemicals for dissolving the ties that bind people to family life. Americans have made "choice" their mantra, and they cannot believe that anything that inhibits choice can be good. As Lawrence Friedman writes (in a book aptly titled *The Republic of Choice*), "Twentieth-century people are inclined to go easy on themselves in another regard: legal arrangements betray a pronounced bias against *irreversibility*—against choices and arrangements that cannot be undone."[11] If a choice cannot be undone, the route to happier alternatives may be barred. If a choice cannot be undone, spontaneity, growth, and freedom itself are crushed.

Thus marriage is redefined to mean a relationship from which both sides feel they currently benefit. When one spouse ceases to feel so, the marriage has ended. Solicitude for the nondeparting spouse is desirable. Financial recompense to balance the books is due. But it would violate one's duty to oneself to stay married in such circumstances, and it would be wrong for one's spouse to impose by asking one to stay. One should not, to be sure, seek to injure one's spouse. But spouses should first look after themselves. Indeed, I have found young professional students in remarkable numbers cannot comprehend how a husband could find language or ideas to deter himself from abandoning his wife even under quite unappetizing circumstances.[12]

## The Fear of Dependence

One measure of the extent to which Americans have come to fear ties that bind is to be found in the rising abhorrence of "dependence." Perhaps no idea in American life has become so convincing as the belief that each of us is entitled to live autonomously. One of the proudest tributes to the power of that faith is that autonomy seems to be undergoing a transformation from an entitlement to a duty.[13] Under this new dispensation, people have not just a right but an obligation to make their own decisions about their important life-choices. This duty makes independence basic, for if those decisions are to be truly autonomous, people must be independent enough to think and act for themselves. Thus as autonomy becomes an ever-more commanding duty, dependence becomes an ever-more degrading state.

The attack on dependence has essentially taken two forms. The first has come from feminism, which has criticized a set of social norms and institutions that channel women into economic, social, and emotional dependence on men, especially husbands. This is not the attack with which I am principally concerned. That attack is directed primarily at what feminists describe as an involuntary system of structural dependence. That is a system women have little choice about entering and few resources for escaping, a system in which power relations between partners are so unbalanced that one person lives at the mercy of the other.

The second attack on dependence comes from more diffuse but quite deep-seated cultural sources. This attack goes beyond a concern for systematic inequality between partners and suggests that dependence itself is an evil. This attack, that is, would be made even when men and women were wholly equal. It is an attack that goes to the heart of our social ideals for personal relations. It is this second attack that seems to me to have such consequence for my thesis.

The extent and depth of the attack on dependence were brought home to me forcefully while reading patients' memoirs about the experience of being ill.[14] A striking number of these patients felt obliged to be on their guard against friends and families. Their friends and families were menacing because they threatened to influence the patients' lives and choices, thereby undermining their independence. The families threatened the patients' independence by offering them too much care and by demanding too much care. One patient, for example, "realized how little recognition I had given to my own needs, how much I had been living other people's lives and needs while neglecting my own. . . . In fact, it was downright mandatory to my well being that I be needed by others. . . . It took a life-threatening, catastrophic illness to force me to be attentive to my own needs, to go within and to listen to what I was all about."[15] Our world so values independence and fears dependence that family life, where independence is inevitably compromised and dependence proliferates, becomes a menace to be kept at a distance and a bondage that must have a ready escape.

Marriage binds. A re-institutionalized marriage would bind more powerfully. Bonds chafe. The bonds of marriage restrain us from following our inclinations. But late-twentieth-century Americans have nurtured their hostility to restraint so that it has become more powerful than ever. They have formulated potent ideological justifications for that hostility. They distrust social forces of all kinds that seek to govern behavior in private life. In short, it is hard to see where we might find the social support that would be needed to re-institutionalize marriage. And without that social support, laws that seek to strengthen marriage are unlikely to be passed and unlikely to work.

## CONCLUSION: WHAT LAW CAN AND CANNOT DO

Ironically, attempts to pass such laws may result in compromises that weaken rather than strengthen marriage. The effort to promote marriage through provisions for "covenant marriage" seems to illustrate some of the contemporary difficulties with trying to use law to improve family life. Its proponents evidently concluded that they could not impose the idea of covenant marriage on the entire population of a state. Therefore they made covenant marriage voluntary. And apparently they were correct in thinking that most people would reject covenant marriage, since few people enlist in it.

The result is that today, in states with covenant marriage laws, most people enter a noncovenant marriage that the state has carefully distinguished from a marriage in which people make a seriously binding commitment to each other. This affects the way people think generally about the obligations spouses accept toward one another. It may suggest that the extent of their obligation is minimal, purely contractual, and entirely negotiable.

I do not mean to suggest that the law and culture are helpless to make lives in families better. A number of suggestions made in the essays in *Promises to Keep*[16] (e.g., Popenoe's) strike me as quite desirable. But improving lives in families and re-institutionalizing marriage are not the same. Before law can be used effectively to promote the latter goal, cultural attitudes will have to change in ways that seem unlikely, at least at this juncture.

I hope it is clear that all this is not a call for inaction among the friends of the family. The law may do things to improve family life even if the law may be helpless to re-institutionalize marriage. In addition, there may well be rearguard actions that will slow the de-institutionalization of marriage. Finally, there may be some profit in trying to publicize and criticize the broader cultural attitudes I have identified. What seems to me unwise, however, is to attempt to re-institutionalize marriage without a clearheaded understanding of the impediments to doing so.

## NOTES

1. Carl E. Schneider, "The Law and the Stability of Marriage: The Family as a Social Institution," in *Promises to Keep: Decline and Renewal of Marriage in America*, ed. David Popenoe, Jean Bethke Elshtain, and David Blankenhorn (Lanham, Md.: Rowman & Littlefield, 1996).

2. See Carl E. Schneider, *The Channelling Function in Family Law*, 20 Hofstra Law Review 495 (1992); Popenoe, Elshtain, and Blankenhorn, ed., *Promises to Keep*.

3. Schneider, "The Law and the Stability of Marriage."

4. Ibid., 206.

5. See Carl E. Schneider and Margaret F. Brinig, *An Invitation to Family Law: Principles, Process, and Perspectives* (St. Paul, Minn.: West, 1995).

6. Schneider, "The Law and the Stability of Marriage," 208.

7. Philip Rieff, *The Triumph of the Therapeutic: Uses of Faith After Freud* (New York: Harper & Row, 1966), 2.

8. On distrust of the government in family law, see Carl E. Schneider, *Family Law in the Age of Distrust*, 33 Fam. L.Q. 447 (1999).

9. See, e.g., Carl E. Schneider, *Moral Discourse and the Transformation of American Family Law*, 83 Mich. L. Rev. 1803 (1985); Carl E. Schneider, *Rethinking Alimony: Marital Decisions and Moral Discourse*, 1991 B.Y.U. L. Rev. 197; Carl E. Schneider, *Marriage, Morals, and the Law: No-Fault Divorce and Moral Discourse*, 1994 Utah L. Rev. 503.

10. Lest this seem harsh, see my attempt to understand morality a la mode in Schneider, *Marriage, Morals, and the Law*.

11. Lawrence M. Friedman, *The Republic of Choice* (Cambridge: Harvard University Press, 1990), 101.

12. I describe the hypothetical I use to raise these issues and the responses it evokes in Schneider, *Marriage, Morals, and the Law*, 503. I have continued to use that hypothetical in my current research among students in and recent graduates of professional schools with similar results.

13. For a full-scale development of this proposition, see Carl E. Schneider, *The Practice of Autonomy: Patients, Doctors, and Medical Decisions* (Cambridge: Oxford University Press, 1998).

14. Ibid.

15. Ibid. at 160.

16. Popenoe, Elshtain, and Blankenhorn, eds., *Promises to Keep*.

# 16

# The Limits of the Law and Raising a Sentiment for Marriage

## Laurence C. Nolan

In the United States, few social questions have in recent years caused more anxiety and elicited more discussion than that of the family. The prominent and startling fact has been the rapid increase of divorce; and it is the investigation of its cause, and to the discovery of means of checking it, that this discussion has been chiefly directed.
                                                                    —Frank Gaylord Cook[1]

## INTRODUCTION

With the dramatic changes that the institution of marriage has undergone in the past three decades and the accompanying surge in divorce rates, it may be surprising to learn that the opening words were written in 1888 in the *Atlantic Monthly*. For the past three decades, marriage rates have plummeted, divorce rates have steadily climbed, and the concern for divorce as a cause for the decline in marriage has remained notable.

But there is another factor in the familiar equation. During the past thirty years, the institution of marriage has been affected by a different phenomenon that has continued to produce a "withering away"[2] of marriage. Not only is marriage becoming less prevalent and the legal constraints of exiting marriage less stringent, but modern attitudes toward marriage are changing. These are fostering a growing acceptance that arrangements besides marriage may fulfill similar purposes without carrying the same legal constraints.

While others have focused ample attention on the influence of divorce on marriage, this chapter concentrates on the impact that alternative lifestyle arrangements have had on marriage and divorce, and the role the law has played in this impact. The chapter develops along three themes. First, society's sentiment toward marriage has changed by virtue of the increasing practice of alternative lifestyles, including divorce. Second, these lifestyles do not produce the equivalent public good that the institution of marriage does. Finally, the law continues to have an interest in the revitalization of the institution of marriage because marriage is a public good, but the law's role in this effort is limited in raising a sentiment for marriage.

### Changing Sentiment Toward Marriage

As the twenty-first century begins, society has changed its attitude and sentiment toward the institution of marriage. In addition to the evidence of high divorce rates, this change is borne out by the increase in alternative lifestyles that may seem to fulfill purposes similar to marriage. The public's acceptance of unmarried cohabitation and premarital parenthood is firmly established. According to recent statistics from the U.S. Bureau of the Census, there are now more than four million cohabiting couples and more than 1.5 million of them have minor children.[3] Premarital parenthood continues at an alarming rate. These numbers are still high in minority communities, but the greatest percentage of growth is among whites.[4] The majority of women who become pregnant for the first time or give birth to their first child are now unmarried.[5] Instead of marriage, cohabitation is typically both the first living arrangement with a sexually intimate partner[6] and the first such living arrangement after divorce.[7] Society's acceptance of cohabitation and premarital parenthood has removed the stigma that was once attached to each of them.

With this change in attitude toward marriage, marriage has lost its status as the only acceptable living arrangement for sexual intimacy, childbearing, or childrearing. Unsurprisingly, the majority of the next generation of adults view cohabitation as acceptable.[8] It is a part of their childhood culture. But their acceptance is significant, because it may greatly affect the revitalization of marriage as an institution.

Changes in attitudes toward marriage support the view that the law mirrors society's sentiments.[9] In many respects, the law's response underscores the limitation of the law in the revitalization of marriage.

In several important cases shaping marriage and divorce law, the courts took note of public sentiment and were, apparently, influenced by that sentiment in arriving at their decisions. In *Marvin v. Marvin*,[10] the court recognized that cohabitants could contract with one another as long as the consideration was not based on the meretricious relationship.[11] Therefore, traditional homemaking services could be valid consideration for promises of economic support. Several times in the opinion, the court noted that demographics revealed "the prevalence of nonmarital relationships in modern society and the social acceptance of them."[12] The *Marvin* court perceived a public acceptance of cohabitation. It is hard to know if this perception influenced the court in fashioning its remedy. Other state courts, though not all, followed *Marvin* in their acceptance of cohabitation. During the last thirty years, state legislation has consistently supported cohabitation as a valid alternative lifestyle. This has been accompanied by the repeal of laws penalizing adultery and cohabitation.[13] Right or wrong, legislation is often viewed as a direct statement of public sentiment.

Similarly, divorce has become completely acceptable, if the actions of state legislatures and courts are an indication of societal sentiment. In *Posner v. Posner*,[14] an influential case allowing that prenuptial contracts may provide for divorce as long as they did not facilitate or encourage divorce, the court noted the change in public policy about divorce. The court reasoned that the state's public policy against divorce had waned with the enactment of no-fault divorce statutes, and therefore settlement of divorce issues was favored—even if the settlement was reached prior to the marriage. Thus, the same agreement planning for marriage could, ironically, include planning for divorce.

Varying and sometimes conflicting public policies become important when changes in society affect large numbers of people. Policies concerning divorce, cohabitation, and premarital parenthood also demonstrate the limits of what the law can do to revitalize marriage. The court's concern about the problems created when many citizens were cohabiting was evident in *Marvin*. For example, alternative lifestyles reflect many of the same problems as marital arrangements when they break up. The courts may question whether the law should mediate the settlement of those problems, especially when citizens normally turn to the courts for dispute resolution and when many middle-class citizens, who influence the law, are participants in alternative lifestyles.[15]

A typical reason given for cohabitation is that the partners can have some of the benefits of marriage but avoid its legal requirements.[16] This suggests that the law is making marriage less attractive than cohabitation. Additionally, the *Marvin* court's indirect concern may have been about enforcement issues when it observed the large number of unmarried cohabitants. A government may not be able to enforce its rules effectively when so many ignore them.

A concern for the welfare of children also demonstrates the limitation of the law in strengthening marriage as an institution. Children need care and financial support whether their parents are married or not. If large numbers of parents have children outside marriage, the law may choose a policy to protect the child regardless of its parents' marital status. The law may accomplish this policy by focusing on the parent–child relationship rather than on the marital relationship (if any) between the parents. Therefore, marriage may be seen as an irrelevant factor when formulating policy regarding the welfare of the child.

Historically, Christianity influenced American marriage and family law as well as public sentiment.[17] As the influence of Christianity and other religious beliefs has waned in America, their influence in shaping family law has lessened as well. Laws affecting adultery, cohabitation, and premarital parenthood have generally stopped imposing penalties. These changes may be attributed in part to the decreasing influence of religion.

The U.S. Supreme Court has continued to broaden its interpretation of individual freedom to make personal choices related to marriage, sexual intimacy, childbearing, and childrearing.[18] Unrestrained liberty is problematic, however. Christianity and other religions were restraining influences. But at the same time the law increased individual liberty to make personal choices, the influence of Christianity was declining. The restraining force of religion to place choices of sexual intimacy, childbearing, and childrearing in the context of marriage no longer seems to work in conjunction with the law.

Technology has also increased the law's emphasis on individual choice in personal matters. Reproductive technology has allowed conception without sex and sex without conception. Marriage may be seen as unnecessary when technology provides the means for sexual intimacy without conception. Conversely, if marriage is the proper institution for sexual intimacy and if reproduction does not involve sexual intimacy, then marriage is not the only setting for reproduction. Moreover, because the law supports the value of individuality, it is the individual, not the state, who under most circumstances decides these matters.

Other social phenomena illustrate the limitation of the law: the increase in life expectancy in the twentieth century;[19] the influence of the women's movement;[20] and the expectation that marriage should be based on more than economic security alone.[21] The 1960s sexual revolution led to greater permissiveness toward premarital sex and to changed views of sexual morality. Economic prosperity brought more affluence, and affluence brought more selfishness. Apart from law, these social changes influenced society's attitude toward marriage.

The relationship between law and other social changes in the decline of marriage is therefore quite complex. How much did the sexual revolution of the 1960s influence the change in attitudes toward marriage, as compared to the decline in the influence of Christianity? The present divorce culture was spawned by no-fault divorce law. Yet no-fault divorce laws were enacted by the state legislatures, and they were responding to someone or something. Whatever the causes and effects, attitudes toward marriage as the only appropriate institution for sexual intimacy, childbearing, and childrearing have changed.

### Are Alternative Lifestyles a Public Good?

Even though attitudes and sentiment about marriage may have changed, most young people still support marriage.[22] Yet their sentiment is often illusory. It is not connected with the meaningful purposes of marriage, because many of these same young people are pursuing sexual intimacy, childbearing, and childrearing outside marriage.

The law has a stake in marriage. The law's interest in marriage and alternatives to marriage stems from three sources: (1) its *parens patriae* power, by which the state protects certain vulnerable citizens; (2) its police power, by which a state has an inherent plenary power to promote the public welfare, including preventing its citizens from harming themselves; and (3) the U.S. and state constitutions, which ensure fundamental constitutional rights to all citizens.

Against this background, marriage has traditionally been regarded as a public good. It has been associated with "positive values of permanence, stability, interdependence, trust and security."[23] Commitment of the spouses to the marriage and to each other was the foundation of these values. Law and social mores also supported these values. Marriage was a fundamental element of the social order. It was looked upon as the primary social institution for the rearing of children and passing on the values of society to the next generation. Marriage was also the primary legal institution to protect property rights. In short, marriage played many public roles.

Recent studies indicate that alternative lifestyles do not offer comparable goods to society. These studies support the relevancy of marriage to the security, protection, and health of children, adults, and of the larger society.

Premarital parenthood, divorce, and often cohabitation result in children being reared by single parents. Empirical studies suggest that children who are reared by both parents are, on average, more successful as adults than children reared in single-parent families or in stepfamilies.[24] Single parenthood is not the sole cause for this difference, but is one of the significant factors putting these children at greater risk for child poverty, school failure, and juvenile delinquency.[25] They are deprived not only of economic support from their parents and the community, but also of the social resources from their parents and the community.[26] Children not living with both parents are at a greater risk for abuse by nonparent caregivers.[27] Empirical studies suggest that parents parent better in a two-parent home than in a single-parent home.[28]

Cohabitation generally does not provide the equivalent levels of commitment, permanency, protection, and stability that marriage does. Social science evidence suggests that cohabiting prior to marriage increases the risk for divorce.[29] Cohabiting women are more than twice as likely to be victims of domestic violence than married women. There are higher rates of depression in cohabitors' households than in marrieds' households. Cohabitors' households are economically poorer than marrieds' homes. Thus, children in cohabitors' households are poorer than children in intact families. As to personal happiness, sexual satisfaction, and sexual exclusivity, social science evidence suggests that cohabitors experience them at lower levels than marrieds' do.[30]

Alternative lifestyles are, therefore, not comparable to marriage with respect to producing comparable public good, based on current social science studies. Instead, they are a significant factor in putting children at greater risk for social problems and poverty. In turn, the negative welfare of children results in a high cost to society, both socially and economically. Societal costs are also high because of the social efforts required to repair the problems caused by these lifestyles, including divorce. Marriage as an institution is better for society.

### What the Law Can and Cannot Do for Marriage

If marriage as an institution seems to be preferred for the benefits it accords society, perhaps government policy should be directed to promote marriage. On the other hand, perhaps government policy should not be directed to promote any lifestyle, in light of the large numbers of nonmarital families. Or perhaps government policy should be directed to focus on the well-being of all children, regardless of their family status, since they are society's next adult generation. Furthermore, if government policy is directed to promote marriage, that may raise an issue of gender equality, because so many single-parent families are headed by women. Similarly, if government policy is directed to promote marriage, perhaps premarital families in minority communities would be further weakened. The task of sorting out how public policy should be directed is difficult because no one knows whether the statistics are revealing a complete breakdown of the institution of marriage or a breakdown that can be arrested and an institution that can be revitalized. Moreover, with any public policy, one must consider its impact on constitutionally protected values such as personal autonomy, gender and racial discrimination, and First Amendment freedoms.

Nevertheless, it is important to continue to make the issue of marriage a part of the public debate. Current social science evidence supports the view that public policy should be directed to promote marriage, as long as part of the discourse in determining the direction of that policy considers its impact on other vulnerable groups.

Any law, however, must conform to the standards of the U.S. Constitution. This conformity is an important issue because it limits what law, as contrasted with the private sector, might do in promoting marriage. This final section illustrates this tension between laws that might promote marriage, but might still fail to conform to constitutional standards.

One direction that government policy might take is to use this social science data to educate the public, especially young people, on the importance of marriage. The mass media is the most effective tool to distribute information to the public. The importance of the media to influence people and establish values has not been lost on the federal government. In a recent endeavor, the federal government was criticized in its efforts to get anti-drug messages as part of the story line in television series because of nondisclosure issues.[31] The subtle approach is usually an effective way to influence people, such as through "designated driver" campaigns and figures such as the Marlboro Man.[32] The greatest criticism of the anti-drug messages was that there was no disclosure of the government's involvement.[33] Along with any needed disclosure, government, federal and state, should pursue this and similar approaches to educating the public on the importance of marriage.

Another direction that government policy might take is a much more active approach to ensure that the tradition of marriage is known to those growing up in a culture of divorce, increased cohabitation, and premarital births. Florida has enacted a comprehensive statute to strengthen marriage, including a program that requires high schools to educate children about the permanence of marriage.[34] It also encourages marriage preparation and parenting classes and permits them to be conducted by religious denominations. This would appear to raise First Amendment issues, but the First Amendment accommodates faith-based principles that further secular public policies.[35] Here the secular purpose is presumably that of protecting children and adults in stable relationships through a better understanding of marriage.

In formulating and implementing policy to encourage marriage, government should consider data showing the effect of the sex-ratio on marrying[36] and data clearly demonstrating that people marry when they can financially afford to marry.[37] This data is pertinent in setting policy to promote marriage in poor, urban, African-American communities. The proportion of young females to young males in these communities is startling. Some of this imbalance has been attributed to the effect of the drug trade on those communities.[38] For example, there is a disparity involving much harsher sentencing for those convicted of crimes involving crack cocaine versus more lenient sentencing for those convicted of crimes involving powder cocaine in the federal courts. African Americans are more likely to be convicted of crack cocaine violations than whites, and whites are more likely to be convicted of powder cocaine violations than African Americans. As a result of this disparity, more young African Americans than whites are serving long prison terms for crimes involving the same drug in a different form.[39] Federal government policy should focus on legislation to eliminate this discrimination and injustice.

Social science data shows a correlation between income and marriage.[40] People are more likely to marry when they think they can afford it. Therefore, government policy might be directed toward facilitating employment training, job creation, and employment placement in poor communities. Currently, Congress is pursuing the latter in legislation with three goals: to promote marriage, to promote better parenting, and to help fathers find jobs to improve their skills.[41] This legislation would provide funds to community and faith-based organizations to develop innovative programs to implement these goals.[42] The U.S. House of Representatives has passed its version of the legislation (Fathers Count Act of 1999).[43] The U.S. Senate has not passed its counterpart (Responsible Fatherhood Act of 1999).[44] This proposed Act has raised issues of gender discrimination by focusing on poor fathers and not poor parents, at the expense of poor mothers.[45] There are also First Amendment concerns because faith-based organizations would be involved.[46]

## CONCLUSION

As the chapter contends, the law is limited in promoting marriage because of constitutional and other public-policy concerns. Therefore, all sectors of the community should become involved in raising a sentiment for marriage. Raising a sentiment for marriage is not in opposition to individual choice. To the contrary, a greater awareness of the benefits of marriage makes it possible for individuals to decide more wisely.

Besides the law, religion has the power to change conduct. The role of religion can be crucial, as when the Christian religion influenced both the law and the people's attitudes toward marriage. Religion can promote marriage entirely from the religious perspective and not be limited as the law would be. Many faith-based organizations have begun actively to promote marriage by providing marriage-preparation classes, counseling, marriage-strengthening classes, and programs promoting sexual intimacy only in marriage, for example.[47] Moreover, other organizations and community programs focus on strengthening marriage and decreasing divorce.[48] Hence, a marriage movement is developing from the grassroots, both from religious and secular communities. The importance of a national marriage movement in raising a sentiment for marriage is that its message will become part of the public discourse. In a democracy, the law often reflects society's sentiment. Covenant marriage legislation is an example of the efforts of a grassroots movement that may be reflected in the law just as the movement for no-fault divorce thirty years ago now pervades the law of divorce. If society's sentiment toward marriage changes, then the law will likely reflect that sentiment.

## NOTES

1. Frank Gaylord Cook, "The Marriage Celebration in Europe," *Atlantic Monthly* (February 1888), 245.

2. This expression is from Mary Ann Glendon, *Marriage and the State: The Withering Away of Marriage*, 62 Va. L. Rev. 663 (1976).

3. U.S. Bureau of the Census, *Statistical Abstract of the United States: 1999*, 119th ed. (Washington, D.C., 1999), table 68, "Unmarried Couples by Selected Characteristics:1980 to 1998."

4. Tom W. Smith, *The Emerging 21st Century American Family* (Chicago: University of Chicago, National Opinion Research Center, November 24, 1999), 3.

5. U.S. Bureau of the Census, *Trends in Marital Status of U.S. Women at First Birth: 1930 to 1994*. Population Division Working Paper, no. 20.

6. Smith, *The Emerging 21st Century American Family*.

7. Ibid.

8. Barbara Dafoe Whitehead and David Popenoe, *Changes in Teen Attitudes Toward Marriage, Cohabitation and Children 1975–1995* (Rutgers, N.J.: National Marriage Project, 1999), 4–5.

9. Victoria Mikesell Mather, "Evolution and Revolution in Family Law," 25 St. Mary's L. J. 405, 406 (1993) ("think that family law tends to follow, rather than lead, social upheaval and adjustment in family decisions and structures.").

10. *Marvin v. Marvin*, 557 P.2d 106 (Cal. 1976).

11. Id. (equitable remedies may also apply).

12. Id. at 122, 109.

13. Id. at 111, n. 4.

14. *Posner v. Posner*, 233 So. 2d 381 (Fla. 1970).

15. William A. Reppy, Jr., *Property and Support Rights of Unmarried Cohabitants: A Proposal for Creating a New Legal Status*, 44 La. L. Rev. 1677, 1681–1682 (1984).

16. David Popenoe and Barbara Dafoe Whitehead, *Should We Live Together? What Young Adults Need to Know About Cohabitation Before Marriage* (New Brunswick, N.J.: National Marriage Project,1999), 1.

17. Stuart Banner, *When Christianity Was Part of the Common Law*, 16 Law & Hist. Rev. 27 (1998).

18. *Griswold v. Connecticut*, 381 U.S. 479 (1965); *Eisenstadt v. Baird*, 405 U.S. 438 (1972); *Zablocki v. Redhail*, 434 U.S. 374 (1978).

19. Alan A. Stone, "Emotional Aspects of Contemporary Relations," in *Contemporary Marriage*, ed. Kingsley Davis (New York: The Russell Sage Foundation 1985), 400; Mather, "Evolution and Revolution in Family Law," 407.

20. Mather, op. cit. 407.

21. Mather, op. cit.

22. Popenoe and Whitehead, *Changes in Teen Attitudes Toward Marriage*.

23. Anne E. Simerman, Note, *The Right of a Cohabitant to Recover in Tort: Wrongful Death, Negligent Infliction of Emotional Distress and Loss of Consortium*, 32 U. Louisville J. Fam. L. 531, 542 (1993–1994).

24. Sara McLanahan and Gary Sandefur, *Growing Up with a Single Parent* (Cambridge: Harvard University Press, 1994).

25. Ibid.

26. Ibid.

27. Catherine Malkin and Michael Lamb, *Child Maltreatment: A Test of Socio-biological Theory,* 25 J. of Comp. Fam. Studies 121 (1994); Leslie Margolin, *Child Abuse and Mother's Boyfriends: Why the Overrepresentation?* 16 Child Abuse and Neglect 541 (1992).

28. McLanahan and Sandefur, *Growing Up with a Single Parent.*

29. Popenoe and Whitehead, *Should We Live Together?* 3–5 (analyzing social science evidence).

30. Ibid., 5–7.

31. Brian Lowry, "White House Tie to Anti-Drug TV Scripts Criticized," *Los Angeles Times,* Part A, National Desk (January 14, 2000), 1.

32. Matthew Miller, "This Is Your No-brainer on Drugs," *Austin American Statesman,* Editorial, A13.

33. Ibid.

34. Fla. Stat. ch. 741.0305 (1998).

35. *Lemon v. Kurtzman,* 403 U.S. 602 (1971).

36. M. Belinda Tucker and Claudia Mitchell-Keinan, ed., *The Decline in Marriage Among African Americans* (New York: The Russell Sage Foundation, 1995); Donna L. Franklin, *Ensuring Inequality: The Structural Transformation of the African-American Family* (New York: Oxford University Press, 1997).

37. Franklin, *Ensuring Inequality.*

38. Ibid.

39. Nkechi Taifa, *Cracked Justice: A Critical Examination of Cocaine Sentencing* 27 UWLA L. Rev. 107 (1996).

40. Tucker and Mitchell-Keinan, ed., *The Decline in Marriage Among African Americans.*

41. Fathers Count Act, H.R. 3073, 106th Cong. (1999); Rep. Nancy L. Johnson, "Q: Should Congress Fight Poverty by Promoting Marriage?" *Insight on the News,* Symposium (December 13, 1999), 40.

42. Fathers Count Act.

43. Ibid. (passed in the House of Representatives, November 10, 1999).

44. Responsible Fatherhood Act, S. 1364, 106th Cong. (1999), reintroduced as S.653, Responsible Fatherhood Act of 2001.

45. Patricia Ireland, "Q: Should Congress Fight Poverty by Promoting Marriage?" *Insight on the News,* Symposium (December 13, 1999), 41.

46. Jim Abrams, "House Moves to Promote Fatherhood in Low Income Families," *Associated Press,* Washington Dateline (November 10, 1999).

47. Michael J. McManus, *Marriage Savers,* rev. ed. (Grand Rapids, Mich.: Zondervan Publishing House, 1995).

48. Ibid.

# 17

# A Marriage Research Agenda for the Twenty-First Century: Ten Critical Questions

## David Popenoe

### INTRODUCTION

The institution of marriage has undergone such rapid and far-reaching changes in recent times that reliable information about modern marriage is sparse. Much new research and thinking are needed if we are to better understand what has been happening to marriage, the social, economic, and cultural conditions now shaping the institution, and how marriage can best be strengthened. The following ten questions have been developed to try to pinpoint some key issues about which a deeper understanding is needed. I address the questions roughly in order of importance and priority to strengthening marriage in the twenty-first century.

### THE TEN QUESTIONS

#### Young Adulthood

1. The age of marriage has been moving upward while the age of puberty has been moving downward, thus lengthening the period of life in which people are sexually mature yet unmarried. The patterns of living during this new and relatively long period of adolescence and young adulthood are often associated with values and behaviors that are antithetical to marriage.

*How can we best insure that the life experiences during adolescence and young adulthood will contribute to, rather than detract from, eventual marriage?*

*Discussion:* It used to be the case that young people, especially women, lived at home in a family-friendly environment until they married. Today, the average American woman reaches puberty at perhaps age 11, and marries at age 25, resulting in a period of about fourteen years in which she could be sexually active yet unmarried. The data for men are similar. If current trends continue, this time period will lengthen; puberty could start slightly earlier, and marriage will probably begin later. In several Scandinavian nations today the average age of marriage for women has nearly reached 30.

At least half of this post-puberty, pre-marriage period typically is lived apart from parents and other family members in a sexually active single's culture that is mainly focused on work, career, and recreation rather than family and children. In America, especially, the nonfamily character of the subculture of young adulthood is accentuated by the entertainment industry in which the serious concerns of marriage and parenthood are seldom addressed. Indeed, a growing number of young people put marriage and children out of their minds during these years and when married family life finally comes it is one of the most stressful times of life, representing as it does a radical shift from the independent and freedom-loving lifestyle that preceded it. The rapidly declining birthrates in all modern societies undoubtedly reflect the difficulty in shifting from young-adult singlehood to responsible marriage and parenthood.

A recent conservative answer to this dilemma calls for earlier marriage. The way to solve the problem, it is argued, is to marry young and thus avoid the singles culture and the temptation for premarital sex. Aside from the fact that this proposal runs directly counter to current trends and would thus be difficult to put into effect, it has some other important failings. Most notably, early marriage—especially in the teen years—has been found by social research to be the strongest risk factor for divorce ever identified.[1] There can be little doubt that modern marriage, which is based on lifelong intimate friendship rather more than the functional relationship of earlier historical periods, depends on the wise and mature selection of a mate. This presumably is more effectively achieved at older ages when personalities have been more clearly formed and work and careers better established.

But if not early marriage, then what? Based on the assumption that the overwhelming majority of young people eventually want to marry,[2] we need as a first step to bring marriage concerns and plans back into the subculture of young adulthood. This might be done through incorporating marriage and parenthood education in the high school and college curricula, re-involving parents in the mating lives of their children, making the workplace more flexible for family concerns, and encouraging the media to portray marriage positively more often. Some messages that could be stressed are the importance of not waiting too long to marry if children are desired, and taking a longer view of life—focusing on the many lifelong benefits of marriage and children for health, happiness, and prosperity. It might also be useful to permit tax-deferred accounts in young, single adulthood that could be used later for childrearing expenses. A careful program of research is needed to evaluate these various policies and programs.

### Sexual Restriction

2. Strong marriage systems of the past have been accompanied by a high degree of sexual restriction, especially of women's sexuality. The sexual revolution has generated unparalleled sexual freedom for both men and women but also probably has lowered the chances for long-lasting marriages and thus harmed children. It is hard to imagine rebuilding a strong marriage system in today's sexual climate.

*Is it possible to move toward a more culturally restrictive sexual system for both men and women and if so, how, and how restrictive should it be?*

*Discussion:* Over the course of history, societies have fluctuated between restrictive and permissive sexual regimes, and we are now pretty far out in the permissive direction. The time may be ripe for a shift back. Despite the sexual libertinism promulgated by the urban elite and the entertainment industry, as well as the widespread proliferation of pornography on the Internet, I believe that most young people realize the explosive downside of unrestricted sex and want to find some way to generate a more humane and responsible sexual culture. Because of the commercialization of sex and the power of new technologies, the achievement of a more restrictive, marriage- and child-friendly sexual regime will surely be difficult to achieve, but does not seem impossible.

First, families probably will have to become countercultural in order to protect their children from the oversexualized culture. If enough families engage in cultural protest and boycotts against the media, insisting that we find better ways to protect children from premature sexualization, it could have an effect. Second, it seems wise to promote sexual abstinence at least through the high school years. This would seem to be an achievable goal, one that is favored by most parents and probably most high school students as well.

A goal that does not seem achievable is the prohibition of all sexual activity until marriage. The weight of evidence from the social sciences suggests that the premarital period now is simply too long and the sexualization of culture too extreme to hold this as a realistic goal, as much as it may be desired by many and held as a moral and religious value. In its place, we should be developing norms in which young adults seek to lead their premarital sex lives with eventual marriage more strongly in mind. The leadership for this probably will have to be taken by women; they are traditionally assumed to be the gatekeepers of sexuality. One such norm is the one our grandmothers thought might be true: if a woman wants a man to marry her, wisdom dictates a measure of playing hard to get. This could mean, for example, that a woman would refuse to cohabit except when marriage is clearly planned, that is, when she becomes engaged. And in such cases the cohabitation should be only on her terms, and usually in her domicile. Another moderate sexual norm that now seems all but forgotten is abstinence from sex until a strong, intimate relationship has been established. The reestablishment of this norm does not seem out of the question, but it would likely have to be reestablished by a large majority of women.

### Father Absence and Paternal Investment

3. The historical record indicates that if women are economically able to raise children without men they will often do so; and that, without marriage, men will stray from their children. In the modern era, more and more women are economically independent and are parenting alone, marriage is weakening, and more men are straying. Thus children lose the benefit of fathers, and society loses the benefit of the civilizing force of marriage and children on men.

*How can we reverse the tide of father absence and ensure that men remain actively involved in childrearing?*

*Discussion*: It is no secret that modern societies face growing fatherlessness. In the United States, for example, the percentage of children not living with their biological fathers jumped from 17 percent in 1960 to more than 35 percent by the century's end.[3] The factors that have led to high paternal involvement in societies throughout history have been fairly well established and they go well beyond economics.[4] Most of these factors are now weakening and, in combination, they represent a most important focus for future research.

First, high paternal involvement occurs when a father has a high degree of confidence that a child is really his. Men are much more willing to make parental investments in their biological children than in children who are genetically unrelated. Given today's sexual climate, paternity confidence must surely be diminishing.

Second, high paternal involvement takes place when alternative mating opportunities for males are restricted, forcing men into a strategy of making higher investments in a few children rather than lower investments in many—the reproductive option they possess far more than females. Today, especially with cohabitation and the ease of divorce and despite our socially imposed monogamy, the alternative mating opportunities available to men are high.

Third, men make strong investments in children if they think that such investments are truly important for child outcomes. Today, with the help of the government, low-income women are at least able to get by, and high-income women are financially self-sufficient—thus diminishing the man's economic importance. Moreover, the cultural perception has arisen that men may even be superfluous to childrearing.

Fourth, high paternal investments traditionally have been accentuated through pressure from extended family members who also have a biological stake in child outcomes, and such pressure has often been contributed as well by peers and through the larger culture. These pressures are notoriously weak today.

Fifth, fathers contribute more if they sense that successful offspring will lead to their own economic enrichment, as, for example, on a family farm or through expected care in old age. Today, children are seen more as an economic drain than an asset (see question 8 below).

Sixth, paternal investments are mediated through the marriage relationship. If the relationship is strong, men will go the extra mile to please their wives through childcare activities. If the marital relationship breaks down, men have tended to leave both the woman and the child. Given the state of marriage today, this phenomenon obviously has serious social implications.

In the face of these six factors, reversing the tide of fatherlessness is surely a daunting challenge. Among the possible solutions, in addition to shoring up the institution of marriage and partially reversing the sexual revolution, are more widely publicizing both the importance of fathers for child outcomes and the benefit to male psychological well-being of close ties to children, and engaging fathers in early childcare so that they will be more likely to bond with their children and stay with them even if their marriage breaks down.

## Marital Bonds

4. Marriages of the past typically were held together by strong bonds of economic dependency between husbands and wives, religious meaning, extended family solidarity, and societal approval, all based around the importance of reproduction and childrearing. Today, in many marriages, the only major bond is adult psychological need, which has proven to be quite fragile in holding marriages together over the long run.

*If modern marriages are to be made stronger and longer lasting, aren't some additional marriage bonds needed? If so, which ones?*

*Discussion*: The primary purpose of marriage throughout history has been the raising of children. The need of every society for successful childrearing is why marriage has been a public institution and a focus of religious concern. In times past, children not reared by a mother and a father who stayed together faced significantly higher risks of negative life outcomes, including early death.

Today, marriage is thought to be more a couples relationship—a friendship between two adults—in which children are an option. Children have been pushed ever more to the sidelines of modern life and are even perceived by a growing number of adults as impediments to the good life. It can reasonably be argued that married people are happier, healthier, and wealthier than single people and that therefore marriage is a social good.[5] But without children, it is much more difficult to envision the institution of marriage as something that requires public attention and regulation. After all, it is a social good for people to have lots of friends, but we don't consider that to be a public issue subject to government regulation.

Frankly, in the absence of children, I do not know what other bonds can be added to the modern marital relationship. And, as marriage becomes increasingly a private relationship between two (or more!) adults, I believe that it will become much more difficult to think of it as a social institution that should be subject to government and religious concern. But this is surely a critical area for further thought and discussion.

### Division of Labor

5. In every society throughout history, except under abnormal circumstances, husbands have been the primary breadwinners and wives have been the primary childrearers. Today, the changing nature of the economy increasingly has blended these marital role assignments.

*To what extent can the traditional marital division of labor be discarded without damaging the success of marriages or the sense of well-being of either men or women?*

*Discussion*: One of the axioms of contemporary evolutionary psychology is that, in mate selection, women prefer men who can provide economic resources whereas men prefer women who are young, attractive, and fertile. This pattern is so common that it likely has a genetic base. That is, it was selected for through adaptation in our ancestral environment. Moreover, throughout history men have been the family leaders—presumably not only because they were the main economic providers but also because they possessed greater size and strength. Yet women today seemingly are in the workforce to stay, more and more families involve joint wage earners, and we see a growing number of couples that break from the common pattern, such as wealthier women with struggling male artists and career women who have househusbands. What do these trends mean for the future of marriage?

It is worth remembering that the extreme marital division of labor—with women serving as full-time mothers and homemakers and not in the labor force, and men serving as the exclusive breadwinners, working outside the home, and remaining somewhat distant from day-to-day family life—dates from the nineteenth century and even then only in the urban middle classes. Throughout most of history, to the degree that childcare permitted, women have shared breadwinning and been in the labor force, mostly in agricultural pursuits. Much of our marital gender-role tension today, then, seems to concern the shift from the "modern nuclear family" of the past century, with its defined roles, to today's nuclear family. This limited time span provides some hope for a successful resolution. Indeed, we apparently have returned to a family situation, not unlike that found in our ancestral environment, in which the predominant family form is nuclear, both husbands and wives are in the labor force and have a relatively egalitarian relationship with one another, and men have a reasonably active and hands-on fathering role.

Still, it is highly unlikely, given human nature, that we will ever see a general role reversal, with women becoming the primary breadwinners and men the primary childrearers. In fact, there is some evidence to suggest that marriages in which this has taken place are unhappy and have a high breakup rate.[6] Unless human nature somehow radically shifts, therefore, we will probably continue to see some differentiation based on women's stronger ties to children with the attendant traits of nurturing and caring, and men's stronger ties to hierarchy with the attendant traits of competitiveness and aggressiveness. But this is obviously an area in which far more knowledge is needed.

### Friendship Outside of Marriage

6. Up until the modern era, no marriage system expected husbands and wives to be each other's nearly exclusive best friend and confidant. In prior periods the close friendships of husbands and wives were much more likely to have been with others of the same sex or close relatives or both.

*To what degree does exclusive marital friendship place a burden on modern marriages, and if a serious burden, how can it best be surmounted?*

*Discussion*: For many people in modern life, especially men, marriage (along with nonmarital cohabitation) has become the only social structure that concerns intimate relationships. This is unfortunate, because it puts enormous pressure on a fragile institution. Just as married women need same-sex friends apart from their husbands, so do men. Because it is more difficult for men to make and keep friends than it is for women, the "isolated nuclear family" is not an especially healthy environment for men. With the reasonable goal of gaining further access to public life, feminism has sought to break down male-only bastions where, in fact, male friendships were once formed. In the future it might be wise to reconstruct some male-only places outside of bastions of public power where married men can seek same-sex companionship and intimacy.

### Sexual Fidelity and the Modern Workplace

7. Historically, in most societies, men and women have been gender segregated in their work lives, and the kin group and local communities have closely controlled their sexual behavior. Married men and women seldom were in situations where intimate contact with others of the opposite sex could occur. Today, men and women are thrown together in the workplace, and their behavior takes place largely apart from the observation and control of relatives and neighbors; married men and women operate in conditions identical to those of the unmarried. Under such conditions, the normal, biological male and female sexual and mate-selection proclivities can be expected to come into play, helping to generate marital breakdown.

*Can explicit norms and workplace policies be developed that inhibit intimate contact among co-workers, especially those who are married?*

*Discussion:* This is a serious problem. The workplace has not only become the venue in which much mate selection takes place but probably also the environment in which many marriages are dissolved. In the absence of gender-segregated settings, a new normative structure will have to be developed if we want to regain some control over the situation. Sexual harassment legislation is one response already in place; the worry is that it will dampen the prospects for successful mate selection. More important, in my view, is the development of a normative code that places married people off limits to sexual approaches. It is hard to see how law could impose this; it would have to arise informally. Shouldn't people at least feel some remorse from going after someone else's wife or husband? The moral obliviousness about this in today's popular culture is as remarkable as it is unfortunate.

### Economics of Children

8. Marriages of the past were heavily based on the fact that both the husband and the wife had a mutual interest in their children's well-being because the children would become part of the family workforce and the

parents would become economically dependent on those children in their older years. In other words, children were enormous economic assets to the married couple. Today, children have become more of an economic liability to parents than an asset, and the economic support of dependent elderly has largely been taken over by the state.

*Is there any way to make children an economic asset to their parents again, and thus strengthen the marriage bond?*

*Discussion:* There is only one way I know of to do this in modern societies, and that is to reformulate social security and old-age pension systems so that a parent's income in old age is based partly on the child's earnings. Economist Shirley P. Burggraf has recently put one proposal forward.[7] Under the current system of collectivized social security, young people pay into a system that provides generous retirement benefits for all older persons, irrespective of whether they have been good parents. As she notes, "People who never have children, parents who abuse or neglect or abandon their children, deadbeat dads who don't pay child support—all have as much claim (in many cases more) on the earnings of the next generation . . . as the most dutiful parents." Under Burggraf's proposal, the parental retirement pension would come from taxes on their children's earnings that had been invested in a trust fund. Parents who invest more in their children might thereby reap the most economic benefits in the long run. The system would not discriminate against the childless; adults without children would be expected to set up their own retirement trust funds; they could, in effect, invest in the stock market instead of in children.

The problem is that turning children again into potential economic assets might be morally unacceptable in today's society. A national discussion of these issues would be useful, but in the end we will probably have to rely on children being psychic rather than economic assets.

### Support During the Transition to Parenthood

9. The arrival of the first child has proven to be a critical time of stress in many modern marriages.[8] There are many reasons for this, but a prominent one is that so many children today are born into households that are isolated from other family members, relatives, neighbors, friends, and supportive services. In the past, childrearing was largely a group experience; mothers had much assistance from others and children were often raised as much by the local community as by the parents.

*How can we bring today's childrearing households into closer contact with others for the provision of mutual assistance and support, or provide such support through other means?*

*Discussion*: It is surely the case that a "village" is an important adjunct to childrearing, and that today's isolated nuclear family is distinctly disadvantageous for children. One answer to this question rests in building communities that are better focused on the needs of childrearing families. In many respects, American communities today are woefully inadequate for children, ranging from the absence of public transportation to the lack of pedestrian access. Another answer is a better network of childcare centers, at least for preschool children.

One outstanding issue is the seeming need for both parents to work when the children are young, thus making childrearing that much more difficult. This problem might be helped through enabling pre-married single people, during the years when they have good incomes and no dependents, to set up tax-deferred accounts to be used for childrearing expenses after marriage. We should also consider expanding parental leave to a longer time period with partial pay, and providing more relief for families with young children from the current high level of taxation. In addition, we need to do much more education for parenthood in high schools and colleges, as well as for couples who are expecting their first child.

### Attachment Experiences

10. There is substantial evolutionary and psychological evidence that the early attachment experiences of infants are related to the intimate relationships and procreational behavior of those infants when they become adults.[9] In other words, weak and insecure early attachment can generate poor adult relationships, including unstable marriages and unhealthy sexuality.

*To what degree are today's high divorce rates and nonmarital birthrates related to inadequate attachment in childhood, and, if the connection is strong, what should we be doing to improve the attachment experiences of today's children?*

*Discussion*: Perhaps the greatest tragedy of recent family decline is the weakening of attachment experiences in children. Because weak attachments in childhood seem to lead to weak attachments in adulthood, and since good intimate relationships are one of life's most meaningful and important attributes, we may be on a course in modern societies in which people become increasingly rich but decreasingly happy. What a sad commentary that would be on human progress. We should be conducting major longitudinal studies to pin down the precise relationship between childhood attachment and adult outcomes, to determine the kind of family units in which attachment is fostered, and to assess the impact of the childrearing process called "attachment parenting."

## CONCLUSION

These questions obviously are framed from broad academic and inter-disciplinary perspectives, including historical, cross-cultural, and evolutionary. Especially for an institution as central and important as marriage, such broad perspectives are essential if we are to have a full understanding of the issues involved. It is clear that marriage issues cannot adequately be addressed by the approach of a single discipline, or even by the social sciences as they currently are established. Marriage is much more than a social institution; it is based in the biological realities of the human species.

## NOTES

1. See, for example, T. C. Martin and L. Bumpass (1989) "Recent Trends in Marital Disruption," *Demography* 26 (1989): 37–51. One recent study has concluded that the increase in median age at first marriage since the 1960s is the most important factor accounting for the recent leveling off of divorce rates. Tim B. Heaton, "Factors Contributing to Increasing Marital Stability in the United States." *Journal of Family Issues* (in press).

2. In the 1996–98 period, 81 percent of high school senior girls and 72 percent of high school senior boys stated that having a good marriage and family life was "extremely important" to them. From Monitoring the Future surveys reported in David Popenoe and Barbara Dafoe Whitehead, *The State of Our Unions 2000* (New Brunswick, N.J.: National Marriage Project, 2000).

3. Calculations from government sources for David Popenoe, *Life Without Father* (New York: Free Press, 1996).

4. See David C. Geary, "Evolution and Proximate Expression of Human Paternal Investment," *Psychological Bulletin* 126 (2000): 55–77; Patricia Draper, "Why Should Fathers Father?" in Alan Booth and Ann C. Crouter, *Men in Families* (Mahwah, N.J.: Lawrence Erlbaum, 1998), 111–121.

5. Linda J. Waite and Maggie Gallagher, *The Case for Marriage* (New York: Doubleday, 2000).

6. Graeme Russell, *The Changing Role of Fathers?* (New York: University of Queensland Press, 1983); Philip Blumstein and Pepper Schwartz, *American Couples* (New York: Pocket Books, 1983).

7. Shirley P. Burggraf, *The Feminine Economy and Economic Man* (Reading, Mass.: Addison-Wesley, 1997).

8. Carolyn P. Cowan and Philip A. Cowan, *When Partners Become Parents: The Big Life Change for Couples* (New York: Basic Books, 1992).

9. See Robert Karen, *Becoming Attached* (New York: Warner Books, 1994).

# Index

Adoption: German law, 121–122; by homosexual couples, 126–130; right to know father, 137; by single persons, 123–125; statutory regulation of, 121; by unmarried cohabitants, 125–126

Adultery, 6, 63

African-American families, 16, 82–83, 87; black churches, 90; decline in marriage, 84–85; gender-role flexibility, 89; high valuation of marriage, 88–89; out-of-wedlock children, 87

Alternative lifestyles, 185–186, 188; as a public good, 189–190

Amato, Paul, 103

American Assembly, 39–40

American Population Society, 30

Amestoy, Justice, 145

Aquinas, St. Thomas, 31, 34–35, 38

Aristotle, 31, 34–36

Arranged marriages, 19–20

Artificial insemination, 136–139; European law and, 124–125

Asian Americans, 17

Assisted reproduction technology (ART), 133; artificial insemination, 136–139; childlessness and, 134–135; cloning, 136–139; donor insemination (DI), 136; equality issues and, 141; infertility, 136; marriage and the family, 134; motherhood and fatherhood, 140–141; procreation for respectability, 135–136; single people and, 139–140; surrogacy, 136–139

Attachment parenting, 204

Autonomy, 16, 65

Bachrach, Christine, 81

*Baehr v. Lewin*, 112, 115, 145

*Baker v. Vermont*, 145; Common Benefits Clause, 146–148; communitarian marriage, 148; community and belonging, 150; Constitution as community, 146–147; importance of case, 145–146, 151; inclusion principle, 146–148; marriage as commitment, 147–148

Barna, George, 18

Becker, Gary, 31

Behavior channeling, 17–18

Biological parenthood, 23

Birth mothers, 138

Black churches, 90
Blood brotherhood, 122
Brandeis, Justice, 171
*Brause v. Bureau of Vital Statistics*, 145
Bryant, Chalandra M., 17
Burggraf, Shirley P., 203

Cahill, Lisa, 37
Cameron, K., 162
Cameron, P., 162
*The Case for Marriage* (Waite and Gallagher), 30
Child abuse, 104
Child support enforcement, 102–103
Childlessness, 134–135
Children, 72, 203–204; attachment experiences, 204; cohabitation and, 103–104; decoupling with marriage, 87; economics of, 202–203; in marriage, 10; parent-child relationship, 187; same-sex parenting, 115–116, 128–129, 155–157. *See also* Father-absent households; Homosexual parenting
Christian religion, 188, 192
Cloning, 136–139
Cohabitation, 9, 51–52, 54, 71, 186, 189; adoption by unmarried cohabitants, 125–126; artificial insemination and, 125; children and, 103–104; low-income populations and, 80–82
Cohen, Jacob, 161–162
Commercial dating services, 53
Common Benefits Clause, 146–148
Common-law marriages, 82
Communication, parents-children, 31
Communitarianism, 145, 148, 171
Communities: arranged marriages, 19–20; behavior channeling and, 17–18; culture and conventions of, 17–18; enhancement to marriage and parenting, 16–22; family autonomy vs., 21; formalized support of, 19–20; investment function of, 17; involvement rationale, 21–22; limits of, 22–24; religious communities, 18–19; size and influence of, 19; as

sources of relationship information, 16; venting and relationship-specific support of, 17
Conger, Rand D., 17
Consortium concept, 6
Conventions, 17–18
Cook, Frank Gaylord, 185
Couple relationships: barriers to overcome, 96–97; community supports for, 93; factors in marriage decline, 83–85; family relationship and, 87–88; low-income populations, 81–83; "magic" moments, 90; strengthening relationships, 90–94. *See also* Cohabitation
Covenant marriage, 16, 22, 61, 182; migratory divorce phenomenon and, 65–66
Covenant marriage legislation, 60–62, 192; political concepts and, 62; as refuge from moral confusion, 64–65; religious assistance and, 63
"Critical" familism, 36
"Critical" marriage culture, 36
Cultural education, 16, 92
Cultural individualism, 30
Cultural values, 64–65, 85, 178
Cultural work, 29
Custody rights, 15

Danish statute on same-sex couples, 127–128
De-institutionalizing marriage, 8–9; legal marriage and, 11; social costs of, 10
Dispute resolution, 17
Divorce, 22, 60–61, 64, 114, 167–168, 170, 187; migratory divorce phenomenon and, 65–66
"Does Marriage Matter?" (Waite), 30
Domestic partnerships, 114–115
Domestic violence, 17, 87
Donor insemination (DI), 136
Double sexual standard, 36–37

Earned Income Tax Credit, 84
Economic individualism, 30
Edin, Kathryn, 85–86, 89

Education, 30, 53–54, 92
Eisenhower, Dwight D., 39
Elian Gonzales case, 15, 24
Equal-regard marriage, 36–38; society
   and, 38–40
Equality, 5; assisted reproduction
   technology (ART) and, 141; same-
   sex marriage, 149
Ethical egoism, 31
European community law, 135
European convention on Human Rights,
   135, 141
Experimentation, 171–172

Faith-based organizations, 63, 192
Family autonomy, 21, 23
Family law: enforcement problems of,
   178–179; federalism and, 168–170,
   172–173; limits of, 178–179; policy
   values of, 170–172
Family policy, 79
Family relationships: couple and, 87–
   88; equality issues and, 141. *See
   also* Children
Family relativism, 105
Family values, racial-ethnic differences
   in, 82
Father-absent households, 101–102,
   198–199; child support enforcement, 102–103; children of, 101–
   102; cohabitating couples and, 103–
   104; visitation, 103
Fatherhood, 140–141; marriage and,
   105–107
Fathers Count Act of 1999, 91, 192
Fault divorce, 70–71, 77
Federalism: communitarianism, 171;
   experimentation, 171–172; family
   law and, 168–170; marriage
   revitalization/law reform and, 172–
   173; pluralism and, 170–171; policy
   values of, 170–172; state expertise
   and shared sovereignty, 172
Female-headed households, 80–82
Feminism, 181
Fidelity, 6–7
Finn case, 15, 24
First Amendment issues, 95, 191

First-generation American communities,
   16
Foster children, 122
Fragile family, 104, 107
Freedom to reproduce, 133
Friedman, Lawrence, 180
*From Culture Wars to Common
   Ground* (Browning et al.), 35, 38

Gadamer, Hans-Georg, 33
Gallagher, Maggie, 30
Garfinkel, Irwin, 104
Gatekeepers program, 93
Gender roles, 5–6, 85, 89
Genesis, 34, 37–38
Genetic paternity, 137
Gilbreth, Joan, 103
Goode, William, 30
Grandparents' visitation rights, 15, 23

Health, 30–33
Heterosexuality, 4
Hill, Robert, 82–83
Himmelfarb, Gertrude, 65
Hindu Americans, 19–20
Homosexual parenting: adoption by,
   126–130; hypothesis testing of, 157–
   163; research findings, 163–164
*Hozhó*, 17
Human Fertilization and Embryology
   Act (1990), 125, 134, 137, 139
Human Genome Project, 137
Hunter, James, 5

Identity, as husband/wife, 2
Illegitimate children, 7, 9
Incentives, 69–71
Inclusion principle, 146–148
Independence effect, 84–85
Individual free choice, 3–4
Individualism, 30
Infertility, 136, 138
Informal communities, 16, 23
Internet dating services, 53
Interracial marriage, 114
Investment, 17

James, William, 177

Jarrett, Robin, 85
*Jones v. Hallahan*, 111–112

Kurdek, Lawrence, 22

Law reform movement, marriage
  revitalization and, 167–168
"The Law and the Stability of Marriage" (Schneider), 177–178
Leeuwen, Mary Stewart van, 37
Legitimacy, 23
Lerman, Robert, 105
Lesthaeghe, Ron, 30
Locke, John, 35–36
Loconte, Joe, 64
Love ethic, 3–4, 37
Low-income populations: aid resources, 91; community supports
  for, 93; couple relationships, 81–83,
  90–94; economic strategies, 91–92;
  external stressors, 88; factors in
  marriage decline, 85–86; marriage
  and, 81–83; public education/culture
  changing in, 92; reasons for study
  of, 79–81

*McCarty v. McCarty*, 169
McLanahan, Sara, 31, 104
Marital bonds, 199–200
Marital community, 21
Marital desirability, 47–48
Marital harmony, 8
Marital matching, 45–46; age factor,
  50–51; in business/employment, 55–
  56; "circulation" factor, 55;
  conditions for optimal matching,
  48–49; education and, 53–54;
  nature and importance of, 46–48;
  obstacles to, 49–53; premarital
  cohabitation, 51–52; religious
  organizations and, 54–55; single
  parent, 52–53; steps to promote
  good matches, 53–56
Marriage, 60; benefits of, 9–10;
  changing sentiment toward, 186–
  188; as commitment, 147–148;
  cultural definition of, 30, 60;
  cultural reconstruction of, 29;

decline in attraction of, 74–77;
  division of labor, 200–201; economies of scale of, 72–74; friendship
  outside of, 201–202; government
  policy and, 190–192; health and,
  30–33; household incentives for, 71–
  72; incentives for, 69–75; income
  and, 192; insurance and risk
  aversion, 72–74; law and social
  changes, 1, 188; macroeconomic
  benefits of, 11; modern workplace
  and, 202; nature of, 111–112; as
  organizing natural inclinations, 33–
  34; personal choice and, 4; as public
  agenda issues, 10, 86–87; as public
  institution, 60; public philosophy of,
  30, 33, 36; purpose of, 115–116;
  reasons for decline in, 83–85; as
  religious reality, 33–34; as sacred
  institution, 59; sexual restriction
  and, 197–198, 202; as social good,
  112–114; as social institution, 1, 3;
  specialization factor, 72–74;
  structure imposed by, 2; as unity, 8;
  young adulthood and, 195–196
Marriage contract, 65
Marriage education movement, 30
Marriage market, 47–48; "circulation"
  factor, 48–49, 51
Marriage movement, 79
Marriage preparation courses, 53
Marriage revitalization: fear of
  dependence and, 181–182; fear of
  obligation and, 179–180; federalism
  and, 172–173; hostile cultural forces
  and, 179–182; institutionalizing of,
  174; law reform movement and,
  167–168
Marriage statistics, 50
Marriage tax, 39
Married Women's Property Acts, 113
*Marvin v. Marvin*, 186–187
Maturity, 4
Mazeaud, Léon, 64
Medicaid, 80
Mexican-Americans, 89
*Michael H. v. Gerald D*, 23
Migratory divorce phenomenon, 65–66

Milbank, John, 32
Milton, John, 38
Modernization, 30
Monogamy, 6–7, 114
Moral education, 62
Moral reason, 31
Moral values, 63
Motherhood, 140–141
Moynihan report, 82
Mutual consent divorce, 75

National Marriage Project, 54
Native-Americans, 17
Naturalism, 34–36
Navajo-Americans, 20
Navajo Peacemaker Court, 17
*The Negro Family: A Call to Action*
  (Moynihan report), 82
No-fault divorce, 61, 63, 66, 69–71,
  75–76, 167
Nock, Steven L., 22
Nonmarital childbirth, 7
Nonmoral goods, 31–32
Normative marriage, 3
Nuclear family, 201

Ooms, Theodora, 105
Out-of-wedlock children, 79–81, 83

*Parens patriae* power, 189
Parent-child relationship, 187; same-
  sex couples and, 115–116, 128–129,
  155–157
Parental obligations, 7
Parenthood, 7–8; transition to, 203–204
Partnerships, 1
Paternal investment, 198–199
Patriarchy, 9, 36, 87
Peer support groups, 94
Person-specific marital desirability, 47–
  48
Personal autonomy, 11
Personal reputation, 2
Personal Responsibility and Work
  Opportunities Reform Act
  (PRWORA), 79
Phillips, Melanie, 141
Physical health, 30–31

Pluralism, 170–171
Polygamous marriages, 112, 114
Pope Leo XIII, 35
Popenoe, David, 54, 182
Posner, Richard, 31
*Posner v. Posner*, 187
Poverty, single-parent homes, 80–81
Premarital agreements, 114
Premarital counseling, 53, 61
Premarital parenthood, 186, 189
Premarital sex, 71, 195–196
Premoral goods, 31–32
Privacy rights, 16, 180
"Privatization" of marriage, 61
Pro-marriage culture, 92
Procreation for respectability, 135–136
*Promises to Keep* (Popenoe), 182
Property, 6
Psychological health, 30–31
Public assistance programs, 80

Race, 81
Rape statutes, 9
Raspberry, William, 106
Rational choice framework, 69–70
Raz, Joseph, 112
Religion: naturalism and, 34–36;
  religious communities, 18–19
Remarriage, 105
*The Republic of Choice* (Friedman), 180
Responsible Fatherhood Act of 1999,
  192
*Reweaving the Social Tapestry:
  Towards a Public Philosophy and
  Policy for Families* (Browning and
  Rodriguez), 39
Ricoeur, Paul, 33
Rieff, Philip, 179
Right-to-life case, 15
Rodriguez, Gloria, 39
*Roe v. Wade*, 180

Same-sex couples: adoption by, 124,
  126–130; assisted reproduction
  technology (ART) and, 134–136;
  child rearing and, 155–157; parent-
  child relationships and, 128–129.
  *See also* Homosexual parenting

Same-sex marriage, 5, 111–116. *See also*
   *Baker v. Vermont*
Sanctions, 2
Sandefur, Gary, 31
Sawhill, I. V., 80
Scalia, Justice, 23
Schneider, Carl E., 21
Scott, Elizabeth, 21
Scott, Robert, 21
*Sex and Reason* (Posner), 31
Sexual activity, 32, 195–196
Sexual fidelity, 202
Sexual harassment legislation, 202
Sexual union, 34
Shared tasks, 5
Singer, Jana, 21
Single parenthood, 80–81, 87
Single persons: adoption by, 123–125;
   assisted reproduction technology
   (ART) and, 139–140
Social costs, 10
Social institutions, 2
Social life, 2
Social networks, as source of informa-
   tion, 16
Social norms, 2
Social obligation, 180
Social relationship: fidelity and
   monogamy, 6–7; vs. institution, 2
Social services, 94
South, Scott J., 19
Sovereignty, 172
Spitze, Glenna, 19
Spouse battering, 8
State expertise, 172
Stephen, James Fitzjames, 179
*Strengthening American Families:
   Reweaving the Social Tapestry*, 40
Structural dependence, 181
Surrogacy, 136–139

Surrogacy Arrangements Act of 1985,
   138

*Tanner v. Oregon Health Sciences
   University*, 145
Team parenting, 104
Temporary Assistance for Needy Families
   (TANF) program, 91–93, 95–96; family
   formation goals of, 95
Testimonial privilege, 9
Treaty of Amsterdam, 141
Trible, Phyllis, 37
*Troxel* case, 15, 23–24

Union building, 17–18
Utilitarianism, 31

Venting, 17
Vermont civil unions. *See Baker v.
   Vermont*
Vermont Psychiatric Association (VPA),
   155–156
Violence Against Women Act, 169
Violent criminals, 101
Visitation, 103

Warnock Committee (1984), 134
Warnock Report, 137
Welfare programs, 80–81, 84
Welfare-to-Work grants, 92
Western individualism, 30
Whitehead, Barbara Dafoe, 54, 103
*Williams v. North Carolina I*, 65
Wilson, William Julius, 84–85
Wolfe, Christopher, 65
Women's sexuality, 197–198
*World Changes in Divorce Patterns*
   (Goode), 30
*World Revolution in Family Patterns*
   (Goode), 30

# About the Editors
# and Contributors

**Brian Bix** is the Frederick W. Thomas associate professor of law and philosophy at the University of Minnesota Law School. He has also taught at Quinnipiac Law School in Hamden, Connecticut, George Washington University Law School, and at Georgetown University Law Center. He is a member of the American Law Institute. Recent writings include "Bargaining in the Shadow of Love: The Enforcement of Premarital Agreements and How We Think About Marriage."

**Margaret F. Brinig** is the Edward A. Lowry distinguished Professor of Law at the University of Iowa, where she teaches courses in family law and alternative dispute resolution. She has taught family law–related courses for more than twenty years, and her recent primary research focus concerns the law and economics of the family. Her book, *From Contract to Covenant: Beyond the Law and Economics of the Family,* was published in 2000, and she is the co-author (with Carl E. Schneider) of a family law casebook, *An Invitation to Family Law* (2nd ed. 2000).

**Don S. Browning** is the Alexander Campbell Professor of Religious Ethics and the Social Sciences at the University of Chicago Divinity School. He is a senior consultant to the Center of Theological Inquiry, Princeton University. His recent publications include *From Culture Wars to Common Ground: Religion and the American Family Debate.* He is co-editor of the ten-volume *Family, Religion, and Culture* series.

**David Orgon Coolidge** is the director of the Marriage Law Project based at the Columbus School of Law, the Catholic University of America. His recent publications are "The Hawaii Marriage Amendment: Its Origins, Meaning, and Constitutionality," and, with William C. Duncan, "Definition or Discrimination? The Role of Marriage Recognition Statutes in the Same-Sex 'Marriage' Debate."

**Ruth Deech** is Pro-Vice Chancellor of Oxford University. She was the Principal of St. Anne's College, Oxford University, 1991–2001, and was a fellow and tutor in law at St. Anne's College, 1970–1991. Recent publications include: "Infertility and Ethics"; "Legal and Ethical Responsibilities of Sperm Banks, in Gamete Donation"; "Family Law and Genetics in Law and Human Genetics."

**Rainer Frank** is a professor at the University of Freiburg (Germany), where he is director of the Institute for Foreign and Private International Law, and where he served as dean of the Faculty of Law (1988–89). He is the immediate past-president of the International Society of Family Law, and currently serves as president of the Commission Internationale de l'Etat Civil (CIEC) and of the International Social Service (ISS). Recent publications include "Recent Developments in the Reform of German Parentage Law in the Legal Relationships between Parents and Children."

**Norval D. Glenn** is the Stiles Professor, Department of Sociology, University of Texas at Austin. He is a research associate of the Population Research Center, University of Texas. His recent publications include: "Closed Hearts, Closed Minds: The Textbook Story of Marriage" and "The Course of Marital Success and Failure in Five American 10-Year Marriage Cohorts."

**Alan J. Hawkins** is an associate director of the School of Family Life, past director of the Family Studies Center, and a professor of Marriage, Family, and Human Development at Brigham Young University. His recent publications include: "Perspectives on Covenant Marriage" and *Generative Fathering: Beyond Deficit Perspectives* (1997, with David C. Dollahite).

**Wade F. Horn** is the Assistant Secretary for Children and Families for the U.S. Department of Health and Human Services, and the former president of the National Fatherhood Initiative, a nonprofit, nonpartisan, nonsectarian organization dedicated to mobilizing communities to increase the number of children growing up with loving, committed, and responsible fathers. He served as the U.S. Commissioner for Children, Youth, and Families. He is a clinical child psychologist and co-author of several books on parenting including the *Better Homes and Gardens New Father Book* (1998) and the *Better Homes and Gardens New Teen Book* (1999).

**Robert Lerner** is a social science statistical consultant in the greater Washington area. His Ph.D. was in Sociology from the University of Chicago. He was formerly assistant director at the Center for the Study of Social and Political Change at Smith College. He has taught at Smith College, Syracuse University, and the Johns Hopkins University School of Hygiene and Public Health. Recent publications include: *American Elites* (with Althea K. Nagai and Stanley Rothman, 1996), and "Family Values and Media Reality" (with Althea K. Nagai).

**Althea K. Nagai** is a statistical analyst and runs a consulting business with her husband, Robert Lerner. She has a Ph.D. in political science from the University of Chicago. She formerly was Senior Research Associate, Center for the Study of Social and Political Change, Smith College and Visiting Lecturer, Smith College. Her recent publications include: *Religion and American Elites* (forthcoming), *Molding the Good Citizen* (1995), and *American Elites* (1996) (each with Stanley Rothman).

**Steven L. Nock** is a professor of sociology at the University of Virginia. His current research includes a five-year study of covenant marriage in Louisiana, funded by the National Science Foundation. His recent publications include *Marriage in Men's Lives* (1998).

**Laurence C. Nolan** is a professor of law at the Howard University School of Law, and received her B.S. degree from Howard University and her J.D. degree from the University of Michigan. She was an associate professor of law at the Detroit College of Law. She currently teaches courses that are all related to the family: family law, wills, trusts and estates, and law and aging, and she has published numerous law review articles and monographs about family law.

**Theodora Ooms** is the past executive director of the Family Impact Seminar, and currently is directing the Resource Center on Couples and Marriage Policy with the Center for Law and Social Policy in Washington, D.C. She is the author of "Toward More Perfect Unions: Putting Marriage on the Public Agenda" and co-author (with Barbara Dafoe Whitehead) of "Goodbye to Girlhood: What's Troubling Girls and What We Can Do About It."

**Allen M. Parkman** is the Regents' Professor of Management at the University of New Mexico. He holds a Ph.D. in Economics from UCLA and a law degree from the University of New Mexico. His research involves economic analysis of public policy issues affecting the family. During 1981–82, he was a senior staff economist on the President's Council of Economic Advisers in Washington, D.C. His publications include *Good Intentions Gone Awry: No-Fault Divorce and the American Family* (2000) and "Unilateral Divorce and the Labor-Force Participation Rate of Married Women, Revisited."

**David Popenoe** is a professor of Sociology at Rutgers University, where he is also co-director of the National Marriage Project and former dean of the college of Social and Behavioral Sciences. He is the author of *Life Without Father* (1996) and *Disturbing the Nest* (1988).

**Carl E. Schneider** is the Chauncey Stillman Professor of Ethics, Morality, and the Practice of Law and a professor of internal medicine at the University of Michigan. His prolific scholarship includes co-editing *Family Law in Action: A Reader* (1999) and "The Law and the Stability of Marriage: The Family as a Social Institution."

**Katherine Shaw Spaht** is the Jules F. and Frances L. Landry Professor of Law at Louisiana State University. She drafted Louisiana's Covenant Marriage Act for Representative Tony Perkins and has written extensively on the subject. Two of her articles on Louisiana's act are "Louisiana's Covenant Marriage: Social Analysis and Legal Implications" and "Covenant Marriage and Conflict of Laws."

**Linda J. Waite** is a professor of sociology at the University of Chicago and former president of the Population Association of America. She is the co-author with Maggie Gallagher of *The Case for Marriage* (2000).

**Lynn D. Wardle** is a professor of law at the J. Reuben Clark Law School, Brigham Young University. He is the current president of the International Society of Family Law, and is a member of the American Law Institute. His recent publications include: "*Loving v. Virginia* and the Constitutional Right to Marry, 1790–1990" and "*Williams v. North Carolina,* Divorce Recognition, and Same-Sex Marriage Recognition." He is co-author of a four-volume treatise, *Contemporary Family Law, Principles, Policy and Practice.*